ONE WORLD OR SEVERAL?

EDITED BY
LOUIS EMMERIJ

DEVELOPMENT CENTRE
OF THE ORGANISATION FOR ECONOMIC CO-OPERATION AND DEVELOPMENT

Pursuant to article 1 of the Convention signed in Paris on 14th December 1960, and which came into force on 30th September 1961, the Organisation for Economic Co-operation and Development (OECD) shall promote policies designed:

- to achieve the highest sustainable economic growth and employment and a rising standard of living in Member countries, while maintaining financial stability, and thus to contribute to the development of the world economy;
- to contribute to sound economic expansion in Member as well as non-member countries in the process of economic development; and
- to contribute to the expansion of world trade on a multilateral, non-discriminatory basis in accordance with international obligations.

The original Member countries of the OECD are Austria, Belgium, Canada, Denmark, France, the Federal Republic of Germany, Greece, Iceland, Ireland, Italy, Luxembourg, the Netherlands, Norway, Portugal, Spain, Sweden, Switzerland, Turkey, the United Kingdom and the United States. The following countries became Members subsequently through accession at the dates indicated hereafter: Japan (28th April 1964), Finland (28th January 1969), Australia (7th June 1971) and New Zealand (29th May 1973).

The Socialist Federal Republic of Yugoslavia takes part in some of the work of the OECD (agreement of 28th October 1961).

The Development Centre of the Organisation for Economic Co-operation and Development was established by decision of the OECD Council on 23rd October 1962.

The purpose of the Centre is to bring together the knowledge and experience available in Member countries of both economic development and the formulation and execution of general economic policies; to adapt such knowledge and experience to the actual needs of countries or regions in the process of development and to put the results at the disposal of the countries by appropriate means.

The Centre has a special and autonomous position within the OECD which enables it to enjoy scientific independence in the execution of its task. Nevertheless, the Centre can draw upon the experience and knowledge available in the OECD in the development field.

Publié en français sous le titre :

UN MONDE
OU PLUSIEURS ?

This volume represents the deliberations of a symposium held to mark the 25th anniversary of the OECD Development Centre. The symposium took place in Paris from 6th to 8th February 1989.

Also available

To be published

Prices charged at the OECD Bookshop.

*THE OECD CATALOGUE OF PUBLICATIONS and supplements will be sent free of charge
on request addressed either to OECD Publications Service,
2, rue André-Pascal, 75775 PARIS CEDEX 16, or to the OECD Distributor in your country.*

TABLE OF CONTENTS

Chapter I

ONE WORLD OR SEVERAL? OBJECTIVES AND CONCLUSIONS

Chapter II

EMERGING FORMS OF GLOBAL MARKETS AND THE NATURE OF INTERDEPENDENCE IN AN INCREASINGLY MULTIPOLAR WORLD ECONOMY

Chapter III

THE CHALLENGE FOR THE NEWLY INDUSTRIALISING ECONOMIES IN THE 1990s: SUSTAINABLE GROWTH WITH EQUITY AND SHARED INTERNATIONAL RESPONSIBILITY

Chapter IV

NATIONAL POLICIES FOR BALANCED AND
SUSTAINABLE DEVELOPMENT IN THE POOR COUNTRIES:
HOW TO AVOID INVOLUNTARY DE-LINKING

Chapter V

INTERNATIONAL POLICIES FOR ASSISTING THE
POOR COUNTRIES IN ATTAINING BALANCED
AND SUSTAINABLE DEVELOPMENT

Chapter VI

TOWARDS A WORLD DEVELOPMENT STRATEGY
BASED ON GROWTH, SUSTAINABILITY AND SOLIDARITY:
POLICY OPTIONS FOR THE 1990s

Chapter VII

FURTHER COMMENTS ON THE QUESTION OF
ONE WORLD OR SEVERAL

Chapter VIII

DEVELOPMENT AT THE CROSSROADS

PREFACE

BY WAY OF PREFACE:
OPENING REMARKS TO THE SYMPOSIUM

by

Jean-Claude PAYE
Secretary-General of the OECD

Since its foundation, the Development Centre has been the OECD countries' window on the developing world. Yet it is far more than a window, something we simply look through; the Centre is a meeting point for people and ideas, and better than any other branch of the OECD it illustrates the readiness to understand, talk together and co-operate which are more necessary than ever in today's world.

The wealth and variety of skills represented here today will, I am sure, make this a meaningful and constructive occasion. The present time of rapid and far-reaching change invites us to pool our thinking on the main factors generating that change and shaping tomorrow's world. We need to consider the opportunities that this change holds out, and the dangers it carries with it, to consider what steps should be taken to grasp the opportunities and elude the dangers. The papers before you provide an extremely rich and varied illustration of these far-reaching changes in our world.

To preface your discussions, I should like to comment briefly upon a few of the questions which occurred to me -- as they did perhaps to many of you -- when reading the papers.

The first question -- included, in fact, in the Symposium's title -- is whether we are embarked upon a two-track process. That would mean some countries proceeding at a rapid pace on the road of economic progress, with the remainder lagging along behind. Dualism is something which arises internationally; it is also relevant within many countries. Any "de-linking" means that strains are likely to develop, and we need to examine that danger, and see what we can do to avoid it.

My second question, which follows on from the first, is whether the development model taken by the advanced countries, those which today are industrialised or becoming so (and here I am thinking in particular of the emerging economies in South and East Asia), is in fact applicable elsewhere. Is it *the* model for development, or is it simply *a* model? Are there others? If so, what are they? In other words, can economic growth, technological development and social progress spread progressively from the advanced countries into the industrialising

11

world, or must we look for other routes, and short-cuts, to help the developing countries catch up?

My third question is tied up with the fact that economic ideologies seem over recent years to have become less aggressive. Today, and perhaps for some time to come, we see fairly general acceptance that the market economy, or at least market mechanisms, in fact hold fewer disadvantages than other forms of economic management. To adapt to economics the famous saying that democracy is the worst form of government except for all the others, we may consider whether the market system is not currently demonstrating that it is in fact less bad than other systems. But that leads us on to a point that needs careful consideration: a tendency in some quarters to think that the market economy means a withdrawal by government; a smaller role for government, or at least a considerably changed one. I am not sure that the effectiveness and successes of the market economy should lead us to the extreme conclusion that government's role should wither away in the economy, or be confined to setting the basic ground rules. It is important, indeed crucial, to weigh up carefully what government's role in tomorrow's world should be.

My last comment arises very directly from the papers before us, and equally clearly from the talks we held a fortnight ago in this very room, with leading figures from what are termed "the four little dragons". It is one of the essential problems in managing the world today. In sum, we can see a gap widening between a world economy that is increasingly integrated and globalised and, if I may employ a semi-Marxist term, an institutional political superstructure that does not mesh very well with the integrated economy. Integration, globalisation, is quite clear in many spheres. Most obviously in financial markets, but the same applies to markets for commodities and manufactures, and on account of lower transport costs, to business strategy which now takes a worldwide view, forming networks that increasingly disregard national borders. A further example of the world's integration can be found in environmental problems. They were first tackled at local level, then within countries. We noticed that frontiers did not hold up pollution, and we are now recognising that collective management of our common heritage, this planet, is of concern to all and a pressing responsibility for policymakers.

Compared with the scale of world integration, I repeat, our institutional superstructure is probably inadequate. Governments are recognising that frontiers have less and less importance. Closer co-operation is accordingly a necessity, and they are striving to achieve that with growing determination and growing success.

At the same time, on account of the disparity between economic integration and institutional superstructure, is there not a danger that, from time to time, people will seek to reject, or thwart, the process of world integration. Is there not a danger of protectionism building up again, of ill-conceived regionalism growing up in opposition to multilateralism? These questions are relevant in the economic sphere, and may give rise to defensive or hostile responses in the political and social sphere.

I am convinced that your deliberations will show that a pooled analysis can be made of the situation in the world today and its problems, and joint efforts can be sketched out so that we can all make our individual contributions to tomorrow's world. We all share the same aim (you will allow me, as a French citizen, to mention in this bicentenary year of the French Revolution) which is the motto of the French Republic: Liberty, Equality, Fraternity.

Chapter I

ONE WORLD OR SEVERAL: OBJECTIVES AND CONCLUSIONS

SOME POLICY CONCLUSIONS (1)

by

Louis EMMERIJ

The 25th Anniversary Symposium of the OECD Development Centre was organised around three major themes: Interdependence, Multipolarity and the Dual-Track World Economy. The discussion was unusual in the variety of elements and disciplines brought to bear in analysing the underlying international context and the nature of development prospects. While considerable attention was focused on economic issues, the breadth of the discussion and range of participants made it clear that an exclusively economic focus is insufficient for understanding and managing national and international economic policies, especially as one looks to the future. Demographic and environmental trends, as well as a growing importance of political, social, institutional and cultural dimensions broadened the discussions in a decisive way.

The fundamental issue addressed at the Conference, as intended, was the dual-track world economy and the fate of the poor countries, especially those of Africa, within it. Whether the poor countries are irrevocably on the slow track while the advanced countries and the first and second generation newly industrialising economies are on a fast track, was a major question of concern and a cause for a serious difference of views. The presence of development practitioners, present and former government officials from developing countries and donor agencies, academics, researchers, writers, private sector executives and members of international institutions from most parts of the world, brought a variety of professional, intellectual and political perspectives to bear. Throughout the Conference, it was repeatedly stressed that a global vision of development was required which would include developing countries from all parts of the world, though the discussion of the dual-track issue emphasized Africa. Among the newly industrialising economies, Latin American debt and East Asian trade and macroeconomic issues were seen more in the context of multipolarity in their connection with major issues affecting North America, Europe and Japan than as development issues.

In the pages that follow, seven major policy issues are presented that might affect the programme of work of the OECD Development Centre, the OECD as a whole, and more importantly, the decision-making of countries throughout the world.

REACTIVATING THE WORLD ECONOMY AS OPPOSED TO ONLY THAT OF THE OECD COUNTRIES

The discussion at the Conference on this theme was implicitly part of a wider debate about the desirability of pursuing international policies that stimulate simultaneous as opposed to sequential world economic growth and development. The sequential approach is based on the locomotive theory: assure growth in the industrialised countries first and that will have positive effects on growth elsewhere in the world later. The debate at the 25th Anniversary Symposium came out quite clearly in favour of stimulating economic development simultaneously in all parts of the globe. A pre-condition for such a policy is an early solution to the international debt crisis. The time was considered ripe to develop a comprehensive set of debt-reduction measures for both the poorest and the middle-income countries. Since then, the Brady initiative seems to be a step in the right direction.

The Symposium baptised as the "Okita Plan" the series of spectacular Japanese initiatives that the world has witnessed over the past few years in order to mobilise international surpluses for world development. The OECD Development Centre has just brought out an evaluation of these initiatives in the publication "Recycling Japan's Surpluses for Developing Countries". An all-out effort must now be made to try to bring this debate a step forward because, according to the Symposium, it is an idea whose time has come.

The Symposium was also presented with the "Stoltenberg Plan for Peace and Development in Africa". This is a plan to avoid involuntary de-linking of an entire Continent from the main thrust of world economic development. It is based on the observation that whereas many African governments have courageously followed international prescriptions for structural adjustment programmes, often at a great social and political cost, concessionary resource flows have not reached the levels promised, while export revenues have dwindled because of the low commodity prices. Moreover, one development obstacle in Africa has been severely underestimated, namely the direct and indirect economic effect of wars and unrest. The OECD could undertake a study which would enable its Member countries to take an initiative in the United Nations to form a Consortium in order to provide funding on the basis of "additionality" for such a Plan. In this connection, it was observed that, with "peace breaking out" everywhere, the reduction of military expenditure and its reallocation to such purposes as the Stoltenberg Plan should now be studied seriously.

GLOBALISATION VERSUS REGIONALISATION

This issue must be seen in the context of the trend towards world economic multipolarity. As the role of the United States of America as a world economic leader is declining, with many countries beginning to challenge this role, it is equally true that there is not yet a single country or group of countries in a position

18

to acquire the mantle of leadership and the title of the next hegemonic power. In other words, as we observe the rise of global markets in the fields of finance, technology, international services, etc., as well as the appearance of global as opposed to multinational enterprises, there is a parallel trend towards the formation of regional economic blocs.

A first subject of attention would therefore be to examine possible tensions between the desirable free trade objective on the one hand and this emerging trend towards regional protectionism on the other. This is obviously related to the ongoing Uruguay Round and to the role of GATT. Indeed, as one participant in the Symposium observed, the GATT jurisdiction only covers 5 to 7 per cent of global economic activity because while it covers 80 per cent of merchandise trade flows, GATT rules do not extend at present to agriculture, services, textiles and capital flows.

In this overall context, different forms of regionalisation, or rather different objectives of regionalisation, must be examined. Regionalisation could mean a policy instrument in favour of voluntary de-linking from the mainstream of world economic development. Several African voices at the Symposium were ready to assume their own responsibilities after having "recognised" that de-linking was a fact. Secondly, regionalisation can be seen as a form of collective self-reliance, i.e. as an attempt to be more autonomous in terms of regional economic development, less reliant on the rest of the world economy, without going as far as de-linking Thirdly, regionalisation can be seen as a variation of the infant industry argument. Behind temporary protectionist barriers, the regional economy and technology are being restructured in order to be in a better position at a later stage to conquer a substantial part of the global market.

Another important topic arose during the Symposium, namely the dilemma of a rapid globalisation of markets and a decline of the Bretton Woods institutions in global management. How can the role of the World Bank, the IMF, GATT, and the OECD for that matter, be made more effective in order to face the challenge and the forces of the global markets in the years ahead?

THE PROBLEM OF GOVERNANCE, ENTREPRENEURSHIP AND HUMAN RESOURCES IN AFRICA

Several African voices at the Symposium "recognised" that de-linking was a fact of life at present. In that connection, there was a difference of views of how the train metaphor (2) should be applied to poorer countries. Some felt that Africa was going backwards, others that all countries were on the same train threatened by internal dualism, and others that the metaphor was inappropriate. Speed may not be the proper measure if all trains are going different places for different reasons. Measuring oneself against oneself was thought to be more salient than comparing oneself with the progress of others. From this perspective, the idea of de-linking implicit in the dual-track economy notion was seen as less problematic, possibly providing a movement to gather forces rather than foreshadowing slower growth.

Compared to other countries, the State in Sub-Saharan Africa is very "soft": formal policies or laws are only followed when they suit the interests of the leaders and their followers. There is often a considerable gap between stated rules on the one hand and action on the other. Politics is seen to be at the root of the African crisis. There is a growing withdrawal from civic participation by the many for whom the political system is a nuisance. This tendency has only grown in strength over the years. The prevalence of "parallel" or "informal" economies in Africa is as much the result of arbitrary politics as it is of official price controls.

There is therefore a growing discrepancy between the civil society on the one hand and the political class on the other. Work needs to be done on how to narrow this gap and how to get "politics right". This may involve work on participatory forms of development programming and policies. There is a need, but this is a general proposition, to enhance the scientific and technological capabilities in the developing countries. Indeed, without a massive and global spread of scientific and technological knowledge and skills, the dependency of the Third World and the gap between North and South is bound to increase, as is their incapacity to develop their own solutions to their own problems. It would be a major error if fear of competition would constitute an obstacle to such an international programme. In the long run, the consequences are likely to be more costly than co-operating with the industrialisation of the Third World, including the industrialisation of the countryside, something that is still in its infancy (see also the contribution of Lourdes Arizpe in Chapter VI, below).

DEVELOPMENT CONTRACTS

Significant divergence occurred at the Symposium over questions of structural adjustment lending, the relative weight of internal versus external factors dampening or disrupting development, conditionality, the development paradigm, the content of economic reform, the nature of the State -- in particular in Africa -- and the kind of dialogue between donor governments, international agencies and developing country governments. The view was expressed more than once that the massive transfer of resources from developing countries to advanced countries in recent years brought into question the credibility of the donor-recipient relationship, suggesting the need for reappraisal and change. The need for developing country governments to have greater control of the process, and the need for donor governments to show results in terms acceptable to their constituencies seem to be in conflict. Reforming conditionality was favoured by many.

It is here that the suggestion made by Minister Stoltenberg concerning "a system of development contracts" comes in. Adjustment programmes must be replaced by more comprehensive "development contracts" which can be defined as comprehensive instruments for the financing of medium and long-term development policies prepared by the developing countries themselves with outside technical support where appropriate. One feature of these development contracts that distinguishes them from adjustment programmes is the commitment to be made by participating donors and banks. But the major difference is that development contracts are contracted between equal partners drawing up a comprehensive agreement relating to debt, financial flows, trade, foreign investments, development aid and so on and so forth, where both partners agree to undertake specific policies and stick to their deal.

THE NEED FOR AN INTERNATIONAL ENERGY REGIME IN THE FACE OF ENVIRONMENTAL CONSEQUENCES

The energy problem, including the technology of its generation and the technology of its use, but also the lifestyles, expectations and values that lie behind each technological choice, has become a global problem. At the present state of technology, there is no hope that at the expected higher levels of energy use the world over, the warming process, for instance, can be halted or slowed down enough for mankind to make the necessary adaptations. The hope that nuclear energy could provide an alternative has lost much of its attraction in recent years, especially now that apparently unexpected problems of finding politically and economically acceptable locations for nuclear waste disposal have emerged.

Account must be taken of the fact that already now China, after the United States of America and the Soviet Union, is the third largest producer of CO_2. Even though industrial countries may embark on major efforts to increase energy efficiency, these efforts will not compensate for the greater fossil fuel utilisation of the industrialising Third World. In addition, one knows how poverty is one of the greatest polluters in the world. It drives millions of people to cut the forests to meet their own energy needs.

It is obvious that the problem of energy needs of the industrial countries and those of developing countries are not separate. There are, of course, quite a number of other environmental problems which require a broad international effort, but there certainly is *a need for an international energy regime* that could regulate the transition of industrial countries and an industrialising Third World towards an ecologically less destructive pattern and organise the research and development effort necessary to that end.

Obviously, additional work is necessary in this area and could consist of examining the feasibility of reaching an international consensus with regard to such an international energy regime. This should include the research and development for energy generation and energy efficiency. Such a consensus should also encompass understanding regarding the effective dissemination of these technologies and policies across the globe, as well as arrangements for the protection of tropical rain forests and for an international system of compensation, incentives and disincentives for those countries in which these forests are located. An effort should be made in this context to develop what could be called a "New Economics" that would relate economic theory to the micro and macro environmental system as well as to new concepts of security if we want a firmer basis for international consensus and international action.

An underlying assumption that came out of the Symposium is that forces such as those mentioned here are creating a new situation in which the future of the rich and the future of the poor can no longer be separated. Given the seriousness of the environmental issues, the world appears to confront the fact that the viability of the two-track world economy may be coming to an end. These perceptions fit in with the view that the viability of the North has been due in part to the ability of the North to absorb the South within it, while now globalisation forces make the North-South dualism as an international relationship increasingly unsustainable.

A NEXT WAVE OF INTERNATIONAL MIGRATION?

Fertility rates are going down almost everywhere, including in most of the developing countries. Nevertheless, the major focus of policy attention remains on numbers of people rather than the qualitative implications of differences in age structures between countries. This applies in particular to those countries that are separated by short distances as is the case, for instance, between Europe on the one hand, and Africa on the other, separated by a narrow stretch of water. It is also the case of the United States of America and Mexico and South America in general, separated by an even narrower stretch of water. The enormous disparities in the standard of living and in age structures, with all the implications on differences in outlook and mentality, tend to become so great that the pressure to migrate to the industrialised countries will turn into an irresistible flood-tide

One will have to choose from three alternatives if one wants to prevent massive and global redistribution of population. Firstly, one could deal with the problem of underdevelopment and international poverty on a scale that does justice to the magnitude of the problem as implied in the Okita plan, for instance. Secondly, one can accept the free movement of people in the way the free movement of capital across the globe has now by and large been accepted. Thirdly, one could identify a combination of the first two options: a much higher level of international development co-operation, a much higher level of immigration from the Third World coupled with policies that aim at increasing the absorptive capacity and the necessary tolerance in the receiving country. This would mean essentially to accept the inevitability of multi-ethnic States in the industrialised world.

In this light, the OECD and other instances could be called upon to look into new population policies as well as defining a new policy attitude towards international migration.

RETHINKING AGRARIAN SOCIETIES

Farming families may well be the most victimised social group on the planet in the decades ahead. They are caught between three advancing bulldozers. The first, biotechnology, is about to change a form of production which is 15 000 years old into something that is, as yet, indefinable and unrecognisable. The second consists of the economic imperatives of world agricultural markets which are making farmers all over the globe go bankrupt. Those in the North, however, have governments who subsidise, regulate, give social security, turn farms into hotels, or otherwise find ways of minimising the damage to farmers. In the South, farmers are blown away like the sand in the desert, thus creating a social desertification of rural areas just as damaging as the soil desertification. The third is ecological depletion which is hitting harder in the South as well. A combination of economic, biotechnological and political factors have taken their livelihoods away from millions of farming families who are now edged towards depleting ecological resources.

This must be a high priority area for policy action in the coming decades and this not only by providing immediate relief. The policy challenge is to rethink the economy of the future in terms of a unified territorial distribution in which the rural form of production can be linked to the mainstream high-speed one. Further research is needed next to political will to achieve this.

* * *

The Symposium came to an end without consensus or formal conclusions. Nor was it intended that such would occur. However, participants seemed most impressed by the fact that discussions of such a wide-ranging nature with strong differences of views occurred within the OECD framework and were hopeful that the Symposium would pave the way for further efforts to achieve a broad integration of themes and issues into a global perspective on the future which seems so essential as we move into the last decade of the 20th century.

I am aware that the present brief note constitutes an incomplete effort to draw policy and programme conclusions from the very rich discussion that took place at the Symposium. It is a beginning, for others, when they have gone through the papers that follow, to draw their own conclusions.

NOTES AND REFERENCES

1. With thanks to Colin Bradford whose input is gratefully acknowledged.
2. See my introductory statement to the Symposium which comes immediately after the present article containing the policy conclusions.

ONE WORLD OR SEVERAL? AN INTRODUCTORY STATEMENT

by

Louis EMMERIJ

The year 1988 marked the 25th anniversary of the OECD Development Centre. Anniversaries are frequently of a retrospective nature, but at the end of this difficult decade, and towards the end of what is clearly a transition period, we ought rather to take a prospective view of where the world economy is, and where it may be moving.

The Council of the OECD is now devoting more attention to OECD's relationship with non-Member countries. This presents an opportunity to focus on emerging issues that are of relevance not only to the Development Centre but to the OECD as a whole.

We seem to be at the beginning of a new era which will mark the world economy well into the next century. It is an era which is likely to be characterized by rapidly changing international competitive strengths and weaknesses as between different countries and regions; increasing economic globalisation combined with growing multipolarity and thus fragmented economic hegemony; growing dualism among (and within) countries in terms of economic participation; and a growing impotence of purely national decision-making It is proposed to celebrate the 25th anniversary of the OECD Development Centre by holding a substantive -- as opposed to a ceremonial -- Symposium to assess:

- i) The probability of these trends;

- ii) The measures to be taken to reverse the trend towards a two-track economic development; and

- iii) To explore the characteristics of a world development strategy based on growth and solidarity.

The identification of the contours of such a strategy would constitute the unifying theme of the Symposium.

If we compare the international economy of the 1960s and 1970s with the prospects for the 1990s, it is clear that the global factors will be much more important. For example, two of the critical ingredients of economic power, the mastery of technology and the availability of capital, are less and less subject to governmental direction. The retreat from rigidity in economic ideology and, indeed, in interstate relations, reflects an adjustment to this reality. National decision-making, even in economically strong countries, will become increasingly impotent in the face of global economic actors and forces which cannot easily be controlled and which are frequently in private hands. A vivid illustration is, of course, the globalisation of financial markets. But the same phenomenon can be observed with respect to technology. And in international trade, global markets, as distinct from bilateral ones, are increasingly important.

It is also now obvious that several developing countries are joining the new international economy and are capturing dynamic areas of global markets for themselves. This is the case today for the first generation of NIEs, and tomorrow it will be the case for the second generation, which embraces bigger developing countries. Several South American countries will also increase their presence in these markets in the 1990s, after the dark cloud of the debt problem has passed over.

Parallel to this economic globalisation, regional centres of economic power, centred on large domestic or regional markets, are also emerging. In addition to the old centres of North America, Europe and Japan, we already see the East Asian and ASEAN countries, South America, and of course the CMEA, with China and India clearly on the horizon. A multipolar global economy seems almost inevitable.

Is there a danger of a period of relatively adverse relations between these economic poles? How can co-operative relations be fostered? This is a first theme of the Symposium.

This dynamic and increasingly multipolar global economy can be seen as a fast train: a TGV in France, or a bullet train in Japan. The OECD countries already have seats. New passengers, the first and second generation NIEs, have got on board or are about to. In the 1990s the train is likely to accelerate.

It appears that during the 1980s a large number of poor countries, mainly but not exclusively in Africa, are becoming involuntarily decoupled from the globalisation process, and have less and less access to the benefits -- and also to the problems -- of the dynamic global markets. They have been left behind on the platform, and seem to have little prospect of getting on board in the foreseeable future. The many existing analyses of the reasons -- both external and internal -- for this situation could serve as a basis for examining the options available for those countries in the 1990s. Will their reliance on concessional assistance increase? How can existing trade arrangements be adjusted in their favour? What internal changes must be introduced to prevent them from losing touch with the main thrust of the world economy?

There is thus a risk, clearly already visible today, of a growing dualism in world economic development, with perhaps three-quarters of the world population in countries participating in a dynamic international economy, and one-quarter in countries either falling more and more behind or steering into uncharted waters -- either way, with the prospect of prolonged marginalisation.

How can such a risk be overcome? This is a second theme of the Symposium.

This scenario raises many questions. For example, why not regard such trends as growing "pluralities" or "diversities" in development, like those observed in the past, rather than in terms of "dualities" and "de-linking"? Historically, since the first wave of industrialisation, we have observed phases during which groups of countries overtook the frontrunners. An initially widening gap turned out to be an incentive for the others, rather than a discouragement: they found other, faster trains. Is this any longer possible?

At least three categories of countries can be distinguished in the developing world: the newly industrialising economies, the middle-income countries and the poor countries. We must, therefore, ask who is really in the fast train today, and who is likely to be in it tomorrow. Is it only much of sub-Saharan Africa plus a few other chronically problematic countries such as Bangladesh and Haiti that are being left behind? What if China and India do not become the economic powerhouses we at present expect? Their problems are totally different from those of Africa. And, most importantly, it must not be forgotten that there are large non-participating groups of poor people in the second-generation NIEs. In terms of world welfare they are at least as important as the poor of Africa, but in terms of international political economy, they are not nearly as visible. While the slow track may apply to perhaps a quarter of the world's nations, it probably applies to half the world's people.

Looking at ways to overcome such internal dichotomies is a third theme of the Symposium.

It is not certain that a growing differentiation, dualism or even polarisation is unavoidable, but the portents are already sufficiently clear for the issue of a two-track world economy to be seriously addressed and possible remedies explored.

Sometimes current discussions give the impression that Africa is anyway not important, does not have the economic weight, to matter much to the rest of the world. This may well be a mistaken view if we think in terms of international peace and stability.

For example, the SADCC region matters both economically and geopolitically, and the OECD countries have to be concerned about the turbulence in Southern Africa. What are the possibilities of reversing the man-made ravages in Ethiopia, Somalia and Sudan? Can Sudan, Ethiopia and Egypt collaborate in the imperative to develop the Nile valley? What further delay can be tolerated in the fight against desertification in Africa? A number of environmental balances are already in danger which it seems may well influence the climate of southern Europe.

Many poor countries, including many in Africa, have weak public structures and the authority of the State is being further eroded by the deterioration of their economies. One could even envisage a lengthy period of drift and disorder before more stable social and political systems emerge, perhaps decades from now, with firmer roots in each nation's culture capable of forging the national cohesion needed for an industrial economy. If one-quarter of the world's nations face a turbulent transition period, this will inevitably have economic and political consequences for the other three-quarters.

The prospects for the poor countries lead to a consideration of their internal conditions, and to a discussion of forward-looking national development strategies and the nature of OECD Members' policies, including aid. Concretely, how will people, and local and national institutions, react to their countries' marginalisation? And what kinds of roles are there for external agents? Looking back, we may conclude that development assistance has had only a moderate effect, at least in those countries which have remained poor. Perhaps these countries' regeneration can only come from within, and the main role of aid should now be to assist those countries going through the difficulties of the transition period. In other words, should aid now largely focus on helping to support minimal levels -- of health, educational services and income, for instance -- in order to prevent these countries' going through the floor, thereby endangering their longer-term strategy of achieving robust and sustainable development?

The exploration of national and international policies that could lead to a world development strategy based on growth and solidarity is the fourth and overriding theme of the Symposium.

In sum, the Symposium will look into the future, addressing important, but as yet unclear, issues:

-- The emerging forms of global markets, and the consequent nature of economic interdependence;

-- The role of first- and second-generation NIEs in the context of an increasingly multipolar world economy;

-- The risks of de-linking of poor countries and poor population groups from the dynamic elements of the world economy, and the dangers of a two-track development path; and

-- The prognosis for the poor countries, and the reactions and roles of external agents.

The Symposium may help to clarify whether international organisations must assume an expanded role in times when global and international factors, largely beyond national control, are becoming more and more important. It ought also to sharpen the conceptual base on which to build new directions in the Development Centre's work, and to strengthen the links with the activities and pre-occupations of the rest of the Organisation.

Chapter II

EMERGING FORMS OF GLOBAL MARKETS AND THE NATURE OF INTERDEPENDENCE IN AN INCREASINGLY MULTIPOLAR WORLD ECONOMY

THE PROBLEM QUANTIFIED

by

Colin I. BRADFORD, Jr.

The challenge before this conference is to seek insights into the underlying dynamics of the world economy today which will shape global economic trends in the future, especially those which will affect the fate of the lower income countries in the coming decade. Louis Emmerij has provocatively focused our attention on the confluence of increasing multipolarity, globalisation and dualism in the world economy as posing the central policy dilemma for the world community for the final decade of the 20th century.

This paper will attempt, in summary form, to highlight aspects of these issues derived from a world trade model constructed under my direction at the World Bank as part of the work of the newly created unit on strategic planning. I will not go into detail either about the model or the statistical results, for these are available in other papers, but rather will try to draw from them the main insights and features of the world economy that are relevant to the issues before this conference.

The paper will address three major themes of the conference. First, the degree to which the world economy has shifted from North-South interactions to a multipolar structure and the consequences for international economic policy will be discussed. Second, the tensions between regionalism and bilateralism, on the one hand, and globalisation, on the other, will be analysed. And third, the degree to which these structural changes in the world economy affect the dualism between rich and poor, dynamic and stagnant economies, will be reviewed in relation to the fate of the lowest income countries in future world growth and trade.

THE MEANING OF INCREASING MULTIPOLARITY IN THE WORLD ECONOMY

The major thrust of international economic policy co-ordination efforts on behalf of greater global growth have been and continue to be focused on the seven large OECD countries represented at the annual Economic Summits, or indeed narrower groupings of the United States, Germany and Japan or even simply the United States and Japan. Whereas these efforts have brought some stability to ex-

31

change markets and interest rates, major economic imbalances and problems remain, not the least of which is that the world's economic growth is slower than it might be.

This continuing focus on industrial countries as the locus of global growth ignores the shifts in world economic structure brought about by the emergence of the highly dynamic, rapidly industrialising developing countries and the potential new role of the socialist countries in the world economy. If instead of focusing on the G-7, G-3 or the G-2, our vision of the dynamic centre of the world economy were to include 36 industrial, developing and socialist economies, over 70 per cent of world trade would be accounted for and a new scope for global economic strategies would be possible (1).

The new structure and dynamism of the world economy derives from the size, openness, and rapid growth rates of nine groups of countries other than the United States, Japan and Western Europe. These are the four newly industrialising economies (NIEs) of East Asia and the four next tier NIEs in South East Asia as well as the three major Latin American countries, the three Southern European economies that have joined the European Community, the six Eastern European states that are part of the Council for Mutual Economic Assistance (CMEA), four Mediterranean economies, India, China and the Soviet Union. These 27 NIE or potential NIE economies account for over 30 per cent of world GDP, roughly equivalent to the size of Japan and the EEC together. The import demand of these nine "NIE blocs" taken together accounts for 25 per cent of United States exports, 30 per cent of Japanese exports, and 15 per cent of total EEC exports.

The size and trade linkages of the nine NIE blocs mean that they have or potentially have a significant impact on the economic outlook of the three major OECD blocs as well as the world economy as a whole. The key to realising the full potential of world growth is to capture the yield obtainable from inclusion of the NIE blocs in global growth strategy efforts.

REGIONALISM VERSUS GLOBALISATION

This increased multipolarity creates a pluralistic as opposed to polarised world economy in which there are multiple centres of economic importance rather than the industrial countries alone providing the growth stimulus on which the rest of the world depends. This multipolar world economy creates new opportunities for globalisation of trade and growth by creating the context in which increased openness to trade and to new trade patterns can generate large gains in global growth.

This increased multipolarity is not the same as, nor necessarily consistent with the highly regionalised patterns of trade also present today. These regionalised patterns often have embedded within them precisely the polarised North-South relations characteristic of the past. The most obvious is the trade relationship between the United States and Latin America, where after some years of a more diversified trade pattern, by the mid-1980s over 40 per cent of the latter's exports and imports were with the former.

The other major regional blocs -- Europe, CMEA, and the Pacific Basin -- run the risk of being at once powerful and relatively self-contained sources of economic growth. Fully half of the trade of the enlarged EEC is within the Community itself. Similarly, almost half of the trade of the Soviet Union and Eastern Europe is trade between each other, with another 20 per cent of Eastern European trade being within Eastern Europe. In the Pacific Basin, the East Asian NIEs, next-tier Asian NIEs, and China import two-thirds of their total imports from each other, the United States and Japan. Between 63 and 77 per cent of the total exports of Japan, the Asian NIEs and next-tier Asian NIEs, and China are within the Pacific Basin region (including the United States).

These summary data manifest a broad pattern of regionalisation in world trade with the dominant flows occurring within the European Community, between the Soviet Union and Eastern Europe, within the Pacific Basin, and between the United States and Latin America. These patterns to a certain degree run against the increased multipolarity of the world economy by retaining the dynamism of growth within regional blocs rather than exploiting the full potential of the new interdependence of a multicentred world. The opening of the socialist economies to the rest of the world, the potential of cross-regional trade (Latin America with East Asia, East Asia with Eastern Europe, India with the Pacific Basin, etc.) and the simultaneous increased opening to external trade by the European Community as it becomes more integrated internally pose significant new opportunities for globalising in the world economy. One of the major questions facing the world community is how the trade and economic growth possibilities of the multipolar world structure can be utilised for the benefit of the world economy as a whole rather than primarily feed the dynamism of regional blocs.

THE DUAL-TRACK WORLD ECONOMY

The redefinition of the world economy from a North-South to a multipolar structure and the simultaneous evolution of more regionalised patterns of trade do not necessarily recast the role of the lower income countries in the world economy. The disparity between rich and poor countries in levels of income has been supplemented by the dualism between dynamic and stagnant economies in rates of economic growth. Multipolarity has added a dimension to the dilemma facing poor countries.

Multipolarity has also made clear that the problems of developing countries are not problems of a single large undifferentiated grouping. Some countries have been able to achieve dynamic development while others have been unable to initiate or sustain the process. The rise of the NIEs have not only added to the sources of global growth, pluralising the North if you like, but have also reshaped the

South, disassociating the problems of the poorest countries from those of the rapidly industrialising developing countries.

These shifts in our understanding of the nature of the world economy do not themselves necessarily lead to solutions to the problem of finding strategies for the viable development of the poorest countries. In fact, they may lead instead to a sharper statement of the problem of the role of lower income countries in the world economy. Faster growth in the United States, Japan and Western Europe and in the nine NIE blocs will not necessarily spill over to the lower income countries.

Trade driven growth is not an easy answer for the poorest countries. The NIEs themselves seem to have followed a model of supply-led manufactured export growth rather than responding to external demand. The dynamism of the East Asian NIEs especially seems to have been primarily internally promoted with external consequences rather than induced by external circumstances. The lower income countries have less linkage with the external world and less compelling internal processes that can be reasonably expected to lead to dynamic trade relations that complement the internal growth process.

As a result, the major structural changes in the world economy do not seem themselves to suggest a strategy for the poorest countries. Rather these changes seem simply to redefine the external context within which the long-standing development problems of lower income countries must be faced, both by their governments and the international community.

Having briefly reviewed the interaction of multipolarity, regionalism and dualism as major characteristics of the world economy today, the next section will discuss some of the quantitative outcomes anticipated from this new global structure in terms of alternative scenarios for the future.

ALTERNATIVE FUTURES FOR THE WORLD ECONOMY

A number of scenarios are possible for the world economy in the future. How the world economy actually evolves will depend on a variety of forces many of which are beyond the direct control of economic policy. As a result, the degree to which the world economy realistically can be guided by strategy towards a prescribed set of outcomes is an open question. Nonetheless, it is worth exploring various options lest the path of least resistance be accepted without knowledge of the "road not taken", to borrow an American poet's turn of phrase.

The most likely path for the world economy is one which results from the continuation of current policies in the major economies and the steady evolution of the global economic structure. Cautious economic policies would lead to modest GDP growth rates in this scenario, imbalances would continue, and openness to trade (import-GDP shares) would remain constant. A second scenario would envision contractionary policies leading to slower economic growth which would force gradual reductions of trade as a share of GDP in the major blocs due to poor export prospects. A third scenario would be based on expansionary policies in the major economic blocs leading to an improved export outlook, higher imports and stronger economic growth. This more dynamic scenario could either occur within the current patterns of regionalised trade or be accompanied by a significant realignment towards increased cross-regional globalised trade. In each of these alternatives the economic growth and export possibilities of the poorer countries can be estimated.

A simple trade model using a 16-by-16 trade matrix of the three industrial country blocs, the nine NIE blocs, three developing country blocs and the rest of the world is used to induce estimated export growth rates, export GDP shares and to calculate GDP for each bloc and the world economy as a whole in 1995 (2). The three scenarios lead to interesting differences in outcomes.

The higher growth, more open economy scenario generates $1.7 trillion more world GDP and roughly $900 billion more in world exports in 1995 than the current policy scenario. This gives some idea of the stake the world has in attempting to move towards a more dynamic and trade-oriented set of economic policies. By contrast, if more cautious policies prevail resulting in slightly lower GDP growth rates and somewhat lower import-GDP shares (2 to 3 percentage points of GDP less than in the current policy base case), world GDP drops by $900 billion and world exports by $600 billion.

GDP growth rates are exogenous variables in generating these scenarios of trade growth. Export growth is more sensitive to changes in the degree of openness measured by import-GDP shares than to changes in GDP growth. Average annual world GDP growth rates for the period 1985 (base year) to 1995 for the three scenarios are 2.7, 3.2, and 4.0 per cent, respectively, while the average annual rates of world export growth for the decade for these scenarios are 1.5, 3.4 and 5.6 per cent, respectively. These results show that shifts in trade growth rates are more than proportionate to changes in GDP growth due to accompanying changes in the degree of openness.

The importance of the nine NIE blocs in generating these outcomes is directly proportionate to their weight in world GDP. Roughly 30 per cent of the increment in world GDP and world exports is due to the nine NIE blocs. Surprisingly, there is virtually no difference in the world totals for GDP and exports in the high growth, open economy scenario as between regionalised versus globalised world trade patterns. There is, of course, a difference in the outcomes by bloc, depending on how the globalised trends are configured. Comparing the two versions of the more dynamic scenario, the United States, Japan, the East Asian NIEs and Eastern Europe have higher export growth rates under the current structure of regionalised trade whereas the two Southern European blocs, Latin America, China, India, the Highly Indebted Economies (HIEs), and OPEC have higher export growth rates under the more globalised pattern.

Not only does the high-growth, open-economy scenario yield higher aggregate outcomes, it also produces better global balance relative to the base case. Not surprisingly, the current policy (base case) scenario results in continuing trade imbalances especially in the OECD blocs but also in the other blocs as well. The high, open scenario in the prevailing regionalised world economy restores balance in the United States, Japan, and the "EEC7" and yields less imbalance in all other blocs relative to the base case. Latin America and the seventeen HIEs run trade surpluses of 3 to 4 per cent of GDP in both scenarios, providing the HIEs do not increase their import-GDP share, while Latin America is able to increase its import-GDP share by 3 per centage points in the high, open scenario.

As a result, the high-open scenario moves towards better balance among industrial countries, adaptation of the rest of the OECD to further EEC integration, an incorporation of the socialist economies into world trade and an amelioration of the world debt problem. All these improvements occur within the G-36.

THE ROLE OF THE LOWER INCOME COUNTRIES

There is much that is hopeful in this analysis. The multipolar world economy provides a structure within which more openness to trade in quantitative terms and more expansionary policies in an enlarged group of key countries, including economies of the developing countries and the socialist world, can make significant differences in the rates of growth and the magnitude of world economic growth and trade. A global strategy of simultaneous expansion of the twelve major blocs would assure export growth prospects which then would permit the increased import growth upon which the strategy itself depends. Unlike the intra-OECD strategy which achieves correction of imbalance in one economy through increased imbalance in others, the broader global strategy moves towards improved trade balances in all blocs as exports and imports increase together.

Nevertheless, this gain by the major players in the world economy by capturing the benefits of their increased interdependence, does not necessarily bring significant gains for the lower income countries of Africa and South Asia. These economies are quite marginalised from the main trends among the other blocs. The 23 African countries, four South Asian economies (Bangladesh, Burma, Pakistan, and Sri Lanka) and Haiti together comprise less than 1 per cent of world GDP and about seven tenths of 1 per cent of world exports (3).

The low growth-closed economy, base case-current policy, and high growth-open economy scenarios assume GDP growth rates for the 1985 to 1995 period for this bloc of 28 Low Income Countries (LIEs) of 2.0, 2.5, and 3.5 per cent, respectively. The export growth rates for the lower income countries induced in these three scenarios are 1.8, 3.4, and 5.6 per cent, respectively. While the export growth rates in the base case and high growth scenario are not dismal, they do not increase the export GDP share sufficiently. Assuming a constant import-GDP share for the bloc of 22 per cent in all three scenarios, the trade deficit as a share of GDP is 7, 6, and 4 per cent, respectively, in the three scenarios.

Against the background of the difficulties of low income countries in the last eight years, especially those in sub-Saharan Africa, these results may appear quite hopeful. But Pakistan, Sri Lanka and Bangladesh account for 40 per cent of the GDP and 25 per cent of the exports of the LIEs bloc; their export growth rates have been around 6 per cent in the 1980s, whereas that of the rest of the LIEs bloc (i.e. Africa) has been closer to zero. With population growth rates of 3 per cent in sub-Saharan Africa, it would be foolish to assume that these results solve the African problem. A high growth, more open world environment is a necessary but not sufficient condition for improving the development prospects of the low income countries.

Perhaps the most trying aspect of the global structure as it relates to the lower income countries is the fact that high GDP growth rates (a doubling in LIEs GDP growth, for example) make virtually no difference in the GDP and export growth outcomes for the twelve groups of major countries. As a result, there is no self-interested rationale that can be developed on behalf of the lower income countries, as can be developed in the case of the nine NIE and socialist blocs, that spurring their growth has positive feedback effects on the OECD economies.

These quantitative structural parameters defining the role of the lower income countries in the world economy seem to confirm the dual track character of the world economy posited by Louis Emmerij in his charge to this conference. They suggest that special and specific policy measures have to be taken by the world community and by the lower income countries themselves to address the problems of stagnant growth and misery in these countries. Whereas the new multipolar character of the world economy presents a structure that can be capitalised on through a global strategy to spur dynamic growth among the 36 significant trade-oriented economies now constituting the centre of the world economy, that structure does not itself lead to a logical strategy for economic development of the marginalised lower income countries. Such a strategy will have to be tailored to the needs of the poorest countries, and its importance to the world community will have to rest on a rationale other than self-interest. This may reduce the likelihood that such a strategy will be adopted but it may ultimately increase its effectiveness.

NOTES AND REFERENCES

1. The 36 countries are:

    i)   The Industrial Country Blocs -- the United States, Japan, and EEC7 (Belgium, France, Federal Republic of Germany, Italy, Luxembourg, Netherlands and United Kingdom); and

    ii) The Mie Blocs -- EEC Mediterranean (Greece, Portugal and Spain), Non-EEC Mediterranean (Egypt, Israel, Turkey and Yugoslavia), Latin America (Argentina, Brazil, and Mexico), East Asian NIEs (Hong Kong, Singapore, South Korea and Taiwan), Next-Tier Asia (Indonesia, Malaysia, Phillipines and Thailand), Eastern Europe (Bulgaria, Czechoslovakia, German Democratic Republic, Hungary, Poland, Romania), the Soviet Union, China, and India.

2. Highly indebted economies (HIEs): Bolivia, Chile, Colombia, Ecuador, Morocco, Nigeria, Peru, Uruguay, Venezuela.

    OPEC: Algeria, Gabon, Iran, Iraq, Kuwait, Libya, Saudi Arabia.

    Low income economies (LIEs): 28 of the 39 low-income countries in World Bank WDR category, except China and India

3. The African countries are: Benin, Burkina Faso, Burundi, Central African Republic, Ethiopia, Gambia, Ghana, Kenya, Lesotho, Madagascar, Malawi, Mali, Mauritania, Niger, Rwanda, Senegal, Sierra Leone, Somalia, Sudan, Tanzania, Togo, Zaire and Zambia.

BIBLIOGRAPHY

BRADFORD, Colin I., Jr. "The NIEs in the World Economy: Toward an Open World Economy in the Mid-1990s," Strategic Planning Working Paper, World Bank, October 5, 1988.

BRADFORD, Colin I., Jr. "A Strategic Perspective on Trade Regimes and Trade Theory", Strategic Planning Working Paper, World Bank, November 2, 1988.

BRADFORD, Colin I., Jr. "Trade and Structural Change: NIEs and the Next Tier NIEs as Transitional Economies," *World Development*, Vol. 15, No. 3, (1987), 299-316.

BRADFORD, Colin I., Jr. and BRANSON, William H., eds. *Trade and Structural Change in Pacific Asia*, Chicago, The University of Chicago Press, 1987.

CENTRE D'ETUDES PROSPECTIVES ET D'INFORMATIONS INTERNATIONALES (CEPII) *Economie Mondiale 1980-1990; la Fracture?* Paris, Economica, 1983.

----- *Economie Mondiale: la Montée des Tensions*, Paris, Economica, 1983.

COMMISSION OF THE EUROPEAN COMMUNITIES "The Economics of 1992: An Assessment of the Potential Economic Effects of Completing the Internal Market of the European Community" (Study directed by Michael Emerson), *European Economy*, No. 35, March 1988.

HARDING, Harry *China's Second Revolution: Reform After Mao*, The Brookings Institution, Washington DC, 1987.

HEWETT, Ed A., *Reforming the Soviet Economy: Equality Versus Efficiency*, The Brookings Institution, Washington DC, 1988.

HOUGH, Jerry F. *Opening Up the Soviet Economy*, Washington DC, The Brookings Institution, 1988

KOVES, Andras *The CMEA Countries in the World Economy: Turning Inwards or Turning Outwards*, Trans. G. Hajdu, Budapest, Akadémiai Kiado, 1985.

LINCOLN, Edward J. *Japan: Facing Economic Maturity*, The Brookings Institution, Washington DC, 1988.

LODGE, George C., and VOGEL, Ezra F., eds. *Efficiency, Stability, and Equality: A Strategy for the Evolution of the Economic Systems of the European Community*, Oxford University Press, Oxford, 1987.

OECD, *The Newly Industrialising Countries: Challenge and Opportunity for OECD Industries*, Paris, July 1988.

SAGASTI, Francisco R. "National Development Planning in Turbulent Times: New Approaches and Criteria for Institutional Design," *World Development,* Vol. 16, No. 4, 1988 pp. 431-448.

POLICY APPROACHES TO THE PROBLEM

by

Saburo OKITA

MULTIPOLAR WORLD ECONOMY

Globalism and regionalism are the two main currents in the world today. Just as strong moves have been made to expand corporate activity across national borders and creating what is called "the borderless economy," advances in transport and communications technologies have made information available rapidly and inexpensively worldwide, and this has in turn made closed national systems less and less tenable. The international flow of information has had a major impact, for example, on the decade-long Chinese shift to more open economic structures and on the reforms opened by Gorbachev in the Soviet Union. Even such closed societies as North Korea, Vietnam and Burma are likely to be pushed into taking part in the international division of labour and economic exchanges sooner or later.

Yet at the same time and as a counter to this globalisation, there have also been increased moves to regionalism. Even if the issues facing mankind are too large for any one nation to solve alone, it is felt that a number of countries might be able to solve them by banding together in regional co-operation. Examples here include the EEC's drive for market integration by 1992 and the United States-Canada Free Trade Agreement that went into effect this year.

Speaking at last October's Minneapolis Symposium on Leading Issues in Pacific Rim Economies, management guru Peter Drucker speculated on the three great economic spheres that are forming: North America, with its 300 million people, Europe, with a common market of over 300 million, and East Asia with its 300 million people in Japan, the Republic of Korea, Taiwan, Hong Kong, coastal China from Shanghai to Canton, and part of Southeast Asia. This East Asian region is now experiencing rapid growth, and it is expected to rival North America and Europe economically before long. In fact, the rise of protectionism in the United States and Europe can be seen partly as an effort by those nations to protect their markets for domestic industries faced with East Asia's insistent rise. Well aware of their importance in the Pacific region, the United States is exploring the possibilities of bilateral free-trade agreements with Japan, ASEAN, and the newly industrialising economies of Asia. The East Asian economies are strong in their support of free and global trade and recognise the inherent dangers in a divided world economy, but it is conceivable that East Asian ties might have to be strengthened if inward-looking regionalism develops in Europe and North America.

The changes taking place in the Soviet Union are an important counterpoint to these developments. Judging from Gorbachev's public statements and other available information, there are a number of factors behind the current drive for *perestroika*, among them the fact that the Soviet Union has been too preoccupied with the United States in its international dealings, that relations with the United States have been tilted too heavily towards the military, that national security is not solely a military concern but also demands perceptive political, economic and other responses, that the Soviet Union now realises it must move away from economic autarky and take an active part in the international division of labour, that the Third World has numerous problems which the superpowers can affect only marginally, and that there is a need for a new awareness of the United Nations' importance in global issues.

If these Soviet changes are real, relaxation of the military confrontation between the United States and the Soviet Union should lead to an alleviation of Western anxiety about the Soviet Union and hence to the possibility of closer economic relations between Western Europe and the Soviet Union and its East European allies. Although the Soviet Union has recently expressed more interest in its Pacific relations and the Soviet Far East accounts for fully 30 per cent of the Soviet land mass, it should be noted that this area contains only 3 per cent of the Soviet population and is of limited economic potential. The Soviet Union remains basically a European state.

As such, it is conceivable that the European economic zone could spread to encompass all of Europe (including the Soviet Union), Africa, the Near and Middle East, and even India and that there could be another economic zone formed of the United States, Japan, China, the rest of East Asia, and Latin America -- with relations between these two great blocs not those of military confrontation but those of economic competition between co-existing social systems.

Another important development in the shift to globalism is in the emergence of global environmental concerns -- a trend that was spurred by the *Our Common Future* report released by the United Nations World Commission on Environment and Development (chaired by Gro Harlem Brundtland, now Prime Minister of Norway) in April 1987. Among the many pressing global environmental issues are the greenhouse effect created by the excess of carbon dioxide in the atmosphere, the destruction of the ozone layer by chlorofluorocarbons (CFCs), the desertification in Africa and Asia, acid rain wafting across national borders, the devastation of tropical forests, the depletion of species, and the continuing population explosion in the poorest countries. All of these have the potential for a grave impact on mankind's future, and it is essential that all of the nations of the world join together in finding and formulating co-operative solutions to these shared problems.

Moreover, as the Brundtland report notes, there are numerous problems that transcend national sovereignty and must be dealt with by all nations in co-operation. These include not only the problems of the planetary ecosystem but also the management of the oceans, space, and the Antarctic. It is imperative that the functioning of the United Nations and its specialised agencies be strengthened and the propensity to international co-operation buttressed to enable us to deal with these problems effectively.

As seen in the strong response that Paul Kennedy's *The Rise and Fall of the Great Powers* evoked last year, there is worldwide concern over the fate of the American-led international system. While there is some erosion in America's dominance, especially its economic leadership, no other country is in sight to replace the United States. As Henry Kissinger and Cyrus Vance argued in "Bipartisan Objectives for American Foreign Policy" (*Foreign Affairs,* Summer 1988), "the United States will (continue to) have the world's largest and most innovative economy, and will remain a nuclear superpower, a cultural and intellectual leader, a model democracy and a society that provides exceptionally well for the needs of its citizens."

Much of the erosion in the United States' international economic leadership is the result of a chain of events in which macroeconomic policy decisions in the early 1980s led to condoning the dollar's hyper-valuation, inviting a sharp increase in imports and enervation of America's export competitiveness, and running long-term fiscal deficits combined with a declining rate of domestic savings to plunge the United States in debtor status. American political leaders exacerbated this by trumpeting the expansion in employment, the quelling of inflation, the sustained economic growth, and other favourable aspects and failing to point out that these developments were made possible only by heavy borrowing from overseas. United States policy is very much influenced by public opinion, and it is very difficult for any administration to implement tax increases or to make other hard choices that are needed when the bulk of the people believe the economy is in good shape. However, given American democracy's realistic flexibility, it should be possible to move quickly once public opinion recognises how much trouble the economy is in.

If the United States can substantially reduce its fiscal and trade deficits, this should contribute to a recovery of confidence in the dollar and a renewal of American economic leadership. However, with United States GNP having fallen to slightly over 20 per cent of the world total, there is much less room than before for the United States to exercise unilateral policy leadership and much more need to strengthen co-operation with Japan and Western Europe.

ECONOMIC DISTORTIONS

The world economy, having hit bottom in 1982, is now in the midst of a sustained recovery and expansion, and the OECD economies have shown an average 4 per cent growth in 1987 and 1988. The problem is the disequilibriums that lurk behind this apparent strength.

Broadly categorising these disequilibriums into three types, the first is the uneven economic growth accompanying the imbalances of payments among the industrial countries, particularly America's massive trade deficits and the surpluses on the part of Japan, Germany, and recently the rapidly growing Asian NIEs (newly industrialising economies). The imbalance between Japan and America in particular, besides causing political and economic friction between the two partners, has become an impediment to stable world economic development.

The second disequilibrium is uneven growth as the developing countries tend to progress at vastly different paces. This tendency has been accelerated in the 1980s, with the result that there are now three distinct groups of developing countries. The first group is made up of the Asian NIEs, some ASEAN countries, China, and other countries that have demonstrated comparatively better economic performance. The economic development of these Western Pacific Rim countries has the potential for becoming a locomotive for the world economy in the 1990s. The second group of developing countries is those countries whose economies are hurting from massive debt or the fall in commodities prices. Included in this group are those oil-producing countries that temporarily experienced high growth rates and the Latin American countries, where the debt-service ratio is extremely high and sustained. The last group of developing countries is the poverty-stricken countries such as the sub-Saharan African countries, where food shortages are widespread and per-capita GNP is declining.

The third disequilibrium is the rapid shift of capital, both public and private, away from the developing countries. This disequilibrium is starkly illustrated by comparing the net $39.3 billion *in*flow in 1980 to the net $31.0 billion *out*flow in 1985 -- a $70.3 billion shift. As a result, the developing countries' total debt outstanding increased from $633 billion (end of 1980) to $1 218 billion (end of 1987) according to IMF statistics. Although the world economy as a whole has been enjoying a modest recovery since 1982, the macroeconomic policy inconsistency among the industrial countries is giving rise to diverging economic structures, which are in turn impeding the recycling of capital to the developing countries, thus exacerbating the uneven growth between the industrial and developing countries.

The issue facing us in the 1990s is basically that of attempting to revitalise the world economy, including the developing countries, by facilitating the international recycling of capital to the developing countries and expanding these countries' export trade. It is imperative that there be a net capital flow from the industrial countries to the developing countries in the form of direct overseas investment, private-bank lending and Official Development Assistance (ODA) to facilitate their economic growth and to enable them to improve their living standards. Yet despite this need, the demand for capital created by the United States deficits seems to be crowding the developing countries out of capital markets, and the negative net capital transfer from the industrial countries to the developing countries is effectively crimping world economic development. If we are to rectify this situation, it is essential not only that the United States work to reduce its deficits but also that Japan and other surplus countries recycle their surpluses to the capital-starved developing countries.

Additionally, both since United States government austerity will inevitably spark a global recession and to avoid snuffing out the hopes of the ASEAN countries, the Asian NIEs, the Latin American countries, and other countries that are dependent on United States imports for their economic growth, it is imperative that the surplus countries step up their capital infusions to, their investments in, and their imports from, these developing countries. This will also alleviate bilateral friction by helping to rectify the imbalances among the industrial countries.

JAPANESE ASSISTANCE: AN HISTORICAL REVIEW

Japan, now considered a world economic superpower, held a total of $1.56 trillion in international bank assets as of the end of June 1988. This figure corresponds to 38 per cent of the world total and 2.6 times the total United States assets. Japan's GNP in 1987 was $2.4 trillion as compared to $4.5 trillion for the United States.

This strength also entails responsibilities. Japanese assistance policy has gone though a number of stages in seeking to discover how Japan can help the developing countries most effectively.

Stage one -- reparations payments: Following the conclusion of reparation agreements in 1954 and subsequent years, Japan paid reparations to Burma, the Philippines, Indonesia, Vietnam, and other countries as part of an effort to make up for the suffering inflicted during the war. Because the payments were in the nature of reparations, there was a conscious policy decision made in this stage not to inquire whether or not the funds were actually contributing to the recipient country's economic development. In fact, this basic "aid by request" policy stance lingers even today.

Stage two -- lending for promoting trade: Beginning with a yen loan to India in 1958, Japan has extended loans and investments as economic co-operation. This form of economic co-operation has covered both sides of the trading process, including both financing for plant and machinery imports from Japan and financing to develop natural resources for export to Japan. As such, it has functioned as an important means of promoting trade. Although there was some criticism that these Japanese assistance policies were weighted heavily toward Japanese industry's own commercial needs and did not pay sufficient attention to the host countries' needs, it must be remembered that Japan's per-capita GNP at the time was only about $80 -- which would qualify Japan to receive assistance under today's standards -- and that there was obvious need for this assistance to consider the economic needs of the donor country as well as the recipient countries.

Stage three -- economic assistance as a part of Asian diplomacy: The third stage, in which Japanese economic co-operation was broadly integrated into

Japan's Asian foreign policy, started around 1965. Economic co-operation agreements were concluded with Taïwan and the Republic of Korea and Japan took an active part in the establishment of the Asian Development Bank, hosted the Ministerial Conference for the Economic Development of Southeast Asia, and otherwise worked to see that its assistance policies were responsive to Asian needs. The emphasis was clearly on development assistance for East and Southeast Asia.

Stage four -- meeting its responsibilities as an economic power: In the 1970s, as the two oil crises and their aftermaths dulled growth rates in the industrial countries and threatened to derail the entire world economy, Japan turned in one of the better economic performances, rising to become the undisputed number two economic power among the industrial countries. Along with these developments, Japan formulated its first medium-term target for official development assistance, vowing at least to double actual disbursements over the three-year 1978-1980. This target was achieved. Moreover, Japan's ODA was expanded to the Middle East, Africa, and Latin America.

Stage five -- contributing as a surplus country: As a result of continuing efforts to expand the ODA volume since the 1960s and the yen's continuing appreciation, Japan's ODA became the second-largest in the world -- second only to the United States -- and accounted for about 17.9 per cent of the OECD Development Aid Committee (DAC) countries' total ODA in 1987.

As Japan scored current account surpluses of $49.2 billion in 1985, $85.8 billion in 1986, and $86.7 billion in 1987, it became necessary for Japan, above and beyond the normal responsibilities accruing to an economic power, to act to ensure an enhanced flow of capital to the developing countries.

This Japanese assistance programme enjoys widespread support from the Japanese public. One recent public opinion poll found that approximately 80 per cent of Japanese people support further expansion of Japan's economic assistance. Asked why, these people cite Japan's obligations in the international community, Japan's status as a peace-loving nation, and Japan's dependence on foreign markets.

Most of Japan's assistance thus far has gone to the Asian countries -- especially the ASEAN countries. In this, Japan differs from the other aid-giving countries, but this tilt is thought to be justified by the close geographical, historical, cultural, and, therefore, political and economic ties that Japan has traditionally had with these nations. Approximately 70 per cent of Japan's total disbursements went to Asia, including China and India, while Africa, Latin America, and the Middle East received roughly 10 per cent of the total each.

Another difference is that Japan's ODA terms are generally somewhat harder than those of other DAC countries -- a difference accounted for by the fact that the economic performances of aid-recipient countries in Asia allows for the low-interest, long-term borrowing rather than grants. Considering Japan's close relations with the other Asian countries and Japan's responsibility to contribute to the economic stability of this region with its huge population and immense development needs, Asia will continue to receive the lion's share of Japanese ODA for some time to come. However, Japan realizes that its interests go beyond its immediate neighbourhood. As the world's second-largest economic power, Japan needs to contribute from the global perspective as well. Accordingly, it is expected that Japan will expand its development assistance to the non-Asian countries, especially to the sub-Saharan African countries.

As seen in this review of the evolution of Japanese thinking on development assistance, the present may be characterized as stage five -- a period in which Japan is called upon to be "unstinting" in its development policies as a major supplier of capital and as a market for imports from the developing countries. It is thus appropriate here to touch on some of the specific initiatives that are shaping Japanese development assistance in this new era.

JAPANESE INITIATIVES

Economic co-operation is commonly thought of as including the flow of private sector capital, and it is especially important that Japan emphasize the complementary nature of private and public sector capital and work to promote more supportive interaction between the two kinds of flows. In so doing, it is imperative that the governments of the industrial countries and the international development agencies do everything possible to encourage the flow of both public and private sector capital to the developing countries.

This need was foremost in my mind when I chaired the Board of the United Nations University's World Institute for Development Economics Research (WIDER) study effort leading to its April 1986 report "The Potential of the Japanese Surplus for World Economic Development" (the Okita-Jayawardena-Sengupta report) and when we wrote the second report of May 1987 "Mobilizing International Surpluses for World Development: a WIDER Plan for a Japanese Initiative". Actually, the idea of recycling Japanese surpluses occurred to me when I was attending the June 1985 conference on "The Challenge of Interdependence" hosted by the OECD Development Centre at Château de la Corniche. Knowing that official flows alone cannot do the job, I have constantly been calling upon the government of Japan to implement new policies to encourage the flow of Japanese and non-Japanese private sector capital and ODA to the developing countries. Thus is was that the second WIDER report urged Japan to recycle its surplus at $25 billion a year for a five-year period.

One difficulty encountered by all these plans is that, at least in Japan's case, the government or official sector is running a deficit and it is the private sector that is piling up massive surpluses. Because this is private sector capital, and because private sector companies seek to get the best return on their money with minimum risk, most of it has gone to purchases of American Treasuries and other forms of investment. If they are to redirect this flow of private sector capital to the developing countries, it is imperative that governments and international development agencies take the lead first in providing insurance and other guarantees to alleviate the risk and second in providing interest subsidies or other means to make the yields more attractive.

I have long argued that Japan should utilize its surplus in a three-pronged effort: one-third to be used to promote domestic demand, one-third for expanding economic assistance to the developing countries, and one-third for supplying capital to the United States and the other industrial countries. Partly in response to this and other similar proposals, Japan has announced plans to recycle a total of at least $30 billion to the developing countries over the three-year period 1987-89 to help them solve their debt and development problems. This $30 billion includes both the $20 billion capital recycling programme announced in May of 1987 and the $10 billion capital recycling programme begun in 1986. As of the end of 1988, about 85 per cent of this $30 billion has been committed. Specifically, the committed portion includes contributions and subscriptions to multilateral development banks; loans to the IMF, expanded co-financing with the World Bank and other institutions by the Overseas Economic Co-operation Fund (OECF), the Export-Import Bank of Japan, and private banks; as well as expanded policy-based lending by the OECF and direct financing from the Export-Import Bank of Japan.

It should be noted that this $30 billion is totally untied, and that the limited government funds available are being used to stimulate the flow of private-sector capital to the developing countries. On 14th June 1988, the Japanese government approved a new Fourth Medium-term Target for ODA that calls for at least doubling the ODA half-decade total -- from $25 billion in the five-year period 1983-87, to at least $50 billion in the five-year period 1988-92. At the same time, this quantitative expansion is to be accompanied by qualitative improvement. At the Toronto Summit in June 1988, Prime Minister Takeshita announced that the Japanese government is prepared to extend $5.5 billion in grant assistance to the Asian and African LLDCs to enable them to repay their outstanding debts -- de facto cancelling those debts.

Apart from ODA flow, Japan's private direct overseas investment has also increased sharply in recent years, from $12 billion in fiscal 1985 to $33 billion in fiscal 1987, of which about 30 per cent was to the developing countries. With these three channels of capital flow to the developing countries -- surplus recycling, ODA flows, and private direct investment -- the WIDER report target of $25 billion a year has already been reached in 1988.

Nevertheless, capital recycling alone is not enough. Japan needs a global strategy for revitalizing the world economy. Together with expanding its ODA and other capital flows to the developing countries, it is essential that Japan promote imports from these countries, for if Japan can substantially increase its imports from the other Asian countries or the Latin American countries, there is a good chance they will spend part of their foreign exchange earnings on imports from the United States or Europe. Such a multilateral approach will thus stimulate Third World growth and at the same time alleviate bilateral friction among the industrial countries.

THE PACIFIC'S IMPORTANCE

As an Asia-Pacific nation, Japan has vital political and economic relations with the other countries of the region. This is a vast region that includes China and the rest of Northeast Asia, Southeast Asia, Oceania, and sometimes even the United States and Canada. Inspired by the formation of the European Common Market, the concept of Pacific economic co-operation was broached in the late 1960s, when the Pacific Trade and Development Conference (PAFTAD) was founded as a forum for discussion among economists from several countries of the region. About the same time, the Pacific Basin Economic Council (PBEC) was established with a primarily business membership. Both of these organizations are still alive, well, and active.

In 1978, Prime Minister Masayoshi Ohira of Japan made the Pacific Basin Community Concept one of his major policy planks and asked me to chair the study group on this concept. Late in November 1979, I was appointed Minister for Foreign Affairs, and in January 1980, I accompanied Prime Minister Ohira on an official visit to Australia and New Zealand. As a result of the discussion between Prime Ministers Ohira and Fraser, it was agreed that Australia would host a seminar on Pacific Community at the Australian National University (ANU) that September under the chairmanship of ANU Chancellor Sir John Henry Crawford. At the same time, there were still fears within ASEAN that the larger countries would dominate Pacific co-operation and that this would be detrimental to the long-term development of ASEAN, which was formed by Southeast Asian countries themselves in 1968. However, Thailand's Deputy Prime Minister Thanat Kohman took the initiative in enabling the second Seminar to be held in Bangkok, at which time the conference's name was changed to the Pacific Economic Co-operation Conference (PECC), and subsequent meetings have been held in Bali, Indonesia (third), in Seoul, Republic of Korea (fourth),in Vancouver, Canada (fifth), and last year, 1988, in Osaka, Japan (sixth).

PECC has 15 countries and regions as full members: the six ASEAN countries (Brunei, Indonesia, Malaysia, the Philippines, Singapore, and Thailand), five Pacific industrial countries (Australia, Canada, Japan, New Zealand, and United States), the Republic of Korea, the Pacific island countries, China, and Chinese Taipei. A tripartite organization of government officials, scholars, and business people, PECC has formed task forces on the economic outlook, trade, investment, energy and mineral resources, livestock and grain, and fisheries. These were supplemented at the Osaka meeting with the formation of study groups on transport, telecommunications, and tourism (the triple-T), forestry resource management, and the Pacific island countries. At present, Chile, Peru, Mexico, and the Soviet Union have applied for full membership in the PECC, but the PECC Standing Committee has decided to defer any decision on new members until the November 1989 meeting in Wellington, New Zealand.

Including the NIEs, China, the ASEAN countries, and Japan, the Asic-Pacific region is one of the fastest-growing and most dynamic economic regions in the world. The general description used for economic development in this region is that it is development in "the flying geese pattern". In that sense, it has been an area of consecutive takeoffs and catching-up, starting with Japan's rapid growth in the 1960s, moving on to the rapid growth of the Asian NIEs in the 1970s, and seeing very rapid growth in Thailand, Malaysia, and other ASEAN countries as well as in China recently. The economies of this region are gradually shifting from a vertical division of labour between the industrial and the developing economies to an horizontal integration in the regional economy. And with this shift, there has been an increase in multilateral trade and investment within the region, with Japan becoming an important absorber for products from the other Asian countries and an important source of capital and technology for them. It is clear that the Western Pacific has the potential, in time, to become a very powerful regional economic zone. However, as I noted earlier, regionalism is not the preferred way to go. Instead, the countries of this region would rather opt for globalism for a number of simple yet persuasive reasons, foremost among them the fact that regionalism could well be devisive at a time when our shared concern with global issues demands co-operation among all peoples everywhere.

GLOBAL ECONOMIC MANAGEMENT IN THE 1990s

by

Mahbub Ul HAQ

While considering the challenge of global economic management in the 1990s, we must take note of at least five distinct trends which have emerged on the international economic scene over the past quarter of a century (1).

GLOBALISATION OF MARKETS

The world economic and financial markets have become increasingly integrated over the last 25 years, thereby increasing the interdependence of nations. During this period, world trade has quadrupled while world output has tripled, implying that the world's economic integration increased by one-third. In the case of the United States, long used to economic independence, its international openness more than doubled: US trade in goods and services as a percentage of GNP expanded from 6 per cent in 1970 to over 12 per cent by 1980. By 1981, developing countries were purchasing 41 per cent of US exports, vividly demonstrating how the prosperity of the United States had become interlinked with the prosperity of the developing world. These trends towards globalisation were even stronger in the financial markets. In 1987, around $420 billion crossed the world's foreign exchanges every day. Economic tremors in one part of the world could easily communicate to all parts of the world. Even the economically powerful nations no longer enjoyed the luxury of making domestic economic policy decisions in isolation; they had perforce to consider the external policy environment and the likely impact of their own decisions on this environment.

DEMOCRATISATION OF GLOBAL ECONOMIC POWER

There has been a major dilution in the central role of a single country's acting as the global economic leader and co-ordinating global management through its quietly accepted hegemony. The United Kingdom played this role in the period between the two World Wars and the United States after World War II. But the US relative economic and financial strength has considerably declined and it has

51

already emerged as the world's largest debtor, with a debt of over $1 trillion. The US budget and trade deficits have been very large in recent years; its currency is weak and unstable; the accumulating "dollar overhang" is a matter of international concern; and the United States' contribution and voice in international resource flows and in Bretton Woods institutions has increasingly weakened. At the same time, other economic leaders have emerged on the international scene with enhanced strength. The European Common Market now encompasses 320 million people, with larger economic output than the United States. The EEC has been seriously considering the setting up of a European Central Bank and common currency and is also committed to the complete integration of its internal markets by 1992. At the same time, Japan has emerged as the world's largest creditor, with net assets abroad of over $300 billion by the end of 1988. OPEC and some newly industrialised economies (NIEs) have also acquired enhanced economic power over the last 25 years, despite their recent troubles. Thus, economic and financial power is more diffused today than 25 years ago, with increased challenges to the US economic dominance. The basic dilemma has been that no country other than the United States is yet strong enough to take over the mantle of economic leadership while the relative decline of the US economic and financial power increasingly inhibits it from playing the role of an economic manager in a world that has become increasingly interdependent.

ENTRY OF THE SOCIALIST BLOC

Another development with profound international implications is the recent entry of the socialist bloc, notably the Soviet Union and China, into the global markets. Both the Soviet Union and China need to import technology and must increase their exports to pay for this technology. One implication of the acceptance of market mechanisms by these countries is that international markets must also adjust to accommodate their interests. Another implication is that global economic management in the 1990s will not be possible without their full participation in such management. While Bretton Woods institutions have not fully integrated the concerns of the socialist bloc in their policies or in their management over the last 25 years, it is difficult to conceive of a successful restructuring of these institutions in the 1990s without the inclusion of the Soviet Union and its allies.

MARGINALISATION OF SOME DEVELOPING COUNTRIES

Contrary to popular belief, the relative income gap between the developed and the developing world has narrowed -- not widened -- over the last 25 years. During this period, the developing countries have managed unprecedented economic growth which has increased their relative share in real gross world product from 15 per cent in 1960 to 21 per cent in 1982. Many of these countries also became major participants in the expanding world trading system: their share of global manufactured exports increased from only 7 per cent in 1965 to over 16 per cent by 1985. However, this economic progress was unevenly shared, with much of Africa and South Asia not fully benefiting from global prosperity. The number of people living in absolute poverty still exceeds one billion despite the spectacular economic growth record of the developing world as a whole in the past quarter of a century. There has been a marginalisation of some developing countries and of a vast number of human beings in the process of global growth. A challenge for global economic management in the 1990s is to ensure more evenly distributed growth and to devise international policies and institutions to bring along at a faster pace those countries and people who are not yet in a position to participate fully in the global market mechanism and the world growth process.

DECLINE IN THE ROLE OF THE INTERNATIONAL ECONOMIC MANAGERS

At a time when world economic interdependence has increased and the need for global economic management is greater, not only the relative role of the United States has declined but there has also been a major weakening of the Bretton Woods institutions which were set up over 40 years ago to perform precisely such a role.

The role of the IMF has been greatly reduced by the breakdown of the fixed exchange rate system in the early 1970s; the impotence of the SDR mechanism, whose functioning was stymied by the United States even when its own role as world's central banker was weakening; the emergence of a separate European Monetary System (EMS) and monetary non-discipline in the United States, as manifested in an overvalued dollar and high interest rates; and the complete inability of the IMF to influence the United States monetary and fiscal policy decisions. It was not surprising, therefore, that the IMF role declined rapidly from a global monetary manager to a somewhat harsh policeman for a few harassed developing countries which had no other alternative but to turn to the IMF.

During the same period, the role of the World Bank has also witnessed a decline, especially in recent years. The developing countries now receive a negative net transfer of resources from the developed world. Yet the World Bank has neither been able to reverse this trend nor to compensate for it through its own spending. In fact, during the 1980s, as the debt problem of Latin America deepened and what started as a liquidity crisis slowly turned into a development crisis, the role of the World Bank was quite curious during this process: its own net transfers to Latin America became negative. Again, while the World Bank is rightly concentrating its limited concessional IDA resources on Africa, it is being obliged to increase the future debt problem of India and Pakistan by offering excessively large hard-term IBRD lending to these countries which are still below a per capita income of $400. The recent role of the World Bank, in a state of negative resource transfers to poor countries, is a far cry from what was originally envisaged.

In the field of trade, the GATT has now jurisdiction over only 5 to 7 per cent of global economic activity. While the GATT covers 80 per cent of merchandise trade flows, its rules do not extend at present to agriculture, services, textiles and capital flows. What is more important, the degree of trade protectionism has increased over the last 25 years, particularly the role of quantitative restrictions (QRs). The share of imports covered by QRs increased from 5 per cent in 1980 to 18 per cent in 1986 in the United States. The average nominal rate of protection for 13 major agricultural products rose from 41 per cent in 1960 to 83 per cent in 1980 in Japan. According to a study compiled by the World Bank, the weighted average prices paid to agricultural producers in early 1980 were 2.5 times the world market price in Japan, 1.5 times in the European Community and 1.2 times in the United States. This kind of agricultural protectionism has been disastrous for the prospects of agricultural exports from developing countries and yet the GATT has been unable to do anything about it. The ongoing Uruguay Round Trade Negotiations seek to change this state of affairs and would considerably strengthen the scope of GATT activities by enlarging it to include agricultural, services, textile, intellectual property and investment flows, but it is too early to predict the success of these negotiations.

Thus the essential challenges for global economic management in the 1990s are:

i) World interdependence has increased, necessitating a greater degree of global economic management;

ii) The role of the United States as a world economic leader has declined, with many countries beginning to challenge this role but as yet not in a position to acquire the mantle of leadership;

iii) Global markets of the 1990s must also accommodate the rising interest of the socialist bloc and special needs of the poorest developing countries; and

iv) When a vacuum of economic leadership is developing, the role of Bretton Woods institutions as international economic managers has also considerably weakened and they stand in need of a fundamental restructuring.

Given this perspective, how best can we manage the challenge of global economic management in the 1990s?

We face a curious dilemma here. The logic of rapid globalisation of markets points towards a greater role for Bretton Woods institutions in global management in the years ahead. Yet the political trends of the 1990s have led so far towards greater bilateralism and less internationalism. If we are to avoid a period of global uncertainty and instability, the logic and the politics must be brought together.

This is the time, I believe, that we should go back to the original proposals of Lord Keynes for establishment of key international economic institutions for global management. Bretton Woods institutions require both a thorough review in the light of their past experience as well as a fundamental restructuring to meet future global challenges.

The purpose of this paper is not to offer a blueprint for the restructuring of the Bretton Woods institutions but only to stress the need for a new vision for the 1990s. However, before concluding, let me define a few questions which must be answered while considering any restructuring of the Bretton Woods institutions:

i) Can we politically convince the United States that its predominant role in the post-war world economy is coming to an end, and that US interests will be better served through the evolution of a greater degree of global management through international economic institutions rather than through periodic, *ad hoc* big power economic summits?

ii) How can the World Bank play a more decisive role in international resource transfers when its own share in these transfers is less than 2 per cent, when international capital movements are largely outside its control and when external assistance is still viewed by many countries as an extension of their bilateral power?

iii) How can the over $1 trillion debt problem of the developing countries be handled without writing off a major portion of these debts, preferably through an International Debt Refinancing Facility under the joint supervision of the World Bank and the IMF? Which countries' lenders are to bear the cost of such a write-off and over what time period?

iv) How can the IMF be strengthened to play the role of an international central bank without exercising more control over exchange rates and interest rates in the developed countries and without having a greater mandate for the creation and regulation of SDRs?

v) How can the GATT become more effective until agriculture, textiles, services, investment flows and all trade-related issues are brought under one umbrella, as is being tried in the ongoing Uruguay Round negotiations?

vi) How are the poorest nations and people to be assisted in a global framework where existing mechanisms often lead to the enrichment of the haves?

vii) How is the socialist bloc to be integrated into the global markets and international economic decision making?

These are not easy questions but their thorough discussion is vital in defining the parameters of global economic management in the 1990s.

No long-term reform is possible without restructuring and strengthening the international institutions.

First, we must go back to Lord Keynes' conception of an international central bank. The United States will not be acceptable in this role for much longer, as the world is becoming too multipolar and diverse (as the increasing significance of the socialist bloc indicates) and many emerging financial powers do not like global financial decisions mortgaged to the national policies of a single country. Nor is it prudent for the United States to accept national obligations -- e.g. to inflate or to deflate its economy -- to suit international compulsions. We should now invest considerable intellectual capital in designing an international central bank that can truly serve global needs.

Second, we need an International Trade Organisation (ITO) on the pattern envisioned by Lord Keynes many decades ago. In a way, the proposed restructuring of GATT under the Uruguay Round will achieve this purpose. Once services, textiles, agriculture and trade-related investment flows are brought within the framework of the GATT rules and the functioning of the GATT system is further strengthened, we would have moved very close to the original concept of ITO. There is presently a shared anxiety on the part of developed and developing economies to move in this direction. The gap, however, lies in the non-involvement of socialist countries without whose full participation the Bretton Woods institutions cannot be restructured to suit the needs of the 1990s.

Third, there is need for considerable restructuring in the role of the World Bank and regional development banks -- much larger resource base, different and more automatic forms of capital replenishment, additional windows for debt refinancing facilities, and so on. At the same time, the United Nations system should strengthen its emphasis on the human dimension in development and supplement the Bretton Woods institutions through national dialogue on investment in achievable human goals.

It is my conviction that institutions, rather than *ad hoc* policy initiatives, shape world events in the long run. We have given too little attention to the restructuring of global institutions even when the globe has "shrunk" and imperatives of global economic management are compelling us in that direction. Let us not wait for another world crisis to inspire our dormant energies or another Lord Keynes to beckon us towards enlightened partnership. Let us undertake this task of reshaping the institutions for global economic management now, in slow, measured steps, before it is too late.

NOTES AND REFERENCES

1. This analysis draws upon the empirical evidence presented in BER-GESTEN, C. Fred *America in the World Economy: A Strategy for the 1990s.* (IIE, 1988) and SEWELL, John W. *et al, Growth, Exports and Jobs in a Changing World Economy* (ODC, 1988).

DISCUSSANT'S CONTRIBUTION

by

Enrique IGLESIAS

The subject proposed by Louis Emmerij is very attractive but also very complex. I doubt that we shall arrive at a final answer today. It will be an ongoing subject for discussion in the period ahead.

In essence, when reading the three very interesting papers by Mahbub Ul Haq, Colin Bradford and Saburo Okita, there is one key word, namely "interdependence". The nature of interdependence, the imbalances of present interdependences, and the organisation of future interdependence are the three major areas in the papers before us. When discussing the nature of interdependence, the new phase that the world of today is passing through comes out quite clearly in the papers, particularly when looking at trade or financial flows -- the most dynamic elements of present global interdependence.

This year is the fortieth anniversary of a very important paper for Latin Americans -- I would say for the whole world -- the Prebisch Report of 1949 which represents a manifesto for intellectual leadership in the region, both for the school of thinkers who follow its ideas and for those who oppose them. It was a major contribution to organised thinking in Latin America and many other parts of the Third World. I remember reading in that paper about interdependence and I wonder what the difference is in the way he saw interdependence in 1949 and how we see it today. In essence, when reading Dr. Prebisch's remarks on the topic, one has to remember that there were two ingredients in his philosophy: that interdependence in the past had made the development of Latin America extremely unbalanced; and that therefore something has to be done to combine interdependence with doses of independence. This was the prevailing view over many years in the closed world of the 1950s we used to live in. Many things came out of this manifesto. One was a line which moved into dependency theory. The other was the continuation of efforts to improve the management of interdependence on the international plane.

I recall that in 1989 we celebrate yet another anniversary: that of the first UNCTAD in 1964 which, incidentally, was very strongly influenced by Third World people and particularly by Prebisch again. One has to remember that an important ingredient of dependency theory in those days was the idea that some kind of international voluntarism should be introduced into international relations in order to narrow the gaps between North and South. I think it is important to remember that we have been dealing with this issue for almost four decades. However, it is obvious that something has changed in the concept of interdependence today.

To my mind, a new aspect of the current way of looking at interdependence is the growing acceptance of its inevitability. *Perestroika* has probably been one of the latest pointers in this direction. Another lesson is that interdependence is not necessarily bad in all cases and some countries have done well in managing it. A third lesson, and one that is very important at a time when we are trying to revise our development approach at the national level, is that the management of interdependence must not be done only through international voluntarism, but that there is an important contribution to be made through the way we handle our internal development models.

There exist disturbing major imbalances in the system of interdependence today. One is the imbalance stemming from different rates of growth. Is "Sustainable" a useful concept when countries are growing at different rates, and particularly, is "sustainable" applicable when there are many Third World countries whose development gap is increasing instead of decreasing.

Interdependence in the area of trade produces another intolerance: large surpluses and huge deficits. Imbalances also arise in the realm of savings: there are countries which save a lot, compared with others who do not save or save very little -- incidentally a major cause of the high real interest rates in the world of today. There is a shortage of savings in the world as a whole and a shortage of the sources where those savings can be tapped, and finally, there are major imbalances in the debt field. This is the major headache for many of our countries.

Looking at these imbalances in an interdependent world, one probably must conclude that not all imbalances are by definition bad. Some imbalances can be good if they provide incentives, as Louis Emmerij says in his introduction paper, for the process of development. What impresses me more is the resilience of the system to live under high risk conditions. This does not mean that these imbalances must be allowed to become unmanageable. For the time being, however, I am neither optimistic nor pessimistic. There is a growing capacity to manage these imbalances in the present situation of interdependence.

Another issue is the organisation of interdependence. There are clear references to two trends which are presently growing in what this Symposium calls a multipolar world. In essence, there is one tendency -- clearly stated in the Uruguay Round -- which is to encourage the building of a world with predictable, open and reliable trade relations, resulting in a more open economy. We all hope that this is going to be the major result of the Uruguay round of GATT.

On the other hand there is a movement towards regional blocs -- the North American bloc, the European bloc, the Asian bloc. The question is, who and what is going to prevail? Is the bloc system an end in itself or is it an instrument for a future integrated world? The answer to this question is crucial, particularly to the countries of the Third World because the forces of attraction of these blocs are very powerful and it is difficult to imagine developing countries, avoiding being drawn into one or the other.

Finally, it would be pertinent to make some remarks on what these three things mean -- the nature of interdependence, imbalances, and the organisation of trade -- for us in the developing world. Perhaps we must organise a seminar in the coming years on: Are we moving to one single model of economic organisation at the national level?" You may ask the World Bank to produce the background paper. In any case, we must all try to revise our development strategies in the light of this inevitable interdependence in which we are operating. My personal feeling is that whatever kind of approach we may have to development strategies there are two or three concepts that have to be stressed if we want to manage our interdependence with the rest of the world properly. One is the question of efficiency -- this used to be a tricky word in past years but I think more and more there is no way to manage interdependence in the world without a maximum level of efficiency, both economic and social efficiency. Put differently, the whole question of limits to voluntarism is something that should be addressed by any economic model in the Third World if we want to build the management of interdependence in a proper manner.

The second question is that of flexibility -- if one has to give a prize to countries in the modern world to manage interdependence it is to those who have the highest degree of flexibility in the management of their relations with the rest of the world, and in that respect I must say that some countries are doing quite well.

The third element is the integration of the countries of the South. I am speaking as a Latin American who has for many many years tried to push integration schemes. I now find that we must redefine our strategies of integration with the rest of the world -- the question of integration takes on a new dimension. This category of analysis which has been so much criticized in many quarters becomes now a new instrument of management in the kind of interpendence we are facing today. It is not the same kind of integration we focused on in the past. It must be more flexible. I believe that this is a time when the three pieces: efficiency, flexibility and integration must take on a more active role in the organisation of our economies in order to manage interdependence in a positive way.

DISCUSSANT'S CONTRIBUTION

by

PU Shan

It is generally recognised that in an increasingly interdependent world economy, globalism and multilateralism are preferable to regionalism and bilateralism, but with the changes of relative strength of the major economic powers, a tendency towards multipolar economic groupings is perhaps inevitable. If these groups increase their openness in external economic relations at the same time as they are more integrated internally, they may well be beneficial to the world economy as a whole, as Colin Bradford has shown in his paper, and thus serve as a useful step toward a more globalised and better integrated world. However, there are worrisome indications that regionalism and bilateralism may instead lead to a more divided world.

As Saburo Okita points out, the world economy is beset with serious disequilibriums in spite of its recent sustained recovery and expansion. The United States has been financing a large part of its huge fiscal deficits by inflows of foreign capital. This has led to a massive trade deficit and a distinct protectionist tendency in the United States. It has also aggravated the debt problems of many developing countries by crowding them out of the capital market and raising the real interest rates, which resulted in an extraordinary reverse flow of capital. Under such circumstances, it is a legitimate concern that regionalism and bilateralism may become more and more exclusive and closed to the outside, and thus have an unfavourable effect on the world economy as a whole and on the developing countries in particular, especially on the lowest-income or the least-developed countries.

In order to alleviate such disequilibriums, it is often emphasized that the United States should reduce its fiscal deficits and the surplus countries, especially Japan, should stimulate their domestic demand. Efforts have been made by both the United States and Japan in the required directions, with Japan perhaps more successful in increasing demand than the United States has been in reducing deficits. In view of the urgent need of developing countries for development capital, however, it seems that more emphasis should be placed on recycling the international surplus to the developing countries rather than on the stimulation of domestic demand in the surplus countries. Mr. Okita has long argued admirably for a Japanese initiative in recycling international surpluses for world development, culminating in the WIDER Report of 1987. He mentions in his paper that the

WIDER Report target of $25 billion a year was already reached by Japan in 1988. The recent efforts of the Japanese government should certainly be fully recognised. But it seems that there are still many excellent proposals in the WIDER Report which have not been fully implemented -- for instance, the proposed target of annual lending and the specific mechanisms for interest subsidies and exchange risk protection. In any case, the WIDER Report certainly deserves more international support, including that of the Japanese government.

The recycling of international surpluses, though extremely important, could not by itself resolve the difficulties faced by the developing countries and restore a virtuous circle in the world economy, as the experience of the recycling of the petroleum dollars has amply demonstrated. It will have to be supplemented by a more favourable international trade and investment environment. This is also essential even for the NIEs, if their further development is to be realised and sustained.

It is true that there has been an accelerated tendency of uneven growth among developing countries, but the vast majority of them are still placed in a disadvantageous position under the present international economic order, as Colin Bradford and Mahbub Ul Haq have both pointed out.

Mr. Okita mentions "the flying geese pattern" of development in which "consecutive takeoffs and catching-up" take place among countries at different levels of development. With rapid technological progress, the possibility of such a pattern of development does exist and since the substantial appreciation of the Japanese yen, some such process can already be observed in the Asia-Pacific region. For such a development pattern to be successful and sustainable, however, it is essential that the developed countries allow better access to their markets, facilitate structural adjustments within their own economies, and provide technology transfers to developing countries on easier terms. The present situation certainly leaves much to be desired. Even the NIEs are seriously threatened by the increasing tendency of protectionism. In fact, with their extremely high dependence on exports, they are perhaps more vulnerable than many other countries if the world is divided into regional blocs.

The world, of course, does not have to be divided into regional fortresses. But there is a real danger, and to prevent such an outcome requires co-operation and co-ordination, not just of the G7, G5 or G2, but of all countries and peoples everywhere, as emphasized by all the three papers presented at our session.

Chapter III

THE CHALLENGE FOR THE NEWLY INDUSTRIALISING ECONOMIES IN THE 1990s: SUSTAINABLE GROWTH WITH EQUITY AND SHARED INTERNATIONAL RESPONSIBILITY

LATIN AMERICA AND THE CHALLENGE OF THE 1990s

by

Helio JAGUARIBE

THE TURN OF THE CENTURY

There is a growing consensus among students of contemporary affairs concerning some basic characteristics of the world as we approach the end of the 20th century. Enumerating these main characteristics, as in all such exercises, requires an unavoidable margin of discretion. Such a list, moreover, will differ according to the focus one has: demographic, economic, political, etc. Considering the question from a broad economic and political perspective I would suggest that most analysts would agree, without excluding other aspects, in stressing the seven following traits:

i) A trend towards peaceful East-West relations since the second half of the 1980s. The stable persistence of a strategic equilibrium between the superpowers combined with the new policies of Gorbachev and the convenience, for both powers, reducing their military expenses, have contributed to a new understanding between the United States and the Soviet Union. The treaty on intermediate strategic missiles and the subsequent developments towards the reduction of armaments and tension, are indications of such a trend.

ii) The gradual emergence of the post-industrial society based on cybernetics, new sources of energy and new materials, in the context of a scientific-technological global economy, in an increasingly interdependent world. This economy is ever more determined by high technology, with the declining importance of the roles of cheap labour or abundant raw materials which formerly presented decisive advantages in international competition.

iii) The trend towards the formation of large regional markets with protectionist implications. The European Community will be a single regional market after 1992. The United States and Canada are rapidly proceeding to form another single regional market. Japan is opening special relationships with the ASEAN countries and the Eastern

NIEs. The Soviet-East European system is trying to develop its own economic integration.

iv) The changing role of the State, reducing the area of its intervention and direct interference in the productive process -- including in the Soviet Union -- and increasing its societal co-ordinating functions (the case of Japan is typical), like the conductor of an orchestra.

v) A more effective transnationalisation of the multinationals, increasing commercial competition among the international branches of the same enterprise and selectively opening their technological black boxes to their more advanced host countries.

vi) Aggravation of the distance between North and South, with the resulting trend towards a two-track world economy, maintaining most of the Third World societies in conditions of stagnation and backwardness and providing fair conditions of development for the advanced societies, including the newcomers to higher development, such as the Eastern NIEs.

vii) Shift to the main centre of economic dynamism from the North Atlantic to the Pacific basin, including the United States (total trade in 1983 in the Pacific of $183 billion, against $113 billion in the Atlantic), with the fast emergence of Eastern NIEs, such as South Korea, Taiwan, Hong Kong and Singapore, in the first generation and, in the second, China and most of the ASEAN countries.

A full discussion of each of these aspects would surpass the limits of this brief study. A quick look at the Eastern NIEs should, however, suffice for our purposes. Not only because they represent the most successful examples of rapid and competitive development but also because since they come from much lower levels in the 1960s than the major Latin American countries, they have achieved much better results.

The successful cases in the Far East are very different, both in size and in their social and political regimes. In Table 1 some basic indicators are presented for six of these countries.

The picture would be far more complex if it were to include China, which achieved annual growth rates in 1970, 1980, and 1987 of 5.8, 7.8 and 9.5, respectively. Its exports , of which 63.6 per cent are manufactures, increased from $2.3 billion in 1970 to $39.5 billion in 1987. China, however, would require a special treatment and cannot be discussed here.

Considering the ASEAN countries (1) -- excepting the Philippines, which has not yet started its development and including the first generation of NIEs (Hong Kong, Singapore, South Korea and Taiwan) (2), it can be observed that from the late 1950s to the early 1960s, these countries have consistently maintained and effectively implemented comprehensive projects of national development.

These projects have included the provision of universal basic education and higher training, in good international universities, for broad groups of selected students. The countries have evolved large projects of social development, from agrarian reform to urban social programmes. They have started, particularly in the case of the larger countries such as South Korea, with selective projects of basic industrialisation. The aim, from the beginning, has been to maximize exports, first of primary products, then gradually, of manufactures, and finally of high-tech electronic equipment. They operate free market regimes, with strong participation of foreign corporations, mostly Japanese and American, but under national guidance and according to a national programme. Most of them have been ruled until recently by enlightened military-based autocracies and are now becoming welfare democracies.

Appropriate development programmes, consistently implemented, supported by hard work, within flexible conditions, combining foreign capital and technology with national guidance, free market practices of production with state controls and until recently, in most of these countries, authoritarian rule, providing discipline and continuity, are the factors that have brought about their success.

Their strong dependence on exports, although supported by very competitive production, is a matter for concern because of the risks of higher protectionism which could follow the consolidation of the regional markets over the next decade. On the other hand, such a trend would compel Japan to strengthen its association with the ASEAN countries and to form an Eastern Common Market with them, preserving their room for export and development.

THE LATIN AMERICAN CASE

Latin America, like Asia, is too large a geo-cultural concept to allow any operational use. An economic and political approach to the region as a whole first requires differentiation between three groups of countries:

i)   The special case of Mexico, inserted into the North American complex;

ii) The case of Central America and the Caribbean, characterized by the diminutive size of the countries concerned, by their generally low level of development and by their broad involvement in what remains of the East-West confrontation; and

iii) South America.

South America, in its turn, is also too broad a cluster of countries to be treated as a whole. For one thing, there are decisive differences resulting from levels of development and size varying from Brazil to Bolivia, in terms of development, or to Uruguay, in terms of size. For another, relatively recent events in some countries have deeply affected national unity and the extent of the effective sovereignty of the national State over its own territory and society. This is the case, to different degrees, of countries such as Bolivia, Colombia and Peru, which have been profoundly disturbed by the perverse alliance between drug traffickers and revolutionary guerrillas. Barely half of Colombia and Peru are under a relatively stable control by the government, with even their own capitals subject to continuous harassment by these forces.

Given such diversity of conditions, a discussion of the Latin American countries must be correspondingly diverse. It would not be compatible with the limits of this brief study fully to deal with each of the typologically relevant groups of countries of the region. For our purposes, it will suffice to consider, in a succinct way, six Latin American countries:

    i)   Argentina, Brazil and Mexico as the three large ones;

    ii)   Chile and Venezuela as two middle-sized ones; and

    iii) Uruguay, as a small but socially advanced and economically balanced country.

These countries present a sufficient number of common characteristics for them to be compared with each other. They are, together with Colombia, the more developed countries of the region. In contrast to Colombia, however, they maintain full control of their national State over their own territory. Table 2 presents some of their main indicators. Notwithstanding their common characteristics, these countries also present important differences, among which three require special mention.

The first feature to be stressed is their level of social homogeneity. At one extreme are two very homogeneous societies: Argentina and Uruguay; at the opposite extreme, we find the case of two very heterogeneous societies, Brazil and Mexico. Chile and Venezuela are intermediary cases situated closer to the homogeneous extreme.

The second relevant difference concerns the political regime. Chile is still under a military dictatorship, although the regime will probably keep its promise, after the recent plebiscite went against Pinochet, to have free elections by the end of 1989. Mexico has been a particular case of partial democracy, based on a dominant party supporting an autocratic presidency. Recent events involving the disputed election of the new president, Carlos Salinas, whose mandate began on 1st December 1988, are likely to introduce a multi-party system. Venezuela is a stable democracy. Argentina and Brazil have recently recovered their democratic systems, the latter still passing through the last phase of its democratic transition, with presidential elections to be held on 15th November 1989.

A final significant difference to be noted in these countries, is their rather different rates of inflation. Brazil is the worst case, followed by Argentina. Mexico has made significant gains against its inflation. Chile, the best case, has 20 per cent per annum while Uruguay and Venezuela have more than twice that.

These six Latin American countries achieved -- although unevenly -- very substantial development from the 1950s to the end of the 1970s. In general terms, they were agrarian societies by the end of the Second War, with incipient industrialisation in Brazil, and became predominantly industrial societies three decades later.

Brazil has been the most successful case. Its huge domestic market -- the largest in Latin America -- was particularly favourable for a development model based on industrialisation by import substitution. Throughout the period, the country has also maintained a consistent policy of industrial development. From 1965 to 1980 industrial production grew at an annual rate of about 10 per cent, with a GDP annual growth of 9 per cent. Its exports have increased from about $2 billion to more than $20 billion, of which more than 60 per cent are manufactures. Its degree of economic self-sufficiency is one of the highest in the world; imports represent only 6 per cent of GDP, and half of this is accounted for by oil. This figure demonstrates how large is the spectrum of domestic production, covering almost all of the necessities of the country.

Mexico and Argentina, at lower levels of industrialisation, have achieved similar results. Mexico's industrial growth, from 1965 to 1980, presented an annual average of 7.6 per cent, with a GDP annual growth of 6.5 per cent, while Argentina had less significant annual growth rates for the same period: an average of 3.3 per cent for industry and of 3.4 per cent for the GDP. Chile and Venezuela, more dependent on mineral exports (copper and oil, respectively) and Uruguay on grains, have obtained less significant industrial development and overall growth. Chile's GDP annual growth has been only 1.9 per cent against 2.4 per cent for Uruguay and 5.2 per cent for Venezuela.

The bright picture presented by these countries, even if it was uneven by the end of the 1970s, was severely damaged through the next decade. The lost decade, as the 1980s are called in Latin America, was a negative one by the unfavourable combination of the effects of international recession and foreign indebtedness, the oil crisis, wrong economic decisions and, with the exception of Mexico and Venezuela, the suppression of the democratic institutions.

The comparison between the six Far Eastern countries and the six Latin American ones is extremely unfavourable to the latter during the 1980s. From 1980 to 1986 the annual growth of GDP was negative for Argentina (-0.8), Uruguay (-2.6) and Venezuela (-0.9). Chile had a zero growth and Mexico only registered 0.4 per cent. Brazil is the only country with some positive growth, but then of only 2.7 per cent against an annual average of 9 per cent for the 1965-80 period.

In contrast to the Latin American countries, the Far Eastern ones, with the exception of the Philippines, throughout the period of crisis have maintained rather favourable annual growth rates: 5.2 per cent for South Korea, 6 per cent for Hong Kong, 4.8 per cent for Malaysia, 4.8 per cent for Thailand and 5.3 per cent for Singapore.

71

The conclusions to be drawn are simple. The Far Eastern countries were able, during the 1980s, to reap the benefits of their former efforts in education and technological development. The Latin American countries, although having achieved a reasonable level of domestic industrialisation continued, with the exception of Brazil, to be primary exporters, severely affected by the deterioration of the terms of trade. As for Brazil, which in any case fared better than the other Latin American countries, the effects and constraints imposed by the foreign debt curtailed the domestic level of the economy, leaving economic growth excessively dependent on exports which did not represent a sufficiently large amount of its GDP to be able to sustain its overall development.

THE CHALLENGE OF THE 1990s

There is a broad understanding, among the elites of the six Latin American countries under study, that they urgently need to resume their development and, to do this, to introduce large-scale reforms. The next decade will determine their future prospects for a long time to come. If serious changes are not introduced, both domestically and in their international relationships, they will not be able to overcome their current stagnation. They will join, for an undetermined period, the backward countries of the world. Worse than that, the five democracies of the group will not be able to manage their social and political tensions in a democratic and consensual way. And Chile's probable return to democracy would lack stability if unaccompanied by a more rapid economic growth.

Economic growth, for these Latin American countries, requires:

i)   Higher levels of savings and investment;

ii)   The general modernisation of their economies and societies;

iii) Participation in processes of high technology; and

iv)   International competitiveness for their main exports, including a predominance of manufactures and a significant proportion of high-tech items.

To achieve such results, however implies, to begin with, the prior solution of their current conjunctural crisis. In addition, important social reforms and relevant changes in their economic policies will be necessary.

We have seen that the conjunctural crisis of the Latin American countries is dominated as a rule by very high inflation rates. Other factors notwithstanding, such inflation is predominantly both a direct and indirect effect of their huge foreign debts. Compelled to transfer about 5 per cent of the GDP annually to foreign creditors, they cannot curb their inflation without provoking dramatic recession. Mexico, under the De la Madrid government which came to an end 1st December 1988, suffered an impoverishment of about 30 per cent and the same rate of unemployment in order to reduce its inflation from about 15 per cent per

72

month to a monthly rate of less than 1 per cent. Excessive public expenditure due to the bad management, particularly of state enterprises, and to clientele politics leading to public appointments of political supporters is also a major factor of inflation.

Controlling the conjunctural problems of such States in socially tolerable conditions therefore consists, on the one hand, in obtaining more favourable conditions for their foreign debt and, on the other, in overcoming their clientele politics in order to eliminate parasitic public expenditures and to attain higher levels of efficiency in the management of the State. reaching such results requires an uneasy combination of sound economic decisions, governmental firmness, broad national support and favourable international arrangements.

The structural problems confronting the Latin American states have become extremely grave because they have been the object, for a long time, of continuous postponements. In the last decade, a protracted conjectural crisis has prevented governments from doing anything other than trying to manage their inflation. Political and social constraints, on the other hand, persistently divert these governments from confronting their social problems. An important place is taken, among these constraints, by ideological views inappropriate for a sound approach to those problems, but still enjoying wide public support.

The left-right controversy, in Latin America, is still heavily loaded with obsolete views. Important sectors of the left, though a minority, still support state forms of socialism and revolutionary means to implant it. Populism, with its easy distributive prescriptions and proposals to maintain and expand inefficient state enterprises, as well as its uncritical opposition to any foreign investment, retains a wide appeal, which tends to grow rapidly in times of crisis. At the opposite pole, a 19th century policy of *laissez faire* proclaims the necessity of reducing the state to its gendarme functions of the past century and, as much for ideological as for pragmatic reasons, opposes any tax reform able to balance the state budget and to provide sufficient funds for indispensable infrastructure and social applications.

Overcoming the structural problems of these countries requires the mobilisation of a new multi-class majority, of a centre-left leaning, able to support a socially concerned project of modernisation and development, based on a socially regulated free market economy, maximising efficiency, within the framework of social democracy. The Latin American problem, therefore, although significantly conditioned by the international environment, is primarily a matter of domestic politics. If this kind of new multi-class majority does not become mobilised in a not-too-distant future, the next decade will be a time of explosive crisis. Uncontrollable expectations, both from the masses and from the middle classes, will not be fulfilled by stagnant economies and inefficient states, generating social and political tensions that will not be manageable by consensual and democratic means.

Alternatively, the institution of modern social democracies in such countries, or at least in some of the larger ones, will provide the socio-political grounds for appropriate reforms and will produce fast rewards. As it can be seen in Table 2, countries such as Brazil, Mexico and Venezuela -- to mention the best examples -- have been able, in the recent past, to maintain very high annual rates of growth through a long period. Such capabilities would be recovered, if perhaps at a slightly lower pace, if these countries are led in socially concerned terms, to a new track of modernisation.

NOTES AND REFERENCES

1. Brunei, Indonesia, Malaysia, Philippines and Thailand.

2. Taiwan is not mentioned in Table 1 because it is not included in the list of countries of the World Bank.

BIBLIOGRAPHY

BALASSA, Bela *Los Paises de Industrializacion Reciente en la Economia Mundial,* translated to Spanish by Eduardo L. Suarez, Mexico, Fondo de Cultura Economica, 1988.

MONETA, Carlos J. "Corea del Sur y los Paises Asiaticos de Reciente Industrializacion en el Contexto de los Cambios del Sistema Economico Mundial -- Reflexiones para America Latina", *Estudios Internacionales,* Ano XXI, Enero, Marzo 1988, N. 81, pp 61-93.

WORLD BANK, *World Development Report 1988,* New York, Oxford University Press, 1988.

-------- *L'Etat du Monde, 1988-1989*, Paris, Edit. La Découverte, 1988.

INSTITUT FRANCAIS DES RELATIONS INTERNATIONALES *RAMSES 89,* Paris, Dunod, 1988.

Table 1

SIX EASTERN COUNTRIES: 1986

Item	Philippines	Hong Kong	Malaysia	Singapore	South Korea	Thailand
Population (million)	57.3	5.4	16.1	2.6	41.5	52.6
GDP (1)	30.5	32.2	27.6	17.3	91.8	41.8
GDP (percent)	5.6	6.91	1.83	7.41	2.37	8.10
GDP (annual growth)						
1965 to 1980	5.9	8.5	7.4	10.4	9.5	7.4
1980 to 1986	-1.0	6.0	4.8	5.3	8.2	4.8
Per cent gross domestic investment to GDP	13.0	23.0	25.0	40.0	29.0	21.0
Industry as per cent of GDP	32.0	29.0	--	38.0	42.0	30.0
Agriculture as per cent of GDP	26.0	--	--	1.0	12.0	17.0
Exports FOB (1)	4.7	35.4	13.9	22.5	34.7	8.8
Imports CIF (1)	5.4	35.4	10.8	25.5	31.5	9.2
Long-term debt (1)	28.2	--	19.6 (2)	2.1	29.1	18.0
Total interest (1)	1.1	--	1.4	--	2.9	1.0
Per cent debt/GDP	72.2	--	77.0	--	36.1	35.2
Service on exports	21.3	--	20.0	--	24.4	25.4
Inflation: annual average						
1965 to 1980	11.7	8.1	4.9	4.7	18.8	6.8
1980 to 1986	18.2	6.9	1.4	1.9	5.4	3.0

1. Billion US dollars.
2. Not including IMF credits and short-term debt.

Source: World Bank, World Development Report, 1988.

Table 2

SIX LATIN AMERICAN COUNTRIES: 1986

Item	Argentina	Brazil	Chile	Mexico	Uruguay	Venezuela
Population (million)	31.0	138.4	12.2	80.2	3.0	17.8
GDP (1)	69.8	206.7	16.8	127.1	53.0	56.0
GDP (percent)	2.35	1.81	1.32	1.86	1.90	2.92
GDP (annual growth)						
1965 to 1980	3.4	9.0	1.9	6.5	2.4	5.2
1980 to 1986	-0.8	2.7	0.0	0.4	-2.6	-0.9
Per cent of gross domestic investment to GDP	9.0	21.0	15.0	21.0	8.0	20.0
Industry as per cent of GDP	44.0	39.0	--	39.0	33.0	37.0
Agriculture as per cent of GDP	13.0	11.0	--	9.0	12.0	9.0
Exports FOB (1)	6.8	22.4	4.2	16.2	1.1	10.0
Imports CIF (1)	4.7	15.5	3.4	12.0	0.8	9.6
Long-term debt (1)	48.9	110.7	20.7	101.7	3.7	33.4
Total interest (1)	3.7	7.5	1.5	7.7	0.2	2.2
Per cent debt/GDP	51.7	37.6	120.1	76.1	47.1	66.9
Per cent service of exports	64.4	41.8	37.1	51.5	22.3	37.4
Inflation annual average						
1965 to 1980	78.3	31.3	129.9	13.1	57.8	8.7
1980 to 1986	316.2	157.1	20.2	63.7	50.4	8.7

---

1. Billion US dollars.

Source: World Bank, World Development Report, 1988.

TRADE AND DEVELOPMENT IN PACIFIC ASIA (1)

by

Yung Chul PARK

Throughout Pacific Asia encompassing ten economies (2) with a total population of more than 1.5 billion on a land mass of 13 132 thousand square kilometres, there is widespread and growing confidence that the economic centre of gravity is shifting to the region and that this shift signals the beginning of a Pacific era. The rapid growth and economic dynamism that the region has been able to generate for the last two decades has been the source of this confidence, and the relative economic decline of the United States has added to this belief.

The Pacific Asian region includes Japan -- a super economic power whose influence on international economic affairs rivals that of the United States -- the most populous nation of the world that is organising itself to develop and industrialise its economy; the four East Asian NIEs (henceforth EANIEs); and the ASEAN countries that have started successfully to promote exports of labour-intensive variety which take advantage of their rich resource base. There has been no letdown in the economic performance of the EANIEs. Since the late 1970s when China embarked on a course of economic liberalisation and market opening, it has recorded a phenomenal rate of growth of over 10 per cent per annum. Despite the slow recovery in commodity prices, in recent years the ASEAN countries have managed respectable rates of growth of 6 to 7 per cent by promoting exports of manufactured goods. Among the industrialised countries, Japan stands out as one of the most rapidly growing and stable economies.

This rapid growth has been accompanied by a number of significant changes in trade and industrial structure of Pacific Asian countries. These changes have in turn created powerful economic forces which may lead to closer economic co-operation and integration in the region. They could also further complicate the management of a global balance of payments adjustment should the United States, Japan, and Europe fail to pursue adjustment policies in co-ordination.

One of the most conspicuous developments has been the universal pursuit of export promotion policies with considerable success in the region. Except for Japan where economic growth has been led by an increase in domestic demand, in particular, investment in housing, other economies have powered their growth through an expansion of exports. Excluding Singapore, the three EANIEs have maintained annual rates of export growth of over 14 per cent for the last seven

years and saw exports grow by more than 35 per cent in 1987. Singapore has recovered from the 1985 recession and registered a 28 per cent increase in its export
earnings in 1987.

Among the ASEAN countries, Thailand has been a star performer, and Indonesia has mounted a successful export drive through a gradual deregulation of
the economy. Even the Philippines seems to be on its way to high and stable
growth as investment demand has been picking up. As in the past, the bulk of the
region's exports has been shipped to the US market. All of the EANIEs, China,
and Thailand have maintained high rates of export expansion to the United States
market ranging from 22 per cent from Hong Kong to 34 per cent from South
Korea in 1987, thereby further increasing their combined trade surpluses with the
United States.

The pursuit of an export-led development strategy requires, and has brought
about, an overall economic liberalisation -- reducing tariffs, eliminating non-tariff
trade barriers, industrial and financial deregulation, and a more realistic exchange
rate policy. This trend of economic liberalisation in the region that is gaining
momentum has been the second most viable development in Pacific Asia. This has
helped break down the ideological barriers that existed between socialist and other
market-oriented economies and subsequently has facilitated a freer movement not
only of goods and services but also factors of production between the two groups
of countries. The most striking results of this development have been the burgeon-
ing trade between China and East European countries on the one hand and Taiwan
and South Korea on the other, and the Soviet Union's growing interest in participating in Pacific trade and economic co-operation.

A third development has been the structural adjustment Japan and the East
Asian NIEs have made and are trying to make in response to the rapid appreciation
of their currencies vis-à-vis the US dollar and to the aggravation of their trade conflicts with the United States. The massive appreciation of the yen against the dollar has triggered a sharp increase in Japan's import demand for manufactures. The
appreciation and the huge current account surplus that precipitates further appreciation coupled with intensified foreign pressure to open its market have made
Japanese firms start moving their production facilities offshore -- mostly to other
parts of the region -- increasing their foreign direct investment throughout Asia,
and making them more co-operative than before in the transfer of technology.
Japan has also been making earnest efforts to improve the quality of life at home.
They are trying to cut down working hours, increase housing investment, expand
the level and variety of consumption, and to augment physical and social infrastructure. In a similar situation, both Taiwan and Korea are seeking, albeit on a
moderate scale, to redirect their investment resources away from the export-
oriented to the home goods sector. In 1987, Japan took in manufactured imports
amounting to $67 billion, representing an increase of 25 per cent over to the pre-
vious year. The EANIEs more than any others were able to take advantage of this
growing Japanese market; their manufactured exports to Japan in 1987 rose almost
60 per cent in value terms, which was followed by ASEAN's 50 per cent. The

United States saw a paltry 0.2 per cent increase in exports to Japan over the same year.

Japanese import absorbing has accelerated in 1989. During the first five months of this year, Japan's imports of manufactured goods rose 51 per cent compared to the corresponding period of 1987. As a group, the ASEAN countries recorded the highest rate of growth of manufactured exports to Japan with a 69.4 per cent increase. A comparable figure for the East Asian NIEs was 60.4 per cent, and for the United States it was 45.7 per cent. Whether this trend will continue into the future is not clear at this point, but so long as the internal-demand powered output expansion is sustained and further market-opening measures are undertaken as expected, Japan is likely to provide an expanding export market for other Pacific Asian countries.

A fourth development has been China's determination and efforts to integrate itself into the world trading system. Since it started seeking economic modernisation through an open-door policy in the latter part of the 1970s, China has emerged as a major export competitor and at the same time provided a fast-growing market to other countries in the region, largely due to the complementarity in trade structures between China and other economies. Between 1970 and 1987, China's exports to the Pacific Asian region rose by 20 times and its imports by 50 times. Although China has been suffering from inflation and plagued by infrastructure bottlenecks and management problems, there is little doubt that it will continue with its liberal trade policy, although periodic relapses are expected. Assuming that China sustains a rate of export growth of about 7 to 8 per cent a year, its volume of exports would be over $100 billion by the year 2000 -- a level that could present a formidable adjustment problem to the rest of the world.

The adjustment efforts made by Japan and the EANIEs to reduce their trade surpluses together with China's open-door policy have contributed to an expansion of intra-regional trade and foreign direct investment, which has further promoted growth, industrialisation, and economic integration in the region. Japanese foreign direct investment to Pacific Asian countries, which has been concentrated in manufacturing, for example, rose by 62 per cent in 1986 and more than doubled in 1987.

Finally, there has been growing concern about European efforts to develop a unified market, the US-Canada free trade agreement, numerous bilateral trade negotiations initiated by the United States, and the stalemate in the Uruguay round of trade negotiations. The concern about the retreat from a multilateral trade agreement and the expansion in intra-regional trade and investment have created possibilities as well as interest in a Pacific Asian-based economic integration in the expectation that such an arrangement would help Pacific Asian countries cope better with the spread of regional economic block formation.

SUSTAINABILITY OF GROWTH PATH

What do all these development means for the future of the multilateral trading system? Do they mean a more harmonious trade relation between Pacific Asian countries and North America and Europe? All countries in Pacific Asia including ASEAN members appear to be bullish about their growth prospects. They are planning or forecasting long-term rapid or moderate growth of GNP ranging from 6 to 8 per cent over the next five years. As an industrialised super economic power, Japan cannot be in this growth league, but it could maintain an average growth rate of over 4 per cent for the next 10 years, which is very high for an industrialised country.

Since all of these countries, including China, have chosen the growth path through export promotion, with the exception of Japan which now places more emphasis on a domestic demand-led growth, it is only logical to ask how they are going to maintain their export competitiveness (supply side) and where they are going to find the markets for their export products (demand side). On the supply side, conditions governing the availability of and access to foreign capital and technology, wage movements, and labour productivity differ from country to country. This, however, is hardly the place to evaluate supply-side issues of Pacific Asia.

In projecting their export growth, however, most of these country plans or forecasts simply assume certain rates of growth for their major trading partners and the world trade volume to estimate the world demand for their exports. These unco-ordinated efforts at planning or forecasting seem to produce two types of fallacy of composition. Even if one does not subscribe to the kind of export pessimism espoused by Cline (1982) and Streeten (1982), it might be worthwhile to examine the direction of trade in Pacific Asia. Our conclusion is that all of the economies promoting exports will be concentrating on North American and European markets, unless Japan makes its market wide open and free to entry. Another fallacy of composition, which is more serious than the former, is that Japan and the EANIEs as a group are likely to run a combined current account surplus of more than $100 billion per year for at least the next five years and possibly longer. Only a fraction of this surplus will be offset by the deficit the ASEAN countries and China are likely to incur.

Many people would agree that such a surplus accumulation is undesirable as it will worsen trade conflicts between Pacific Asia and the rest of the world and serve to generate strong protectionist pressures to block East Asian exports from entering the markets of the United States and Europe. It is certainly in the interest of the Pacific Asian economies to reduce tensions in their trade relations with North America and Europe by making policy adjustments within a bilateral as well as multilateral framework. What then could they do individually and collectively? Before addressing the question, it would be worthwhile to examine whether the continuing expansion in intra-regional trade in Pacific Asia would not only change the direction of trade but also help reduce the East Asian surplus.

It is evident that there are economic forces developing in the region that will bring Pacific Asian countries together to integrate their economies through an expansion of intra-regional trade and foreign direct investment. As an economic superpower with a potentially large market and ability to supply finance and technology, Japan is at the centre of this integration process. The EANIEs play the role of a second locomotive pulling the ASEAN and China to expansion and industrialisation. How far will this economic integration progress over the next five to ten years? The answer to this question will to a large extent depend on whether the countries in the region could overcome through policy co-ordination some of the forces and regional characteristics that could interfere with or at least slow down the integration process.

Economies in the Pacific region differ from one another not only in terms of their resource endowment but also their cultural backgrounds and economic and political systems. This diversity could serve as a source of complementarity that helps bind the countries in the region together, but it also makes it difficult to define common economic and political objectives. In recent years, rapid growth and increased flows of goods and services and factors of production have contributed to narrowing down the differences in trade and industrial policy. Yet, Pacific Asian countries have a long way to go before agreement on any plans for the proposed integration is reached. For example, the ASEAN as an economic association boasts of its long history, but since its inception, Member countries achieved little success either in mutual trade liberalisation or policy co-ordination. There are few indications that they could improve their rather unimpressive record on promoting intra-ASEAN trade in the future.

For a successful integration, the Pacific Asian countries must find ways in which they can expand intra-regional trade by promoting intra-industry and intra-firm trade among themselves. The economic integration would be facilitated if the Pacific Asian economies take measures to liberalise further their trade regimes and Japan could increase its capacity to import manufactured goods from its Pacific Asian partners. The prospects for these changes are not promising, but even if these changes could be brought about, the proposed economic integration centring on Japan could at best be a gradual process stretched out over a long period of time.

Because of the striking similarity of their industrial and trade structures, which limits inter-industry trade, the volume of trade among the EANIEs has been insignificant as a proportion of total Asian trade. The endowments of the ASEAN countries are also competitive rather than complementary. This feature, together with the inability to reduce trade barriers, explains the lack of success of the ASEAN Preferential Trade arrangement in stimulating intra-regional ASEAN trade. Although the intra-EANIEs trade has been growing rapidly recently, it is too early to tell whether this trend will continue. They could of course specialise along lines of comparative advantage within industry which will help expand intra-industry trade. This would require a mutual openness of markets and more important a close co-ordination in industrial policy. Since they are not competing with one another in their own markets, but in third markets such as the United States and the

European Economic Community policy co-ordination has been more difficult than otherwise. Partly because of severe competition among themselves in the third markets, they have been more protective of their domestic markets to each other than they have been to other trade partners.

Not only are their trade structures similar but the EANIEs also share poor resource endowments in common which require them to rely heavily on imported oil and other raw materials. This is also true for Japan. In order to pay for these imports of primary commodities, while maintaining their overall trade in balance, they must obtain a surplus on their trade in manufactures with the countries outside of the Pacific Asian region. The ASEAN countries with a rich resource base have maintained a deficit on their manufactures trade with Japan and the EANIEs. Through the promotion of labour-intensive products, however, the ASEAN countries and China are trying to balance their manufactures trade. This means that as a whole the Pacific Asian region may be developing a structural characteristic that could produce a persistent trade surplus with the rest of the world.

Even though the prospects for intra-ASEAN and intra-EANIEs trade expansion are not promising, would not the growing volume of trade among the ASEAN, EANIEs, Japan and China develop a regional market large enough to absorb the bulk of Pacific Asian exports? In Pacific Asia, it is true that different countries have different initial conditions and start exporting at different stages of development. As Ranis (1985) points out, this means that different countries arrive at a substantial manufactured goods export capacity at different points in time. It is also possible that the interdependence in trade among the ASEAN, EANIEs, and Japan, which will promote inter-industry trade, combined with Japan's market opening measures could expand intra-industry trade large enough to accommodate the growing volume of exports (mostly labour-intensive) produced by China, ASEAN, and the EANIEs. However, this type of argument -- a version of the flying geese pattern of development -- does not seem to stand up to scrutiny (3).

One reason for this pessimistic view is that the flying-geese pattern of development seems to require, to be sustained, a large export market outside of the region. To elaborate on this argument, let us assume that Japan will remain as the most innovative economy, inventing continuously new technology and products and that the markets of North America and Europe will remain open as they have in the past so that the Pacific Asian economies can continue to export to them. According to this scenario, all countries including Japan are moving up the ladder of comparative advantage, thereby integrating their economies on the export side through the penetration of third markets. That is, as their labour costs rise continuously and their currencies are further appreciated, the EANIEs would gradually lose out in competition to the ASEAN countries and China in supplying textiles and electronics to North American and European markets. The EANIEs move on to the production and export of more sophisticated and technology-intensive manufactures by displacing Japanese suppliers in these markets so that they could make room for the EANIEs and China to move in. As a result, the export share of Pacific Asia in North America and Europe may remain unchanged, although the commodity composition of the exports of these Asian countries is likely to change.

Aside from the question of whether the United States and Europe will be prepared to receive Asian exports as much as they have in the past, this argument does not answer whose exports to, or which domestic suppliers, of the United States and Europe Japan is going to replace. Since the EANIEs, ASEAN, and China have only a limited capacity to import those Japanese exports of sophisticated high-technology products, it is logical to assume that Japan is going to invent, develop and export new products to the markets of the United States, Canada, and Europe or to replace further domestic producers of other existing products such as automobiles, computer-related products, and general machinery in these countries. This mode of trade expansion and structural changes suggest that the existing trade imbalances between the United States on the one hand and Japan and the EANIEs on the other would remain unchanged or could even increase with the consequence of worsening trade tensions on the two sides of the Pacific.

In presenting the preceding argument, we have ignored the crowding-out problem that the catching-up development process could create in Pacific Asia. At present, trade relations between Japan and the EANIEs are both complementary and competitive. However, the speed and the catching-up process in Pacific Asia is likely to accelerate in the future as the EANIEs as well as Japan are expected to increase their foreign direct investment and technology transfer throughout Pacific Asia. Korea's foreign direct investment in the ASEAN jumped to $130 million in 1987 from less than $2 million per year on average during the preceding five years. Reliable statistics for foreign direct investment by other EANIEs are not available, but a recent estimate places the total foreign direct investment by EANIEs in the ASEAN at about $550 million in 1987 which was almost four times as large as it was four years before (Chen, 1988).

The catching-up process could then substantially expand the range of manufactured products in which Japan and the EANIEs will be competitive suppliers in both Asian and third markets. An important question is whether Japan will be able to adjust to this catching-up problem. Trade relations between the ASEAN and the EANIEs will also create a similar tension as the ASEAN moves rapidly up the ladder of industrial and technological development. As a major innovating nation at the top of the ladder of comparative advantage, Japan is bound to slow down whereas the pace of catching up by lower-tiered countries will increase along with intra-regional expansion of foreign direct investment. The EANIEs will find themselves squeezed by Japan at one end and by the ASEAN at the other. The efforts to overtake the countries in upper tiers will generate strong competitive pressures among the Pacific Asian economies. These pressures will in turn induce the EANIEs, ASEAN and China to penetrate the markets of Northern America and Europe while keeping their markets closed to one another. This pattern of development could then enlarge the trade imbalance and hence worsen trade conflicts between Pacific Asia and the rest of the world, in particular North America.

So far we have assumed that the markets of North America and Europe would remain relatively large and open as they have been in the past. This is a rather unrealistic assumption as the United States would make trade and policy adjustments needed to bring about a large decrease in its trade deficit. The proponents of the flying geese pattern of development argue that this US-initiated policy adjustment would not create any serious adjustment problems to the EANIEs and ASEAN, if Japan is going to open up its market as expected. That is, pushed out of the US and European markets, exporters from the EANIEs, ASEAN, and China would now move into Japan as an alternative market. Chinese and ASEAN exporters could also move into the markets of the EANIEs.

This scenario has a number of problems and at least in the short-run it is as unrealistic and troublesome as is the first one. First, the second scenario focuses only on import-side adjustment on the part of the United States, implying a trade contraction and a possible worldwide recession. Second, it implicitly assumes that the Japanese export market share in the United States would remain unaffected or at least would not decline as much as the market shares of the EANIEs and the ASEAN would as a result of a US trade deficit reduction, because Japan has not as many competitors for its export products as the EANIEs, ASEAN and China do. Most important of all, this pattern of adjustment assumes that Japan could supplant the United States market enough to allow Pacific Asian economies to continue with export promotion policies. This is at best a highly questionable assumption.

In 1987, the total volume of Pacific Asian exports to the United States was larger than the total value of the intra-regional trade in Pacific Asia. Japan purchased less than 10 per cent of total manufactured exports of the EANIEs, ASEAN, and China, while the United States absorbed more than 30 per cent. The United States imports from all of the EANIEs, ASEAN, and China in 1987 were six times as large as the Japanese imports from these countries. Even if Japan were capable of tripling the volume of its imports of manufactured goods over the next five years and imported only from its Pacific Asian partners, it could at most absorb one-half of their total manufactured exports. It is simply unrealistic to expect Japan to grow into an export market for other Pacific Asian economies large enough to supplant the US market in the near future no matter what it does to transform its economic policies and lifestyle.

Over the next five years, Japan's earnings on their holdings of foreign assets will begin to pile up, and in fact the interest income will be growing so fast that by 1995 Japan's invisible trade will record a surplus of almost $60 billion. By the year 2000, this will have risen to $80 billion. This means that Japan could run a huge current account surplus even if it succeeds in balancing the trade account. This development also means that Japan will have plenty of room to run a deficit on its manufactures trade, although it is entirely different matter whether Japan would actually do so.

In order to run a deficit on the manufactures trade, Japan should be able to induce a shift of labour from declining industries to competitive and expanding ones. According to one estimate (Okumura, 1988), foreign direct investment will cause a loss of half a million manufacturing jobs by 1995, the steel industry will reduce its work force by one third, and shipbuilding by almost one-half in Japan by the year 2000. It is predicted that growth in service sector employment will make up for the decline in manufacturing employment. As a result, the share of the service sector will rise to 29 per cent of total employment from 24 per cent in 1987.

It is not clear whether by 1995 Japan will be able to generate such a large number of job opportunities in the service sector, and if indeed it does, whether it will adjust to such an abrupt structural change in employment in a country known for lifetime employment. There is also another macroeconomic characteristic which may interfere with Japan's structural adjustment efforts. Japan has maintained one of the highest savings rates in the world and in all likelihood will continue to do so for some time in the future. Only after the mid-1990s when the percentage of the population over 59 years of age starts to increase rapidly is Japan's savings rate projected to decline (Okumura, 1988). For the next six years, therefore, Japanese households are not likely to increase their spending on luxuries and holidays despite the expected reduction in working hours. Unless investment demand rises enough to exhaust domestic savings, the saving-investment balance will persist, hold back its imports demand, and hence complicate Japan's current account management.

THE DANGER OF REGIONAL ECONOMIC BLOCS

This paper has, perhaps, been more pessimistic than is warranted in forecasting the future growth in the inter-regional trade in Pacific Asia. It may also underestimate the role Japan could play in promoting growth and industrialisation in Pacific Asia. Japan is certainly in a position to facilitate and speed-up Pacific Asian integration without necessarily creating any formal co-operative institutions or agreements. It could do so simply by exercising its financial power as the banker for the world economy, disseminating and making available its technological know-how, and opening up its market for imports from other Asian countries. Few countries in Pacific Asia would support such a mode of integration centring on an economic superpower, however. As it is, most of the Pacific Asian economies acquire capital and technology from Japan; they do not cherish the idea of depending also on the Japanese market for export of their manufactures.

There is, however, a more fundamental question as to whether Pacific Asian countries will be able to gain from the creation of formal institutions and structures designed actively to promote economic integration in Pacific Asia. Given the overwhelming diversity in social, economic, and political systems and differences in trade interests from country to country, it is difficult to expect that they could even agree on any agenda for mutual co-operation, let alone co-ordinate their industrial and trade policies vis-à-vis the rest of the world. Establishing an institutional framework will not strengthen the bargaining position of Pacific Asian economies; it will instead create a visible target for trade retaliation and protectionism by other countries in different regions.

The rapid growth and industrialisation in Pacific Asia has been achieved not through any formal agreements and creation of new institutional arrangements but through competition in the market. In the long run, through this competition an integrated Pacific Asian market would evolve. Any intervention in this process by the governments of the region would not only delay the process but could complicate the existing trade relations among Pacific Asian countries and potentially worsen trade tensions between Pacific Asia on the one hand and the United States and Europe on the other.

However, if the EANIEs, China, and ASEAN countries are forced out of United States and European markets by means of protectionist policies, or lose out as the United States successfully reduces its current account deficit, then Pacific Asian countries will have no choice but to integrate themselves with Japan, both on the import and export sides. Seizing the opportunity to reassert and consolidate its economic and political power in Pacific Asia, the Japanese public may become more susceptible and go along with the idea of opening its market to other Asian countries.

If indeed such a development took place, and Europeans came to construct a fortress Europe, the world economy would be divided into three competing economic blocks and trade relations among these blocks would be marketed by greater trade conflicts and harsher protectionist policies directed against one another. If, on the other hand, the United States continues to accumulate trade deficits and to keep its market relatively free to enter, then there is the danger that the East Asian trade surplus would remain unchanged and China and ASEAN could develop a trade pattern in which they import mostly capital and intermediate inputs from Japan and export consumer goods and assembly products to the United States. The Pacific Asian share of the United States trade deficit is then likely to remain unchanged; only the composition by country would change.

Neither outcome is desirable, and it would be in the interests of Pacific Asia as well as North America and Europe to avoid dividing the world into a number of blocks, or leaving global payments imbalances unattended. Japan, Taiwan, and Korea must change their policies to bring about further trade liberalisation and re-orientation of domestic investment to reduce their surpluses to a level acceptable to the rest of the world as much as the United States has the responsibility to correct its trade imbalances. The failure to do so would mean proliferation of more bilateral trade deals and regional groupings which would in turn lead to the collapse of the multilateral trading system, which has already been paralysed for some time.

NOTES AND REFERENCES

1. This paper was written during the author's tenure as Visiting Professor of Economics in the Department of Economics and as Research Associate at the Harvard Institute of International Development during the fall term of the 1988-89 academic year.

2. They are: Japan, China, Korea, Taiwan, Hong Kong, Singapore, and the ASEAN countries other than Singapore.

3. See Okita (1986) and Yamazawa (1988) for an analysis of the flying geese pattern of development in Asia.

BIBLIOGRAPHY

CHEN, E. "Asian-Pacific Co-operation in Trade and Investment in a Changing International Economic Environment", (mimeo), 1988.

CLINE, W.R. "Can the East Asian Model of Development be Generalised", *World Development,* Vol. 10, No. 2, 1982.

OKITA, S. "Pacific Development and its Implications for the World Economy", *The Pacific Basin: New Challenges for the United States,* The Academy of Political Science, J.W. Morley, eds., New York, 1986.

OKUMURA, H. "The Development of Structural Changes in the Japanese Economy", NRI and NCC Co., Ltd., Tokyo, April 1988.

RANIS, G. "Can the East Asian Model of Development be Generalised?: A Comment", *World Development Review*, Vol. 13, No. 4, 1985.

STREETEN, P. "A Cool Look at Outward-Looking Strategies", *World Economy*, September 1982.

YAMAZAWA, I. "Trade and Industrial Adjustment", *Review on Pacific Cooperation Activities*, The Japan National Committee for Pacific Economic Cooperation, the Japan Institute of International Affairs, May 1988.

DISCUSSANT'S CONTRIBUTION

by

Antonio M. COSTA

The two papers, by Professors Jaguaribe and Park, are very valuable. Many previous speakers made reference to the European community: therefore I will compare what is happening in Europe and in other countries in terms of the problems mentioned earlier in the discussion.

Let me look at the recent past.

First, we must resist a temptation: to accept a cliché whereby two regions, Latin America and Asia -- two regions so different culturally, in terms of policy and performance -- lead us to conclude that in the recent past one region did everything right and the other region did everything wrong. This is a fallacy. Of course, we know that import substitution in the Latin American continent did systematic damage. We also know that export promotion in Asia did quite some good during the 1980s. Yet, if we cast our eyes beyond the 1980s and go back to the 1960s and the 1970s, we see that the performance of these two continents was quite comparable. Growth was very strong in both regions, external trade was in balance in both regions and capital kept flowing: bank lending in Latin America, together with foreign direct investment; while development aid poured into Asia.

Secondly, in the 1980s things changed. First of all, because the two development strategies had different payoffs; but also because external circumstances changed worldwide, and the changing parameters worldwide impacted the two regions differently. In a sense one region was better positioned and better prepared to take advantage of the evolving situation in the 1980s -- an evolving situation which we have to scrutinise carefully to judge whether it will last or not.

Several changes occurred -- one is well known: the decline of primary commodity prices and in particular oil prices. We know that one of the two regions (Asia) is a net importer of primary commodities -- and in particular oil -- while the other (Latin America) is a net exporter. The biggest change occurred in the United States and in its economic policy during the 1980s. It is legitimate to ask how much the economic performance of these two regions would have changed or would have been modified had the two Reagan administrations behaved differently. Two sets of policies characterised the Reagan Presidency. The first one, very serious monetary tightening, took place at the beginning of the decade and was sorely needed after a long period of negative real interest rates. That was welcome although it caused havoc to heavily indebted countries like those of Latin America. The second set of policy changes -- in fiscal policy -- was not necessary. The crowding out of domestic resources in the United States, the dollar appreciation, the loss of competitiveness because of the dollar appreciation, the enormous external debt of the United States, all that was not necessary and was not welcome. It should not last. In the event this policy very seriously and positively affected one of the two regions -- Asia. The other region was less capable of benefitting from these changes. One could well imagine that the world would look quite differently today in terms of the surpluses of the Far East had the United States behaved differently, especially in fiscal terms.

The third element of my retrospective is the two different types of capitalism which exist in the world today. This is a point which economists perhaps tend to forget too easily.

There is one type of capitalism (the European and North American variety) which is similar to that of Latin America. This type of capitalism is rooted in the philosophy of the 18th and 19th centuries and has been characterised by hedonism and atomism. Hedonism means a maximisation of welfare, which essentially means maximisation of consumption. Atomism essentially means competitive conditions: a large number of producers, a large number of consumers, supply and demand meeting at the marketplace to establish the appropriate price.

Then we have the Far Eastern capitalism. I have two words to describe this, which are more attuned to the sociologist than the philosopher -- solidarity and parsimony. Solidarity means a very cosy relationship between the public and the private sector, cosy relationship between the social partners, a cosy relationship between producer and distributors in particular. Parsimony means savings, which means looking towards the next generation -- what counts is not today, not tomorrow, but the day after tomorrow or perhaps beyond that. In the 1980s, these two types of capitalism reacted differently to evolving circumstances. With the dollar's value increasing, the excess savings of very parsimonious Asia turned into a staggering net export surplus to the United States. With higher interest rates, rather hedonistic Latin America following the pattern of North America and Western Europe entered into a debt crisis, into social strife and capital flight. All sorts of social conflicts emerged over who should suffer the burden of adjustment.

Fourth element of this retrospective analysis: *frontier states which are no longer such*. The Asian NIEs border very big neighbours, neighbours who have been very militant until very recently: China, North Korea, and Vietnam. They have been forced to face, in the 1950s, 1960s and even the 1970s, potentially very dangerous situations. That prompted movement of capital into these countries from the United States for humanitarian as well as for strategic reasons. This promoted the national effort to prepare and survive in a difficult environment, creating a sort of social tension, which indeed kept economies going and kept capital flowing. In the 1980s, and especially very recently, things have changed: tensions have abated. As a consequence, the machines which were set up for conflict -- the human machines and equipment -- have been turned to peaceful purposes, which means export, which means surpluses. (By the way, there is another country in the world which geographically finds itself in a very similar relationship with its neighbours; a country which was able to turn desert into gardens, Israel. Please do think about the analogy and what it means to be the neighbour of a very powerful country which may or may not behave properly.)

I come to the second part of my statement: what do the two papers say about the future. Let me begin with a general consideration on a point made by the Chairman about the transition to the decade of the 1990s occurring in rather favourable conditions. Peace is replacing hostility in many parts of the world. At the same time, the economic momentum -- in the second half of 1987 throughout 1988 and according to the OECD estimate in the biennium ahead -- looks very favourable.

So, if you allow me another catchy sentence (which is not very original), it looks like *the transition from the 1980s to the 1990s is going to be in a climate of peace and prosperity*. This is quite a change with respect to the conflicts -- with respect to inflation, with respect to the social strife -- which we know characterised the transition from the 1970s to the 1980s.

Now what do the authors say about the next decade? First a word of warning: let us not extrapolate too easily. If we fit an exponential function to the Latin American debt or if we fit an exponential function to the Asian surplus, we get numbers which are simply meaningless.

Second, take the prescriptions which the two authors suggest. Jaguaribe claims (and I think correctly) that the way ahead is very difficult and indeed very complex. He claims that if Latin America is to grow out of its debt, it has to promote exports, has to stop the capital flight and bring back the $450 billion worth of Latin American capital which is located abroad (at least according to our and IMF estimates). It has to engage in social and political reforms, it has to modernise the economy with high-tech orientation, higher competitiveness, and so forth. Indeed, if this happens, as staggering a job as that may be, there is no reason to believe that Latin America in the 1990s should behave any differently from the way it did in the 1960s and the 1970s, namely very successfully.

What about the Asian model? Park's assessment is in my view acceptable. These countries need to bring their export surplus under control because the absorption capacity of the rest of the world has a limit. These countries have to engage in greater intra-trade, namely within the Asian region: NIEs, with Japan, and *vice versa*. At present, neither the level nor the structure of trade within the region is adequate; we shall see in a moment what I mean by that. It is hard to see how in the 1990s, unless these measures are undertaken, growth in these countries can be as good as in the 1980s.

In other words, comparing these two parts of the world and comparing the analysis presented in the two papers, we can conclude that both regions need to reduce the large imbalances, the financial imbalance -- the debt of Latin America -- and the commercial imbalance, Asia's surplus. Both need social reforms: Latin

America to increase savings and, therefore its investments, while Asia needs to reduce its net savings and, therefore, its net exports. Both have to find sustainable, more balanced, sources of growth: more Latin American growth abroad and more growth of the Asian countries at home, or at least in the region.

I now enter into the third part of my observations.

Again, two words of caution. First, the transition to the decade of the 1990s: it is right that the present prosperity seems to bode well for the next biennium, but it is well beyond the next biennium that we have to master events better than we have done to date. Europe has 16 million people unemployed. The United States is indebted to such an extent that it has become a problem: 180 per cent of the American GNP is the amount of resources which would be needed to cover the domestic and external debt of the United States, including the private and the public debt. Latin America has a development constraint which is caused by the servicing of the debt, and Asia has accumulated such a financial asset surplus that it has made the surplus structural -- and we know the difficulty of reducing a structurally unbalanced balance-of-payments.

Second note of concern: flow imbalances, deficits and surpluses, have turned into stock imbalances and therefore into problems which have to be resolved with structural policy. Look at the convergence of ideology worldwide. Totalitarian regimes have collapsed almost everywhere around the world. There are very few of them left and we can almost count them on the fingers of a single hand. Worldwide, there has been a growing emergence of economic and political democracy. We vote by the ballot periodically, but even more significantly, an increasing number of people worldwide vote daily; buying, selling, producing, and investing.

There is more. During the 1980s, a massive process of worldwide liberalisation took place. During this process of deregulation, an equally massive amount of sovereignty has been surrendered by governments to the marketplace. This is fine to the extent that we realise that markets do not lead; markets only pass judgment on leaders. Therefore, to the extent that financial intermediation has become worldwide, with markets fully integrated in terms of commodities, services and factors (especially capital) shared responsibility has become necessary. There are those who use a different expression. They say, "Let's create a mirror image of the world economy into a world government". Now this does not a mean an operational superstructure of a United Nations-type, but it does mean sharing responsibilities East-West, North-South and in the trilateral area of the OECD. The recent G7 meeting is important to show how the major industrial countries of the OECD can meet *ex ante* before events develop, rather than *ex post* in crisis management.

What is the role of the major players in this context? Today, I want to leave out the United States. In my life, I have given lots of advice to the United States and we all have done so at the OECD for quite some time. I want to address the other two regions of the world, Europe (the Community in particular) and Japan. Pointing out with regret to some of the statements which Yung Chul Park made, I want to say that we should differentiate any countries which have their house in order from those which do not: the United States and Japan do not; Europe does.

The Chairman has made reference to the internal market drive, to the efforts of European communities to create a fully homogenious economy consisting of 320 million citizens by 1992. That is an enormous effort and the results have so far been remarkable in terms of the legislation which has been approved well on target with respect to the 1992 objective. Now the economic situation in Europe is changing for the better. Of course it is very difficult -- I would say impossible -- to deny that there is a relationship between the two. In the past 24 months in the Community economy there was the best combination of price and output growth, the highest level of job creation (1.65 million last year) for a long, long time, and the best trade and investment performance ever. Prospects for the next biennium are very similar.

The Community situation, and especially the trade situation, is perfectly under control. The house is in order. Of course, we know that Italy has a very large fiscal deficit; of course we also know that Greece has a very high inflation rate; but if you take the Community at large, you realise that the house in the Community is in order. Yet the papers I see and some of the statements I hear, point to problems with the Community; they point to "fortress Europe". To correct this misunderstanding, I will give you some numbers just to square the records and make sure we understand each other.

In 1988, the European Community purchased $400 billion worth of goods from the rest of the world. The same as the United States and three times more than Japan. In 1988, Europe exported $400 million worth of goods and services -- the same as imports since our accounts with the rest of the world are in equilibrium. The United States had much less than that (80 per cent). Our house, in terms of external relations, is in order. To talk about fortress Europe sounds very peculiar when the stakes for us -- selling and buying $400 billion worth of goods every year -- are very high.

Of course, the emergence of regional blocks is a problem, or at least is something that we have to look at. In the European Community economy, growth forces are indigenous -- or if you prefer, are endogenous -- they are given by and related to an internal EEC process. Trade between the Community and the rest of the world is in equilibrium which means that faster growth in Europe, faster growth in the Community in particular, turns into greater opportunity for the rest of the world.

Instead, in Asia, according to Yung Chul Park, there is very limited intraregional trade. There are very limited indigenous forces of growth and there is a continuing dependence on net exports to the rest of the world. If this is right, it would make Asian growth different (from the one in process in Europe) and it is something worth looking at.

There may be a fortress Europe building up as some people claim, but let us look at the fortress of the Pacific before looking into the continent where we are located at the moment. Let us look at Japan.

Professor Park used this very interesting statement, "the head goose of a flying geese formation". That is a very nice metaphor. Yet despite remarkable accomplishments -- growth, competitiveness, technology -- one just wonders where the goose is going. One also wonders how sustainable that growth performance is, given the extraordinary unbalanced nature of the growth performance of Japan. Both Europe and the United States are in deficit with the Asian NIEs and the ASEAN countries, and so is Latin America, but the developing countries in Asia are strongly in deficit vis-à-vis Japan. Therefore, one just wonders how the developing countries in Asia -- in bad need as they are to improve their growth performance, to improve their standards of living -- how well positioned these developing countries in Asia are to perform better and to lower their external surpluses vis-à-vis Latin America, Europe and North America unless their deficit vis-à-vis Japan is brought to zero, or at least reduced substantially. At the moment, there is very little evidence of this.

Some interesting numbers have emerged very recently, proposed by the Economic Planning Agency of Japan. The savings which have accrued to the Japanese economy due to the halving of world prices and the dollar exchange rate have amounted to something like $230 billion. Because of lack of deregulation and lack of perestroika in Japan, lack of indigenous forces, the distribution of the terms of trade savings has been as the following: only one-third were passed to consumers, two-thirds being kept by firms as profits. They are being turned into foreign direct investments (in the Unites States, which is the wrong place), as well as in a very powerful machine for international banking. This of course will perpetuate the surplus problem structurally.

I will close with two consequences of all this for today's debate.

We have nothing against export-led growth. Our system grew because of export-led growth. But we are against a surplus-led growth, surplus which cannot, and should not, last. What we are witnessing in the Pacific is a less acceptable form of integration. It is potentially disruptive and it may eventually lead to resistance -- politically or otherwise -- elsewhere.

The Asian model is not at all appealing for the rest of the developing countries, at least in its present form. Do not forget that surplus-led growth means that somebody's surplus has to be somebody else's deficit. With the kind of external deficit in the United States and with the kind of unemployment in Europe, it is hard to believe that either Europe or the United States can intake more of the surplus of Japan or of anyone else. We know the limited capability, carrying capacity of the Eastern European countries. I suspect that a surplus-led growth of the Pacific cannot really last in the 1990s.

DISCUSSANT'S CONTRIBUTION

by

Paul R. JOLLES

The excellent papers presented by Professors Helio Jaguaribe and Yung Chul Park deal with the challenge presented for and by the Newly Industrialising Economies (NIEs) at the threshold of the 1990s. The North-South dialogue, which was institutionalised 25 years ago with the creation of UNCTAD in Geneva is taking place in a new context. The issues to be resolved are no less important today for a healthy world economy, but they are placed in a different political and economic context. Among the basic changes that have occurred since the de-colonisation period after World War II, let me recall the political drive for a new international economic order in the United Nations followed by the oil shock, which more realistically highlighted the global interdependence of the world economy. Since then, the positive developments in East-West relationships have reduced the political prominence of North-South tensions, and some of the North-South issues have been transferred into a regional frame, both in the European-African region and in the Western hemisphere. The emergence of Japan as a principal world economic power (1964 also marked the accession of Japan to the OECD) and the entrance of the NIEs into world trade created an increasingly complex and differentiated picture. Against this general background, both authors although speaking from widely different vantage points -- Brazil and Korea -- are dealing, among others, with five similar key issues, on which I should like to comment from a Swiss and an industrial point of view.

1. The trends toward regionalism with its promise and its conflictive potential: neither in the Pacific nor in Latin America, does there seem to emerge an explicit option in favour of regionalism though this is not being excluded as a defensive strategy against the possibility of protectionist policies by other blocks like the United States or a fortress Europe. Regionalism is thus associated with bilateralism. The analysis of the authors clearly points towards their preference for a global approach, which would better correspond to the multiple interdependence of their regions with the rest of the world -- in terms of trade and finance in particular with the US and European markets.

2. The changing role of the state in relation to the investment activities of the domestic and foreign private sector. Jaguaribe, in particular,

spoke about a more effective transnationalisation of the international companies and of their positive economic impact. The influence of the state in the productive process is more limited and can be more narrowly circumscribed and better focused on specific social objectives.

3.   Both authors stress the importance of domestic economic policies for growth in order to close the remaining North-South economic gap. They consider efficient mobilisation of resources and improvement of productivity a far more important form of leverage than exclusive reliance on either export orientation or import substitution.

4.   The persistent microeconomic disequilibriums existing in the global market -- surpluses and deficits, foreign and domestic debt problems and their effects on inflation, interest rates and exchange rates -- which have a direct bearing on growth, raise the question whether the international institutional framework is still adequate to deal with this situation. The Secretary General, Jean-Claude Paye, asked us very forcefully in his opening speech whether the time had come for a reform of this superstructure.

5.   Both papers have engaged into some speculative thinking about whether the entry of new players of continental size into the world economy -- the Soviet Union of Mr. Gorbatchev and the People's Republic of China -- will tend to aggravate or alleviate these disequilibriums.

First the issue of regional versus global strategies. The two approaches need not be considered as alternatives; they can be considered as successive or even complementary conditions, provided they point in the same direction of liberalising trade and investment flows. Co-operation on a regional level can become an instrument for promoting global approaches by testing the ground and leading the way to broader international solutions. Our experience with regional groupings has been positive; increasing the size of the market has stimulated growth. Liberalisation on regional basis has increased competition, promoted structural adjustments and led to greater economic efficiency.

The reason why today regionalism is considered such an interesting phenomenon is its success in Europe. It must, however, be recalled that it has taken more than 25 years for European integration and the European free trade system encompassing both the European community and the EFTA countries to become such a positive factor. It is, moreover, based on highly industrialised and export-minded countries with similar cultural and political values and traditions adhering to market economy policies. Despite these favourable conditions, the negotiating process to develop appropriate methods of co-operation has been long and cumbersome and is still not complete. It would, therefore, be an illusion to consider regional integration as practised in Europe as a short-cut model for other areas of the world to use to catch up with European levels of productivity and growth.

Moreover, there is a protectionist danger, which arises from the discriminatory effect of regionalism on outsiders. Members of regional groupings share advantages, privileges and corresponding obligations on a contractual basis. The negative effect on non-regional partners can be alleviated by openness and conscious efforts towards globalisation, or it can be exacerbated by inward looking and purposely protectionist policies.

Globalism, on the other hand, is a true reflection of the actual state of economic interdependence and of present entrepreneurial strategies. We have heard that global firms are striving for a borderless economy and that some multinational enterprises have become so international that they don't even remember which national origin they have. From the point of view of Nestlé, I would go one step further and say that they have become *multidomestic* because of their decentralisation and integration in the respective local environments.

Any conflicts between regional and global policies could present a real risk of splitting up the multilateral framework of world trade, financial flows and investment activities. This would be unfortunate for everybody, but may be avoided through parallel progress in the Uruguay round of GATT and the creation of the European internal market of 1993. Today there is a generalised interest, shared by the NIEs, in a successful Uruguay round and an extension of this global framework to new subject matters, such as services. All participants in the world economy must ensure that GATT is not lost sight of. To say that GATT is dead would be a deadly assumption indeed!

The second point relates to the changing role of the state and of the private sector. The trend over the last 25 years has been to reduce the voluntarist and interventionist policies of the state in the productive process to make more room for market forces. The spectacular success of the NIEs is, in large part, due to this shift of emphasis, and the room they have created for market forces to produce their dynamic effects on development. In the meantime, governments have moved in the direction of deregulation reducing administrative impediments and the burden of bureaucracy. This is also, to a considerable extent, the course underlining the programme of Europe 1992 in order to increase the competitive strength of European industry.

This is not to belittle the indispensable role of the state in the developing world for supplying the necessary infrastructure, for fulfilling the basic needs of the population, for providing education and proper health facilities and for caring for marginalised social groups.

International companies like my own operate primarily in the newly industrialised economies and middle income countries. That is where they can contribute to economic development and efficiency, to the integration of these economies in the worldwide economic system.

By assessing how business strategies can help in reconciling regional integration with the maintenance of an open world trading system, one must distinguish between three different activities of international companies:

--   Their role as world traders, importing raw materials and supplying processed or manufactured goods;

--   Intra-company trading, such as decentralised stockpiling, the export of bulk products from one productive centre to another in another country, thereby adding value in different places through successive stages of transformation;

--   And, finally, as foreign direct investors for what I have already described as multi-domestic operations.

The foreign private sector can thus show that global approaches work, that regional ones are too narrow; it can abstain from advocating protectionist measures or artificial stimulation of exclusively export-oriented industrialisation (e.g. double pricing) or rigid import substitution, which are dangerous alternatives because of their adverse internal price effects and the risk of retaliatory reactions by foreign trading partners.

These artificial incentives and special privileges should be avoided because they are not sustainable and tend to distort the normal price and cost structure, on which international competitiveness must be based. International companies, however, can contribute decisively to what should be the main objective: the creation of an efficient and competitive local economy. By demonstrating flexibility to seize new market opportunities, they can indicate which factors are relevant for successful competition; by their international contacts and exchanges of personnel, they can promote international understanding; they can introduce new products in new areas and generate positive spill-over effects to other sectors (in the case of Nestlé to agricultural production and distribution, research about plants and crop varieties and seeds, etc.); they must accept the burden of structural adjustments in the interest of long term efficiency, explain the working conditions for a market economy, and develop local human resources through, for example, training programmes and technology transfer. I believe this is what we, the international companies, generally do.

This leads to the third point: the importance of the right domestic economic policies in order to close the remaining North-South gap. Both authors emphasize the relevance of domestic economic policy choices and establish an interesting correlation between the advance of democratic forms of government and the success of economic reforms. Other speakers have pointed to the reverse problem. Patel quotes the phrase: "More democratic governments in Latin America find it more difficult to introduce and implement, over a period of time, economic policies which are not necessarily popular in the short run." It is, indeed, more difficult for them to pursue consistent economic policies over any length of time, if they are not sure of being able to maintain the necessary support of their voters. Patel addressed the issue of urbanisation as a case in point. Our experience confirms the risk of a vicious circle: where the majority are urban voters, and export orientation is the main economic policy objective, competitiveness is sometimes artificially promoted on the cost side by low food prices which tend to depress the domestic agricultural price level and lead to further migration from agricultural areas to urban centres. The ensuing need for increased food imports can then become an additional charge on the foreign exchange balance.

Rather than dwelling on domestic policy choices in general, however, I would like to limit my remarks to factors determining the investment climate. Since foreign direct investment is considered desirable, and since investment activities tend to decline rather than increase in developing countries (this does not apply to Nestlé in absolute terms, but the tendency also exists in our group with respect to relative shares of total annual investment growth), it may be useful to clarify these points.

The key economic criterion for investment decisions is, of course, the demand potential of a particular area: do the purchasing power and the assessment of productivity increases reach adequate levels of added value. Equally important is a positive attitude of the government towards foreign direct investment as an economically valuable form of capital and know-how transfer, education and training of local workers, employees and management, and the creation of an industrial mentality and discipline including a sense of efficiency, hygiene, punctuality and quality. Moreover, there is a need for a basic legal framework with respect to intellectual and physical property rights, labour legislation etc. The expansion of the domestic private sector through policies of privatisation is also considered as a positive element. On the other hand, the weight of a subsidised public sector, unfavourable demographic trends (more than 50 per cent of the population under 18 years old), the effects of inflation on the middle class and of debt and austerity programmes on local demand are considered to be inherent constraints on long term perspectives.

The debt problem as a key word leads me to the fourth issue: the adequacy of the existing international institutions to manage macroeconomic disequilibriums. Is their efficiency so low that the use of bilateral leverage is the only answer or should we devise some new international superstructures? These are somewhat rhetorical questions, if one recalls the successful efforts of the OECD in this very room to promote a horizontal approach to the closely interlinked macroeconomic problems. It is here that, as a result of the Smithsonian link, the REY report was created in 1972. It is here, where it became apparent that the interrelations between trade, finance, development, investment and energy had become so close that effective policies could no longer be developed in isolation. I think, this is still what is required from international organisations today, which need not be multiplied but must be rejuvenated into a new generation better adapted to the present economic realties. Efforts to this effect are undertaken in GATT and have, for some time, been a central concern of the Bretton Woods institutions. As to the usefulness of the economic analyses by the OECD, let me just recall two pertinent examples: the persuasive reasoning for a trade pledge during the oil crisis and Professor Jolly's report about the positive trade effects of the breakthrough of the NIEs into our markets. The consideration of this report has prevented counterproductive protectionist reactions.

One aspect will require increased consideration, namely the consultation procedures between the private and governmental sector. If the private sector is playing an increasingly important role internationally, this should be better known by the public sector and vice versa. This symposium provides a valuable forum in this regard, an example to be followed.

For a final comment, I would like to turn to a fifth point, relating to new players on the world economic scene: the Soviet Union and the People's Republic of China.

There has indeed been a tendency towards a multipolar world over the past 25 years. Whereas the great political achievement of UNCTAD in 1964 was the solidarity of the Group of 77, economic progress in the North-South relationship has since led to economic differentiation. Both OPEC and the NIEs have emerged as powerful new groups on the world market. The question now is whether the Soviet Union and China will have as much of an impact on the world economy, which they are about to enter, as Japan. This seems unlikely for quite some time. Both countries are markets of a continental size with a tremendous potential of internal demand. They seem, however, reluctant to overspend and will, therefore, require some time to develop their own export drive. Moreover, their adaptation to a market economy is likely to produce serious internal tensions. Especially in the Soviet Union, the internal political consequences of the plans for economic reforms are very fundamental. The pressure for increased autonomy of the different national, cultural and religious groups and republics might split rather than integrate the present market structures and give rise to a new surge of subregional protectionism. This uncertainty is added to the question of the extent to which market economy methods will be compatible with a centrally planned economic system. It seems to me, therefore, too early to visualise the outlines of a new international division of labour -- but the challenge is there.

The multipolar world, which has altered the context in which the traditional North-South dialogue takes place, has become a fact. The weight of the different economic centres of gravity and their relation to each other remains, however, an open question -- and a very pertinent one, in the light of the global and interdependent character of the international market.

DISCUSSANT'S CONTRIBUTION

by

I.G. PATEL

It is a tribute to the remarkable progress achieved by NIEs that a whole session of this symposium is devoted to their problems and prospects; but what exactly are we seeking to distinguish when we speak of NIEs? If we adopt Louis Emmerij's admirable description of the theme for this symposium, one can certainly say there is a group of countries now in the middle-income range which have been, for the most part of the last 30 or 40 years at any rate, on the high-growth track. These are also countries for whom it matters a great deal whether the international environment is supportive and outward-looking or contentious and inward-looking.

These countries also do not constitute -- not as yet anyway -- one of the poles of the multipolar world, so that while their stake is great, their ability to mould the external environment is not correspondingly so. Is there not some over-simplification in referring to all of them as industrialising -- with perhaps more than a hint that manufactured exports do and will play a large part in their future? Would it not be appropriate to refer to newly modernising countries in order to isolate those, which, unlike the recently over-rich oil kingdoms, have a reasonably good infrastructure of modernity in the sense of skilled labour and other economic and financial infrastructure of a sophisticated character?

The question is not altogether academic. Even if we look at the two sets of countries discussed in the excellent papers before us the question arises why the EANIEs have managed a sustained economic growth better than the LATINIEs. The standard explanation -- leaving aside for a moment the recent debt crisis -- is bad economic policies. More precisely, that EANIEs followed an export-led strategy whereas the LATINIEs carried import substitution too far.

There is, I am sure, some truth in this conventional wisdom, but an added factor could well be that resource-rich countries are in a different position from labour-surplus countries. The former have the opportunity of earning high incomes in primary production which keep real wages high and this might make it more difficult and less necessary for them to rely on exports of manufactures. Of course, all high- or middle-income countries develop a sizeable industrial structure because it is natural for a great deal of industrial activity to be located at home -- and the infant industry argument has some validity after all. My simple point is that the term NIEs needs careful delineation if we are not to prescribe standard remedies that may not apply to all middle-income countries that have enjoyed high rates of growth in the past. After all, Australia, New Zealand and Canada may be closer models for Argentina or Chile or even Brazil than Korea or Taiwan.

I agree with Helio Jaguaribe's main conclusion that resumption of sustained economic growth in the major Latin American countries requires both a reduction in the debt burden and a programme of reform towards greater equity which goes beyond what are often described as orthodox or heterodox approaches to stabilization and adjustment. We know now that after a prolonged period of inflation, mere monetary and fiscal adjustment is not enough. Some unorthodox remedies like temporary wage and price fixation and currency reform may also be necessary. The reverse is also true.

Even with the best programme containing orthodox and heterodox elements, success can only be guaranteed if it does not require the generation of too large an export surplus which is bound to be inflationary. This is the basic reason for debt reduction in terms of some reasonable figure of debt service beyond which payments should be postponed or written off -- incidentally, this approach provides a guide for future prudence, also, as the debtor country would be expected not to transgress these limits in future. If a parallel is needed, it was provided as long ago as the Anglo-American loan agreement soon after the war. A general principle like this is also not inconsistent with a case-by-case approach.

Jaguaribe however, makes a more important point which is seldom considered: for sustained growth we need some steps towards greater equity in these countries. Without that, the discipline implicit in sound fiscal and monetary policy can at best be short-lived. I wish he had said more about what exactly he has in mind when he says that these countries require "the mobilization of a new multi-class majority, of a centre-left leaning, able to support a socially concerned project of modernization and development, based on a socially regulated free market economy, maximizing efficiency within the framework of social democracy." These words ring true to Indian ears. After all, we have been uttering them for a long time, but we are still awaiting a happy ending after several decades of lost or out-of-reach opportunities. The question is: how do we get there? And what exactly does a centre-left government do in detail? It is easy to say it will follow the Scandinavian model, but how long a road will it be before we can reach that goal? We do not also want mere redistributive equity. We want equity that equips the poor better with productive capabilities. How do we do it? Incidentally, can it not be -- and this goes back to my first point -- that unlike in India, there could be much greater scope in Latin America for land reform, giving land to the poor who generate a new wave of more equitable growth through diversified agriculture?

Coming to the EANIEs, Yung Chul Park whets our appetite so much that I do not know how best to restrict my remarks. Let me say -- at least to provoke discussion -- that I am less pessimistic than he is. I agree with him that the United States will not allow an even larger deficit with the Far East to develop. Nor can Japan take the place of the United States as a market -- and to the extent that it does, the NIEs will be under pressure to import more from the United States and from the next generation of NIEs in the Far East. Why then am I an optimist? First, because I believe the United States will force the NIEs to appreciate and open the doors wider even if it does not help the bilateral imbalance a great deal. Others can walk through the wider open door -- and I am sure Park agrees that that is a good thing. The EANIEs, like Japan, have shown in the past a remarkable capacity to adjust to adverse shocks from abroad and they have even greater resilience now.

Second, I believe a better solution than the NIEs' increasing domestic consumption or investment is possible. After all, Hong Kong and Taiwan are only extensions of China, and with the Chinese policy of "one country, two systems" we can foresee a huge investment by at least these two NIEs in China -- and there need be no return other than ownership of property in the motherland. For Korea also, similar opportunities may soon arise in North Korean and the Mekong region -- not to speak of the Philippines and Indonesia, although obviously the relationship is different. Where the world is so hungry for capital, it is rather strange to think that we have to adjust by reducing savings anywhere rather than by diverting investment to where it is needed. If we are talking of shared international responsibility, there is surely much that the EANIEs can share in terms not just of capital but technology and management, at least with their immediate neighbours; and this need not be done on commercial terms only. The EANIEs can play a greater part in providing concessional finance also -- particularly in respect of technical and managerial assistance.

My third reason for optimism is that if the EANIEs experience somewhat slower rates of growth after a long journey on the fast track, it is not really a disaster for them or for anyone else. Japan too is slowing down. Perhaps this may not be so bad for the environment; and perhaps it will be good for the psychological health of the passengers on the slow train.

I have assumed that the EANIEs have no serious domestic equity problems which might justify more consumption at home and the fiscal and other reforms that may go with this approach. This may not, of course, be wholly true. It is certainly not true of Thailand, Malaysia or Indonesia, which are also resource-rich. Does the Latin American remedy for equity have relevance for them?

I have refrained from commenting on China and India -- but I hope this symposium does not exhibit the same forgetfulness towards India which I have witnessed increasingly in so many international gatherings. If you want something else, however, to divert your attention, I suggest we devote some attention to Eastern Europe. Here are the SOCIALNIEs who are also challenging the rest of us to make room for them in an interdependent world: will they find it in a European bloc as the EANIEs may find in a yen bloc and LATINIEs in an American bloc? I hope not. For where will South Asia and the Middle East seek their salvation then?

Chapter IV

NATIONAL POLICIES FOR BALANCED AND SUSTAINABLE DEVELOPMENT IN THE POOR COUNTRIES: HOW TO AVOID INVOLUNTARY DE-LINKING

AFRICA: THE CHALLENGE OF GETTING POLITICS RIGHT

by

Goran HYDEN

THE GLOBAL CHALLENGE

The changes that are sweeping the world these days are stunning: the collapse of communism as an economic model and the rise of a radical reformer in the Soviet Union; the new ascendancy of economic power, rather than simply military strength, as a measure of national security and well-being; the global spread of democratic and free-market forces; and the palpable reduction in the threat of war between the super powers. Peace is breaking out, too. The bloody and seemingly endless wars in the Persian Gulf and Afghanistan are finally winding down. Conflicts in Angola, Namibia, Cambodia and Western Sahara that have been raging for more than a decade may also be ending, as the exhausted combatants face reality and decide to negotiate.

If the military conflict is receding, economic warfare seems to be on the rise. From Asia, the economic challenge from Japan and a half-dozen mini-Japans is growing daily. Meanwhile, Western Europe is organising itself into a trading bloc that may prove as tough and unyielding as Japan. In these circumstances, the risk of growing protectionism in the United States is real. Add to this the possibility that CMEA countries, as a result of the liberalisation of their economies, will emerge as yet another trading bloc within a single, integrated global economy, and we have the rough contours of the power constellations that will determine international politics in the 1990s and beyond.

Contemporary events often tend to look more overwhelming than those which have been "massaged" and "re-packaged" by historians. Thus, caution is warranted. Current trends may prove to future historians to be nothing but parenthetic. History is not surprise-free and we far too often tend to forget it. The point is that our rapid train may encounter mechanical problems -- even derail -- although we believe that we have taken all the necessary steps to pre-empt such mishaps or disasters.

This caveat notwithstanding, it is hard to escape the impression that we are on the verge of entering a new phase in global politics. We are in the process of leaving behind us the relative certainty of a bipolar world held in check by a balance in military strength and entering an uncertain multipolar world in which economic power will determine the equilibrium. This is a whole new ball game, or perhaps better put: it is like shifting the game from chess to poker. Being a master at chess is going to prove increasingly irrelevant as the world is turning to poker, where the rules differ and other skills and qualities, including the readiness to take risks, are needed. The challenges of tomorrow are likely to be quite different from those of yesterday.

At first glance, this "new" world looks more attractive as the spectre of nuclear destruction and prolonged wars appears to recede. The optimism and sense of relief that currently prevails in the United Nations and many other quarters, however, must not lull us into a false sense of security. Though tomorrow's challenges are less immediately threatening, they will prove elusive and often difficult to come to grips with. As, for instance, the market mentality takes greater hold in the East and in the South, the many different ways to a better life are implicitly reduced to one single track: that of pushing production and multiplying output. Yet such a trend is only likely to reinforce the pollution of the atmosphere with gases that prevent the Earth from reflecting solar heat back into space and trap it in the lower air, thus accelerating the global warming that a growing number of scientists already view as the principal threat to humankind in the 21st century.

The new world is also going to witness tension along two other lines. The first is between the rich and poor countries. While countries in the "South" will most probably continue to grow in economic strength, many will remain in poverty for the foreseeable future. The international community is going to be faced with the task of ensuring that these countries are not involuntarily de-linked from the faster growing parts of the globe. This implies finding means of enabling these countries to develop "from within", yet be beneficiaries of global integration. The second tension is likely to be between institutions and people. The task of global integration will have to be managed from above, by institutions that are far removed from the day-to-day concerns of ordinary people. As governmental and inter-governmental agencies engage in the difficult pursuit of managing and developing an increasingly diverse and multipolar world, the patience of people will be put to test. If politicians fail to legitimise their actions, people will show suspicion towards the very institutions on which successful global efforts depend. The risk of a backlash in terms of a growth of parochial sentiments should not be underestimated.

The challenges to tomorrow's political leaders are going to be no smaller than those facing the governments of the world today. In fact, if anything, they will become greater as the global economic environment turns increasingly fluctuating and uncertain. The concept of governance is bound to take on a new meaning, as prevailing models of policy-making will be questioned. Neither the marginal, incremented mode of policy-making derived from a rational choice model -- so prevalent in the United States today -- nor the more *dirigiste,* yet fine-tuning mode of policy-making associated with a corporatist Western Europe is likely to prove adequate for tomorrow's issues. This may prove to be particularly true in the industrialised world which has become used to operating according to two mottos: "more of the same" (Adam Smith) or "more to achieve the same" (John Maynard Keynes). As we move into the 1990s both these maxims will prove not only too conservative, but also increasingly out of touch with the emerging challenges of global integration; one because it is too economised, the other because it is too bureaucratic.

While the lure of social revolution no doubt will continue to be strong in societies affected by inequality and uncertainty, its image as providing a viable alternative to gradual change has been seriously compromised by the performances of Communist states. Although the record of states affected by religious fundamentalism is much shorter, there is little to suggest that it provides more than an escapist response. Revolutionary romanticism is going to prove no more beneficial to humankind than managerial incrementing.

Fortunately, there is a sizable middle ground between these two extremes that a new approach to governance can occupy. This middle ground gives leaders the opportunity to make the "big" decisions that pave the way for new opportunities for people to engage in productive and rewarding reciprocities. Governance becomes something more than just "running the system". It refers to the ability of leaders to mobilise the best in politics: to overcome its tendency to become libertarian, totalitarian, parochial or dirigiste. In a multipolar world where economic variables are particularly salient, more refined political skills will be needed. New rules of the game may have to be initiated and existing ones adjusted quite often to accommodate challenges caused by uneven distribution of resources or benefits, one-sided pursuit of narrow interests, destruction of a common resource, etc. Somewhat paradoxically (at least for some), the world is going to be more, not less, dependent on political intervention as it turns increasingly to the market.

With economic factors becoming increasingly important in international relations, it may not be out of place to refer to parallels in business. As recent literature, e.g., Peters and Waterman (1982), indicates, those companies fare best where managers can rise above the ordinary and provide the opportunities for employees to motivate themselves to do better. Companies do well when managers become leaders ready to make the big decisions. The same is true for societies: those that fare best have leaders with the ability to see beyond the status quo and make decisions that inspire people to new levels of collective action.

The creative aspects of politics, then, will be put to special tests in a world where economic factors are replacing military strength as measures of "national security" and well-being, but do so in the context of growing multipolarity and thus a fragmented economic hegemony; growing dualism both among and within countries in terms of economic participation; and a growing impotence of purely national decision-making. But if this challenge is universal, its articulation is bound to differ from country to country and from region to region, depending on the nature of its economy and society, and its place in the global "division of labour".

If this challenge of "getting politics right" is universal and applicable to international as well as national governance, Sub-Saharan Africa provides a particularly grave challenge for two related reasons. The first is that African governments since independence have by and large failed to perform the role of engine of development that everybody expected at the time of independence. The second is that in spite of a massive resource transfer from particularly Western donor countries, the international community has failed in its effort to boost African development. In analysing the current predicament in Africa, this paper addresses three questions:

i) Is Sub-Saharan Africa, in a comparative development perspective, a special case?;

ii) Is the "new" world a more congenial place for peripheral development?; and

iii) What need African leaders and the international community do to ensure a stronger position for these countries in the global economy?

AFRICA: A SPECIAL CASE?

In contrast to other Third World regions, Sub-Saharan Africa has shown consistently weak economic performance over an entire generation. To make matters worse, during the 1980s per capita income has fallen about three-quarters of the level reached by the end of the 1970s (World Bank, 1988). In Tanzania, for instance, the real income of an urban resident today is less than 40 per cent of what it was 20 years ago; for the average rural resident it is two-thirds of what it was in 1969 (Collier, 1987). A combination of external and domestic factors have contributed to this. Africa's poor economic performance has now begun to erode the region's productive base and human resources. By the end of the 1980s gross investment levels in many countries were too low to maintain capital stock, and health care and education are now deteriorating. Although these trends are not exclusive to Africa, a growing number of observers treat the continent as a special case. In the briefing for this symposium, Africa is singled out as the most probable candidate for "involuntary de-linking from the globalisation process" and thus, by implication, for falling behind the rest of the world even further.

It is only 20 years ago that Gunnar Myrdal (1968) made a similar prediction for India and other Asian countries -- an assertion which was proved to be wrong only a few years later. The difference between now and then is of course that Myrdal's domesday prophecy never became anything but a minority view while today's premonitions about Africa constitute the conventional wisdom. Thus, it is hard to escape the point that Africa is a special case. In what respects it is special, however, matters.

One school of thought argues that Africa's resource endowment is worse than that of other continents. Andrew Kamarck (1976), for instance, suggests that the poor quality of soil, irregular quantities and frequencies of rainfall and a multitude of pests and disease make agricultural development particularly difficult in Africa. While it is probably correct that tropical agriculture is more hazardous and time-consuming than agriculture in the temperate zones, many countries in the tropics, notably in Asia, have made great progress using the agricultural sector as the engine of growth. Even soils poor in nutrients can be developed and accommodate large numbers of people. For instance, Eastern Nigeria has some of the highest population densities in Africa on some of the poorest soils on the continent; yet, it is also one of the more prosperous places. A poor resource endowment, then, can hardly be used to argue the case of African exceptionality.

Others take the view that Africa's problem has little to do with its resource endowment but much to do with its economic management. This view is embraced particularly by economists in the leading international agencies concerned with development. The World Bank (1988) comes back to this set of problems in its most recent report on the state of the world economy. If anything, the managerial concerns have grown in recent years, not only because of development trends in Africa but also as a result of continued uncertainty in the global economy and an accelerating depletion of common resources. We must be able to get more out of less, according to a growing number of international institutions, the Brundtland Commission (1987) being perhaps the most important pacesetter. There is an increasing inclination to sound the alarm: to alert us against the threat to the survival of the planet. While sounding the bell to draw our attention to this global challenge is important, the strategy becomes more questionable when Africa is being singled out as the most urgent case because more people are living on the brink of disaster there than anywhere else.

The overall effect of this thinking is to reduce Africa to being a "welfare" case, constantly at the receiving end. It becomes a special case because of the particular lenses we use to examine reality. By reducing the African condition to a management problem, we tend to overlook the significance of local skills and local institutions.

Africa should be treated as special more because of its untapped potential than its deteriorating performance. This will only be achieved if we accept the historical anomaly of Sub-Saharan Africa as the only region in the world where the indigenous producers on the land haven't yet been effectively captured by other social classes. This does not mean that pre-colonial Africa was the home of the "noble savage" or "idyllic communitarianism". African society had its fair share of both rich and poor, but wealth did not translate into relations of production whereby one group of people owned the land and others tilled it. Social stratification was less the result of control of land than control of trade, particularly long-distance trade. Africa's pre-colonial empires and kingdoms earned their revenue foremost from such trade. When trade routes shifted in the 16th century as a result of European expansion, these political entities began to crumble.

Thus, the concept of state, as it is understood in the West, never survived in pre-colonial Africa. The notion of the state as a set of impersonal institutions created to serve the interests of a ruling class (as Marx and Engels not inappropriately described it) was unknown to Africans when it was first introduced by the colonial

113

powers some hundred years ago. Ethiopia was the only possible exception to this rule. By forcing Africans to produce for the world market and pay taxes the colonial powers changed the relations between rulers and ruled. Yet, with the exception of a few places where numerous Europeans settled, land was not alienated. It remained in the hands of local clan and lineage groups. The latter is significant because control of land never became, as it did elsewhere in the world, the prerogative of corporate villages. Even in colonial days, the state never really captured local institutions for its own ends.

A major reason for this was that the colonial state not only served external interests but also remained the preserve of European officers. African chiefs and notables were incorporated into the lower echelons of the service to make it more effective but, with the exception of a few countries in West Africa, hardly any African rose to a position of senior responsibility. Similarly, only a very small number of Africans were accepted into the ranks of the elite outside the civil service. Those who were had to do so on the conditions set by the colonial powers. Furthermore, colonial rule in Africa (unlike other regions of the Third World) was comparatively brief. For instance, Kenya's first president, Jomo Kenyatta, was born before the British established control of the territory. Before passing away, he ruled his country for 15 years.

For all these reasons, African countries at independence lacked two historical prerequisites that had been crucial to economic development in other parts of the world: i) a system of rule based on differential control of land; and ii) a concept of the state as a public realm with its own norms and rules.

To the extent that African public servants may have articulated such a concept they were vigorously fought by the continent's new political leaders in whose populist perception of things it was anathema.

This historical anomaly was ignored in the 1960s and 1970s because of the generally held assumption that development could be socially and politically engineered. In this technocratic scheme of things, capital transfers and manpower development programmes were going to make the difference. Official development assistance in the form of government-to-government transfers of funds led to a rapid expansion of the public sector in African countries without there being a real understanding of the role of the state in society. As a result, every effort to improve public management ran into serious difficulties as it encountered the tentacles of an all-pervasive system of patrimonial rule.

Following the so-called Berg Report (World Bank, 1981), even the ODA community has come to accept the limits of African governments. There are, for instance, growing pressures on these governments to turn state-owned corporations over to private shareholders. Privatisation, however, is only addressing the symptoms of a much larger problem that has been allowed to develop in Africa since independence without objections from either domestic or international sources: the increasingly personalised control of state funds by a small group of political leaders. This tendency, which is found in both "capitalist" and "socialist" countries, among honest as well as dishonest leaders, can only be explained with ref-

114

erence to the absence of the historical prerequisites of national development mentioned above. As Ali Mazrui has reiterated several times in the past three years: the real challenge to African economic development in the years ahead is how to de-privatise the state, i.e. how to reduce the influence of personal interests in the management of the state.

Africa is a special case but not necessarily or foremost for the reasons advanced in the international development community today. The implications thereof need to be examined in relation to its potential for advancement within the global economy.

IS PERIPHERAL DEVELOPMENT POSSIBLE?

This was the question that both analysts and policy-makers in the Third World seriously asked themselves two decades ago. Beginning with the "historical dependency school" in Latin America, a growing number of scholars suggested that as poorer countries in the periphery of the capitalist world economy are incorporated, they end up increasingly dependent on the metropolitan core countries. This argument came in different shapes. The *dependencistas* (e.g. Cardoso, 1973) accepted that capitalist development in the periphery had led to increased industrial output, gross national product, and aggregate national income, but inasmuch as these economies do not produce their own capital goods or technologies, they are "structurally incomplete" and must maintain a "dependent articulation" with a world economy dominated by transnational corporations in order to function at all. Under capitalism, the transnationals are the only source of the "missing" inputs to the productive process and therefore have the monopoly power to decide what shall be produced, and how. The decisions of the transnationals result in a form of local industrialisation that overemphasises the manufacturing of goods that, although massively consumed in the metropoli, are luxuries in the "periphery".

Following Lenin, others (e.g. Frank, 1969; Emmanuel, 1972; Rodney, 1972; and Amin, 1973) reasoned, in a neo-imperialist fashion, that international capital, centred in the metropolitan core of the world economy, imposes hierarchical, externally rooted structures of control upon the less developed "periphery" so that it may be more readily exploited. Exploitation consists in the extraction of surplus from the national economies of the "periphery", which cripples locally focused development. The less-developed countries are compelled by economic necessity to import capital, technology, and machinery, thereby becoming dependent upon foreign suppliers, financial institutions, and transnational corporate managements. Their conclusion was that only by voluntarily disengaging from the capitalist world economy is development feasible.

It is important to remember that this was not only an academic argument. It penetrated radical political circles in the Third World, particularly in Latin America and Africa, because it made sense. The periphery was sensing the full pressures of the global ambitions of capitalism in the 1960s. There was available

115

to governments in these countries an alternative economic model -- socialism -- that held out real promise for realising the ambitions of national development. In Africa, the optimism associated with the newly gained independence reinforced the desire to cut the ties with the metropole.

Although no government ever seriously contemplated a complete de-linking, the argument had a radicalistic effect on policies in the periphery. The responses in Latin America and Africa, however, differed. In Latin America, industrialisation had already proceeded thus reflecting the integration of these countries into the world economy. The dependency argument never became a "mainstream" political position, though it was translated into action in Chile and Peru.

In Africa, by contrast, with no real domestic industrial base nor an entrenched social structure, but caught in an ongoing liberation process, the anti-capitalist flavour of the dependency argument permeated the political leadership more easily. It manifested itself in a series of nationalisations and related policy interventions that drastically cut the flow of private capital to Africa in the early 1970s. Tanzania and Madagascar are only two of many cases in point. After these measures were taken, capital provided by international finance institutions and individual donor countries constituted the sole inflow to the continent. Such capital was preferred because it could be controlled by the leaders and it provided badly needed revenue. The extensive dependence on "soft" money that developed in Sub-Saharan Africa in the 1970s enabled the political leaders to avoid the question of how to expand the local revenue base and how to bring about an endogenous form of development.

The euphoria that spread in radical political circles in Africa in the wake of the first OPEC hike in oil prices created false expectations about new capital inflows to the continent and only reinforced the outward orientation of African leaders. Third World solidarity, however, fell far short of African expectations and when the "petro-dollars" began circulating, they were invested primarily in Asia and Latin America, leaving Africa increasingly peripheralised. Attempts by leaders like Julius Nyerere of Tanzania to rectify this situation through active participation in international fora like the Brandt Commission failed.

Although the African region has always been weaker than either Asia or Latin America by virtue of its heavy reliance on export of primary commodities, its position in the world economy was further weakened by the measures taken by many radical governments to nationalise foreign private capital. Thus, there is a connection between the voluntary measures taken in the late 1960s and early 1970s at least partially to de-link Africa from the global economy and the current state of affairs in which the continent is slipping so far out into the periphery of the world economy that talk of an involuntary de-linking is not out of place.

In the early 1980s, the Berg Report urged the African countries to "export themselves" out of their economic difficulties. By giving priority to export of cash crops, the downward trend could be broken. With world demand for these commodities going down or remaining stagnant, however, increased production has only led to declining prices and reduced earnings for the exporting countries. The problem has become particularly serious for cocoa-producing countries like the Ivory Coast. This frustration has been further exacerbated by the growing debt burden. There is a double irony here. Compared to Latin American countries, the debt service burden for African countries is much heavier -- in the extreme cases reaching over 100 per cent of export earnings -- yet the total debt per country is so small that it gives Africa virtually no leverage *vis-a-vis* their creditors. In the case of the larger debtor countries in Latin America, the creditors have as much to lose as the borrowers. These countries constitute important markets and money is tied down in long-term manufacturing investments. As a result, these countries have some say in negotiations with their creditors. The African countries, by contrast, have virtually none. Even if they join hands together, they achieve little. In addition to the fact that their loans are "light weight" to the creditor community, the Africans suffer because these loans are primarily with international finance institutions which lack operational flexibility and because they have often helped finance projects which have failed. The heavy debt overhang under which Africa suffers does raise serious concern not only in terms of the levels of human misery that it causes but also in terms of how it might be constructively resolved.

It is understandable that in this situation many African leaders are losing faith in the institutions managing the global economy and that, as a result, they implement IMF and World Bank agreements only with a moderate measure of enthusiasm and commitment. Behind the surface of apparent African compliance with demands for structural adjustment by these institutions is a crisis of confidence in the relations between Africa and the international community. It is exacerbated by both "aid fatigue" and a growing impatience in the West with the corrupt and tyrannical character of some African governments. Although aid agencies are under constant pressure to demonstrate that their "business" works, there is also a realisation that they cannot keep "throwing good money after bad". With the settlement of regional conflicts in areas where the West or the East have a strategic interest, as in southern Africa, another reason for outside interest in the continent is losing its importance. Furthermore, with biotechnology permitting the production of substitutes for crops that currently earn Africa foreign exchange, e.g., cocoa, sugar and vanilla, the continent's trade options are also being circumscribed. The new world, therefore, is not necessarily a more congenial place for peripheral development than the old one.

An involuntary de-linking, then, is a possibility that cannot be discounted. Although the strategic interest that more powerful nations have in Africa won't disappear completely, there is a growing risk that the prime reason why the rest of the world will interact with Africa is because of charity. In fact, we are already a long way in that direction. There is nothing developmental in such interaction, however, and it will only reinforce the image of Africa as a helpless continent.

WHAT CAN BE DONE?

In this context, voluntary de-linking has become an increasingly attractive alternative to some African intellectuals. Amin (1985), for instance, argues that it is the only way that Africa can ever get its economic house in order. With Africa currently getting so little in return for its incorporation into the global economy, this is the time for such a voluntary de-linking. The costs are no longer forbidding. Such a measure might also provide Africans with an opportunity to "find" themselves, i.e. to develop a new sense of confidence that can help the continent forward on its own in the longer run. This was the message, for instance, at a meeting of African scholars of varying disciplinary backgrounds held at Kericho, Kenya in 1987, the proceedings of which are about to be published (Achebe, Magadza and Pala Okeyo, 1989). Although there is a lot to be said for considering de-linking in the interest of enhancing the cultural dimension of development, this approach is associated with tremendous costs of its own. In Africa's highly import-dependent economies, any attempt at voluntary de-linking would bring the modern sector to a halt. It would lead to tremendous hardship for urban residents. In addition to a probable decline in living standards, African governments would have to engage in an increasingly "primitive accumulation", causing relations between government and people as well as between rich and poor to become more rather than less exploitative and oppressive. It can be argued, of course, that this is how societies elsewhere in the world developed and became strong. But are Africans going to accept the costs involved in this approach and will the rest of the world let it happen? The answer is almost certainly no and thus voluntary de-linking must be considered an improbable scenario.

Regional integration is actively advocated by African heads of state through the Lagos Plan of Action and related documents. Various steps have already been taken in this direction: ECOWAS in West Africa, the Preferential Trade Agreement (PTA) in Eastern and Southern Africa, and SADCC in Southern Africa. On paper, ECOWAS is the most ambitious with full economic integration as the ultimate objective. PTA is more akin to EFTA. SADCC is motivated by the common threat from racist South Africa. The fact that crucial national interests are at stake makes SADCC the strongest of these entities, but its significance to member states would considerably decline the day South Africa comes under majority rule. PTA remains a weak organisation in spite of attempts to promote it. Like ECOWAS it is struggling against heavy odds, foremost of which is the limited complementarity of member economies. Only those states with already more advanced economies like Nigeria, Ivory Coast, Kenya and Zimbabwe really benefit. Regional integration, then, is not going to make much of a difference in the short to medium term, as others, e.g. Ravenhill (1987) have also concluded. In view of the frustrations Africa has encountered in terms of promoting closer co-operation, it is significant that there is slowly emerging a debate about the validity and relevance of Africa's boundaries. Like the Holy Alliance in 19th century Europe, the Organization of African Unity has so far defended the sanctity of the colonial borders. Now this is being challenged by some prominent Africans. Nigeria's former head of state,

Olesugun Obasanjo, for instance, argues in a recent book (1987) that Africans ought to question the artificial divisions created for them by the colonisers in the 19th century. His own vision of Africa in the 21st century is a continent divided into six political confederations. Although large size is not a panacea, the initiation of a debate that transcends the integration by trade approach is being met with approval in many quarters.

Many have suggested that the only meaningful solution to Africa's current problems is to allow the writing-off of its foreign debts. Given the suffering that the debt burden has imposed on Africans, such a proposal finds a quick response. Some bilateral donors, and some private banks, have already taken steps in this direction. It must be recognised, however, that the debt is as much a symptom as a cause of Africa's woes. To a considerable extent, it is the result of poor investment decisions by the creditors themselves, but it is also the consequence of the backward nature of the African economies. Thus, even if the debts were to be written off without any conditions attached, so as to give Africa a fresh start, the basic social and economic structures as well as its unpredictable political setup would still be there.

Another proposal is to increase the flow of foreign aid to Africa. It must be remembered, however, that the conventional aid strategies have failed to engender equitable and sustainable development largely because they did not correspond to local realities. Implicit in these strategies is the belief that poverty can be successfully addressed in the Third World by outsiders -- whether they be international donors or national public officials -- lacking associations with and understanding of the poor and their communities. Donors have helped to create a modern institutional infrastructure in Africa that did not emerge from the local reality and that has little relationship to it. Aid agencies work through these structures because, being near mirror images of Northern institutions, they are easily identified and accessible and often share short term donor interests. Furthermore, these structures provide development and project information of a kind and in a form that generally corresponds to the needs of their Northern counterparts rather than those of the poor. The size of these structures is also a factor, for they appear to have the capacity to absorb large sums of aid monies. Usually, however, this capacity is lacking. This situation has helped to perpetuate the myth that Africa needs and can effectively utilise even greater financial resources than it presently receives. Quantitative goals for aid funding, such as one per cent of GNP, have been pursued without any practical demonstration of how this would be translated into more rapid, more extensive, or more relevant development among the poor.

As a recent report in the United States emphasises, we are at a crossroads (Hellinger *et al.*, 1988). We have a choice. The donor agencies in the North can continue the absurd task of defining development for the people of Africa, wrapping it in the rhetoric of a familiar cliché, or we can let go and allow the poor to define their own needs and support them as they take their own initiatives. We need to change the paradigm, turn it upside down, and build respectfully from below. If we listen to the voices of the poor, recognise and underwrite their own institutions as engines of social change, and withdraw support from those structures that are not impeding that change, the North can play a role in the engendering of equitable, broad-based, self-sustaining development and new democratic structures. There is little, if anything, to support the notion that larger quantities of aid lead to more development. On the contrary, with great amounts of money around, the donor community is only likely to continue supporting questionable projects and the already oversized "aid industry" with its own institutions, officials and consultants. Foreign aid in Africa needs to be reduced to what it is in Asian countries where it works quite well: only one, and a relatively small component of all public funding for development (Cassen, 1986).

If Africa and the world are serious about development, it must be recognised that it is society not the state, the people not the bureaucrats, that bring it about. The role of governments and donors must be to create an enabling environment, as an international conference organised by the Aga Khan Foundation in Nairobi, 1986, acknowledged. Given the nature of donor-recipient government relations and the attitude of African government leaders towards their own societies, this is an enormous challenge, because it involves major changes in political relations. Yet, if Africa is going to be able to develop using its own resources, there is nothing short of "getting politics right".

The revolts in 1988 against the one-party governments in Algeria and Burma are not necessarily indicative of what will happen in Sub-Saharan Africa but they can hardly go unnoticed. One took place in a country that has suffered the consequences of a rapid modernisation and integration into the global economy, the other in a country that has come as close to voluntary de-linking from the global economy as possible. Although the situation in both countries is still unsettled, the authorities have been forced to concede pressures for greater political openness. Events in the Soviet Union and China are also being watched in Africa. In some countries, there is an emerging debate using *perestroika* and *glasnost* as points of reference.

Political reform in Africa does not necessarily mean a move towards a liberal, multiparty democracy. It does, however, imply greater openness for actors other than those in control of government. African leaders are still captives of a high-risk patrimonial patronage politics. The vast majority of the continent's leaders insist on personal loyalty and unquestioned support of their own positions. The result is not only the stifling of public debate -- and thus often bad policy-making -- but also a futile effort to reduce societal conflicts to a single dimension: for or against the leader. Post-independence experience shows that this archaic form of rule, in spite of the use of an extensive -- and expensive -- secret police literally to spy on and occasionally intimidate people, only increases the arbitrary and unpredictable character of African politics (Wunsch and Olowu, 1989). As long as African leaders can treat politics as their personal realm with the ensuing confusion about what is *private* and *public,* and about what constitutes a *right* and an *obligation,* the climate for development is extremely hostile. Few, if any, individuals will make long-term investments in productive ventures; few individuals will consider it worthwhile the risk of starting or joining organisations with an objective to make an independent contribution to national development; few individuals will be interested in developing the communications media, etc.

In this respect, Sub-Saharan Africa differs from other Third World regions, where more advanced class differentiation has already put in place more institutionalised, and thus systemic, forms of rule. Class interests have crystallised in ideologies that give the political systems a more permanent character. Policies are being implemented and laws are being followed because there is an institutional machinery in place to accomplish these things. Compared to these countries, the state in Sub-Saharan Africa is very "soft": formal policies or laws are only followed when they suit the interests of the leaders and their followers. There is often a considerable gap between stated rules, on the one hand, and action on the other.

Politics is at the root of the African crisis by producing two tendencies that limit the ability of these countries to solve their problems: i) a servility, often bordering on sycophancy, among those few who can be made to benefit from this archaic form of rule; and ii) a withdrawal from civic participation by the many for whom the system is a nuisance.

The latter tendency has only grown in strength over the years. The prevalence of parallel or informal economies in Africa is as much the result of an arbitrary politics as it is of official price controls (Azarya and Chazan, 1987).

Three scenarios are possible for Sub-Saharan Africa in the 1990s and beyond. The first is that the present system of rule continues. This is almost inevitably a recipe for doom. Even those countries that are currently not on the list of "worst cases" will suffer stagnation and decline as politics continues to corrode the social fabric and leaves the international community with few, if any, meaningful ways of assisting these countries to reverse their predicaments. The end result is, almost by definition, involuntary de-linking and, at the least in the short to medium term, greater suffering.

The second scenario presupposes a growing opposition within the African countries to arbitrary rule. This is already apparent in the economically more advanced countries where class forces are beginning to crystallize. Demands for greater openness and for respect of human rights have been articulated with increasing vigour by professional and religious associations in countries like Kenya and Zimbabwe. This opposition may be quelled and critics co-opted into the system, in which case the country may reverse to the logic of the first scenario. Or, the opposition may succeed in transforming the political system in the direction of greater openness and respect for human rights. In that case, the outcome could become either voluntary de-linking or closer integration with the global community.

The third scenario implies that the political leadership in Africa realises the cost of the present system of rule and takes steps to transcend it. Structural adjustment policies may be supportive of this transition provided the leaders can see the benefit to the country and themselves and they can get a handle on them. To that extent, new economic policies are necessary but certainly not sufficient. At least four other measures must be seriously considered by African leaders in the immediate future.

The first is to redefine the role of the state in such a way that its scarce resources are truly employed in a fashion that supports national development. This does not imply rolling the state back in a neo-liberal fashion, but clearly making cuts where other organisations can be encouraged to do better what the state is doing now. The state is already oversized and in most countries a heavy burden on society. A large number of government employees can be expended particularly since salary only constitutes a small part of their total income today. If offered a meaningful sum of money at the time of being retired, they ought not to have any difficulty in making a transition to another occupation.

The second measure is to provide incentives for the government bureaucracy to become more client-oriented. Development policies must stop coming from a small group of top officials, or even worse, from expatriate consultants and advisors. By "lifting the ceiling" inside the public service, i.e. by encouraging different views and a real debate within government organisations, officials, even at lower echelons, may be encouraged to listen more carefully to what ordinary people suggest.

The third measure is a necessary corollary to the second. Citizens must feel free to organise themselves into associations to promote development, whether locally or beyond. Voluntary organisations are not just convenient mechanisms for implementing projects. They are an integral part of the institutional infrastructure of civil society. To be sure, freedom can be abused but if combined with responsibility it can enhance the strength of society as well as the state. Above all, institutional diversity has the potential of engendering cross-cutting loyalties that reduces the risk of politics becoming -- as it currently is in Africa -- an expensive and non-productive "zero-sum" game.

The fourth measure is to ensure that a greater reliance on the market forces becomes beneficial not only to a small number of individuals but to society at large. African countries badly need private investments in agriculture and industry but with the uncertainty that surrounds politics today, foreign investors are reluctant to move their capital to Africa and local investors find quicker returns in trade or real estate. Grooming a business class that is not dependent on the state for its strength and that is encouraged to act responsibly on its own may prove to be the single most important measure to be taken in the near future, because such a group of people, more than any other, may be powerful enough to demand greater reliability and greater efficiency from the state sector.

These measures would set in motion social forces that are contradictory but that is what development is all about. No society has ever developed without social contradictions. Africa's problem is that these contradictions have yet to crystallize. They need to be nurtured if Africa is going to develop and find itself on the same track as the rest of the world.

This is an enormous challenge to Africa's political leaders, but they have little choice. Sharing power has been seen in some circles in Africa as a sign of weakness, but it doesn't have to be viewed that way. To the extent that such an impression still prevails, it is the outcome of the way the first generation of African leaders have behaved as despotic rulers. The exercise of power can be changed in the direction of greater sharing and respect for the rights of others. It can be done incrementally or with a sense of historical drama as long as it is considered and presented as a necessary and positive step towards progress. Political leaders, courageous enough to take these measures, stand to gain a lot of personal legitimacy therefrom. Such a shift in governance may be precisely the kind of thing that will inspire Africans to re-dedicate themselves to national development and to make Westerners and others abandon their impression of Africa as the "doomed" continent.

"Getting politics right" should be an exclusively African affair, but the international community cannot take comfort in the assumption that African leaders will necessarily initiate this process, however compelling the reasons for such a move appear to be. It is quite possible that African government leaders will complacently let things continue the way they have evolved since independence. In this situation, where it is going to be even more evident than today that the African peoples really are victims of the way their countries are being ruled, the international community can hardly sit idly by with good conscience. To avoid having to cope with a situation that may be impossible to reverse, it must already now begin to consider what constructive measures can be taken to make African governments more responsive and accountable to their own peoples. Everybody knows that this is a move of both moral and practical problems, but even if these may seem forbidding, a debate about the possibility of political conditionalities should be started. At a time when the international finance institutions are already exercising considerable influence over financial and economic policy-making in Africa, such a debate may in fact be a step forward.

As a contribution to this debate I am proposing that the real challenge facing the international community and the African countries is how to convert their foreign debt into an asset for development. Repaying these loans in foreign currency is beyond the means of African countries. Unilaterally writing them off, as some countries, e.g., West Germany, Netherlands and the Scandinavian countries have done, may be an appropriate political gesture but, as suggested above, it is not going to alter the basic development equation in Africa. An alternative way forward may be to create a responsible system for allowing the African countries to repay these loans in local currency, provided certain conditions are met that enhance the prospect for sustainable development. This is not a totally new idea. Debt conversion into repayment in local currency is already being practised on a limited scale. For instance, UNICEF has been instrumental in such a move in the case of a loan from a private British bank in the Sudan. Susan George (1989) is advocating something similar in her book, *A Fate Worse than Debt*.

If the assumption made in this paper that a major reason for Africa's failure to develop is the frailty of its private and voluntary sectors, an agreement to convert debt repayment into local currency could be meaningfully pegged to the condition that African governments take the necessary steps to strengthen non-governmental organisations that have the potential of making a contribution to national development in a responsible manner. A specific proposal would be to create, e.g., a system of regional development funds within a country to which government treasuries are encouraged to pay off their foreign debt in local currency. The purpose of these funds would be to finance local development carried out by domestic voluntary agencies and community-based organisations. These African development foundations would be independent in that nobody currently active in a ruling party or government agency is eligible to serve on the board of these funding agencies. This would limit the risk that they would be captured by political patronage networks that may divert them from their original objectives. Board members would be individuals respected in their communities because of their integrity and commitment to public service. To avoid that these boards come under the control of only a certain type of persons, membership of certain categories, e.g., women, may be prescribed in the constitution. As a way of monitoring the progress of these funds, creditors might be awarded one seat. This way, there is no risk that the indigenous nature of the funds will be lost.

African governments might find such a proposal more acceptable if there is a chance for them to participate in this debt conversion scheme. As Susan George also proposes in her book, debt repayment in local currency may be pegged to creative projects initiated by the African governments with the aim of protecting or reviving the continent's threatened culture and ecology. In these cases, it might be difficult to assign a given pecuniary value to a project but an appropriate amount could be deducted from the debt as a reward for a successful implementation of such a project. Examples of what could be considered are projects to rehabilitate the physical environment and to restore a country's cultural heritage, e.g., languages, art forms or technologies.

Debt conversion into local currency on conditions such as those proposed above has two very strong advantages over existing measures. The first is that it gives the African governments an option. In the present setup, representatives of these governments are only told what to do and, as a result, they always find themselves on the defensive side. In the scheme proposed here, African governments that are uninterested in sharing responsibility for development decision-making with other institutions are allowed to continue paying off their debts in foreign currency. It gives African governments an opportunity to demonstrate how far they are capable of transcending the limitations of patrimonialism and thus introduce more open and constructive forms of governance, perhaps the most important prerequisite for a sustainable development on the continent. The second advantage is that funds will be made available in response to specific local demands. Rather than operating in an environment in which the lure of foreign aid distracts policymakers from critical institutional development concerns, the scheme proposed here stands the chance of enabling development to come from within and from below rather than from outside and from above.

To be sure, this is only a rough proposal and any attempt to take it seriously would involve careful consideration of a number of both economic and political issues, e.g.:

i) What time horizon should be adopted for a scheme like this?

ii) What quantities of debt might be converted at any particular time in order to avoid causing inflation?

iii) What criteria might be used in order to ensure that progress towards a responsible use of this approach is being made?

It should also be noted that many previous efforts to apply political conditionality, as for instance in the case of the United States putting political pressure on the governments of Liberia and Zaire, have not been very successful. The reason for this failure, however, is that these two African states have been clients of the United States. It has been very difficult for the US administration to apply pressure effectively in this situation. Constructive political conditionality of the type proposed above standards a much better chance of working in the 1990s, particularly if the East-West conflict subsides. Steps could also be taken by the international community that this debt conversion scheme would be administered by multilateral as opposed to bilateral agencies, thus reducing the probability that individual donor interests might undermine its original objectives.

There might still be those, not the least in African governments, who find this kind of scheme objectionable. After all, it does imply a certain infringement on national sovereignty. Yet, in the world that we live in today, such infringements are inevitable. The global challenge in a multipolar world dominated by economic factors is how such infringements can be redefined in positive and constructive terms, e.g., as necessary compromises to achieve a more prosperous and equitable world. In this sense, what is being proposed above is not exceptional to Africa. Yet, it is clear that the notion of political conditionality might be particularly objectionable to African leaders, who still remember the indignities associated with colonial rule and whose countries are the least incorporated into the global economy. That is why the task of avoiding Africa's de-linking from the global economy in the decades ahead is likely to be a painful process both for the continent's own governments and the international community.

BIBLIOGRAPHY

ACHEBE, Chinua, MAGADZA, Christopher, and OKEYO, Pala Achola *Beyond Hunger in Africa: The Conventional Wisdom and an Alternative Vision*, Heinemann Kenya, Nairobi, 1989.

AMIN, Samir *Accumulation on a World Scale*, Monthly Review Press, New York, 1973.

AMIN, Samir *La deconnexion*, La Decouverte, Paris 1985.

AZARYA, Victor and CHAZAN, Naomi, "Disengagement from the State in Africa: Reflections on the Experience of Ghana and Guinea", *Comparative Studies in Society and History*, Vol. 29, No. 1 (January, 1987).

BRUNDTLAND COMMISSION, *Our Common Future*, Oxford University Press, London, 1987.

CARDOSO, F. Henrique, *Dependency Revisited*, University of Texas, Austin, 1973

CASSEN, Robert, *Does Aid Work?* Clarendon Press, Oxford, 1986.

COLLIER, Paul "Aid and Economic Performance in Tanzania," paper presented to the Aid and Development Conference, Talloires, France, 13th-17th September 1987.

EMMANUEL, Arghiri *Unequal Exchange: A Study of the Imperialism of Trade*, Monthly Review Press, New York, 1972.

FRANK, André Gunder *Capitalism and Underdevelopment in Latin America*, Penguin Books, Harmondsworth, 1969.

GEORGE, Susan *A Fate Worse than Debt*, 2nd Edition, Pelican, London, 1989.

HELLINGER, Stephen *et al. Aid for Just Development: Report on the Future of Foreign Assistance*, Lynne Reiner, Boulder, Colorado, USA and London, 1988.

KAMARCK, Andrew M. *The Tropics and Economic Development*, Johns Hopkins Press, Baltimore, 1976.

MYDRAL, Gunnar *Asian Drama*, Random House, New York, 1972.

OBASANJO, Olesugun *Africa in Perspective; Myths and Realities*, Africana Publishing Corporation, New York, 1987.

PETERS, T.J. and WATERMAN, R.H. *In Search of Excellence: Lessons from America's Best-Run Companies*, Harper and Row, New York, 1982.

RAVENHILL, John ed. *Africa in Economic Crisis,* Columbia University Press, New York, 1987.

RODNEY, Walter *How Europe Underdeveloped Africa,* Bogle l'Ouverture Publications, London, 1972.

WORLD BANK *Towards an Accelerated Development in Sub-Saharan Africa,* Washington DC, 1981.

WORLD BANK *World Development Report 1988,* Washington DC, 1988.

WUNSCH, James and OLOWU, Dele *The Failure of the Centralised State in Africa,* Westview Press, Boulder, Colorado, USA, 1989.

NATIONAL POLICIES FOR DEVELOPMENT IN POOR COUNTRIES

by

Philip NDEGWA

One point I would like to make at the outset is that it is fitting that exploration of the important subject before us is being undertaken in a symposium organized by the OECD Development Centre. In modern times the countries in the OECD have dominated the economic and political affairs of the world, particularly since the beginning of this century. Political domination included other parts of the world; in fact in the case of Africa the dismantling of colonialism began only 32 years ago. Even where colonialism did not exist, economic domination assured the countries exercising it a great deal of political influence on the poor countries. It is true, of course, that in certain international issues, especially peace and security, the Soviet Union has been exercising the "superpower" role alongside the United States in recent years, especially since the Second World War. But in economic and finance matters, it is really the OECD group of countries which wield the clout. For example in those areas the Federal Republic of Germany and Japan are more influential than the Soviet Union.

The significance of these observations is that the circumstances now facing the poor countries are partly a result of the policies and practices of the OECD countries. Therefore discussion of the themes set for this Symposium under the auspices of an OECD organization is fitting for at least two reasons: first, it shows, one hopes, some recognition that the policies of OECD countries must also be looked into when discussing the economic future of the poor countries. Secondly, it is clear that whatever the poor countries do to promote their development will not provide a "sufficient condition" for achievement of that objective; in other words, action in the industrial countries and internationally in general is also necessary. This last point should be stressed because, realistically, the necessary changes at the international level, for example, in the area of trade, could only be achieved if the developed countries agree to such changes. It is these countries which have the power and economic flexibility to initiate such changes within their own economies and internationally. This is not to say that the countries of the Third World should not use whatever "bargaining strength" they might have to prod the industrial countries to agree to the necessary changes. However, although the developing countries absorb 27 per cent of the industrial countries' exports of manufactured goods, their bargaining strength is still too modest for the task.

Moreover, a truly collective and undivided approach by all developing nations appears an unrealistic expectation. In any case, instead of confrontational strategies, a better and more efficient approach would be an enlightened and truly international management of the existing situation in the world economy -- an approach in which those countries now with political and economic power should take the initiative. I believe that a deliberately and objectively *managed* world economy is not only feasible but would produce a more efficient and better world than the one which would evolve through unrestricted *market and natural forces*.

THE WORLD WE LIVE IN

As part of the necessary background and also as a way of indicating some of the elements in the prevailing international politico-economic environment, I want to make a few personal observations about the present world as I see it. First, there can be no doubt about the existence of a "two-track economy", although some might argue that a "three-track economy" would be more accurate. This is because while the industrial countries, including a handful which in 1960 were poor, have continued to grow in terms of material or economic wealth, the poor countries, particularly those which are very poor, continue to stagnate and in some cases actually experience negative growth rates. What will happen in the future? The analytical framework of a "multipolar and two-track world economy" suggested by Louis Emmerij is therefore a very useful one.

Secondly, while the world is becoming more severely divided economically, it is also becoming more interdependent in many ways. Transport and communications reveal a visible aspect of this phenomenon; but equally real and perhaps more fundamental are developments in the area of *environment*. Recent studies on, for example, climatic changes and consequences of the increasing loss of tropical forests show that all the countries of the world are really in "one boat" in which what happens in one part of the world, whether poor or rich, affects the rest of the world directly sooner or later.

Thirdly, our world is not a *peaceful* world. Those in the OECD countries can boast about the extended period of peace and prosperity since the last World War, but for the poor regions of the world it continues to be a period not only of poverty but also of armed conflicts and social upheavals of one sort or another. Let it be remembered that about 17 million have died since the last World War, most of them in the poor countries, through the so-called regional conflicts. It should be stressed that the prevailing situation is truly serious. For example, it is now estimated that war and war-related deaths in the South African and proxy-force wars against Angola and Mozambique amount to over 1 500 000, including over 800 000 infants and young children.

Fourthly, in terms of *leadership* the present world appears very different from the world of the 1960s. In those earlier years commitment to internationalism and belief that development in the poor countries was possible existed in many de-

130

veloped countries. As a result, aid programmes and other measures to support development efforts in the poor countries were actively pursued, although not on the same scale and nature as the Marshall Plan for the rehabilitation of Europe after the Second World War. Today in those same countries there is a so-called "aid fatigue", and increasing doubt concerning the feasibility of economic development in African countries, Bangladesh, etc. In my view, the negative attitudes created by the conservative governments in the North in dealing with the development problems of the poor countries -- whether those problems be external indebtedness, instability in commodity prices, or increasing unavailability of external markets and capital -- have been remarkably costly to the development commitment. In some of these countries the big international issues in the last eight years or so have been build-ups in defence programmes, summit meetings to discuss matters essentially of interest only to the developed countries, and economic adjustment programmes in which the poor countries have borne the biggest burden. Indeed one of the most serious worries about the future is whether political leadership in the North will change its attitudes and place the required importance on the truly global issues instead of concentration on national concerns often pursued through selfish strategies in which the poor of the world are ignored.

Fifthly, the present world is one in which *regional groupings* are becoming clearly established, even if not always through formal agreements and procedures. Reference has already been made to the growing tendencies within OECD to concentrate discussions about international matters, on those aspects of direct benefit to the members to the exclusion of non-members. This tendency has been strengthened by the equally growing tendency amongst these countries to harmonize their foreign economic policies and political stances in dealing with non-members. For example, in the international trade area the approach within OECD has been to promote a kind of share-out of benefits amongst the members. A good example here, in addition to the discriminatory trade practices against the developing countries, is world trade in agricultural products. In recent years discussions between the United States and the European Community in this area have concentrated on how the United States could regain what it has considered to be its rightful share in world trade. In those discussions no attention has been given to how the so-called primary producers (the poor countries) could be assured of their share in this trade (on which they are extremely more dependent than the industrial countries for foreign exchange earnings, employment, government revenues, etc.) (1). These tendencies in the OECD to discuss global matters "internally" with the main objective as promoting the interests of its members are likely to be strengthened by the recently concluded trade agreement between the United States and Canada, and the efforts being made in the European Community towards the establishment of a "single European market" by 1992. It seems clear that as the industrial countries devote their time to such discussions the interests of the poor countries will be progressively more marginalised

EXISTING WORLD REALITIES AND THE AFRICAN COUNTRIES: RESPONSES AND ADJUSTMENT

These are some of the realities of present world. They provide the context within which to look at the poor countries. The important question now is: How should the poor countries react to these realities? Here I shall not say much about Latin America and Asia; my concentration will be on Africa. This is for a number of reasons including the fact that Africa, especially sub-Saharan Africa, faces a more awkward development situation than the regions of Latin America and Asia even if some countries in those regions face contexts more similar to Africa than to the general ones of their own region. In fact, it should be recognized that while the interests of Latin America and Asia and Africa coincide in many cases in matters relating to desirable actions at the international level to promote these regions' development, the circumstances facing Africa are very different from those of the other two developing regions. Indeed, most of the countries of Latin America and Asia should be able to join the "fast moving train" if the right actions were taken to give these countries unhindered access to the markets of the industrial countries, more international capital and money markets, equitable and practical measures to deal with these countries' external debts so that they can grow out of their indebtedness; and unrestricted access to technologies available in the industrial countries. Initially most of these countries are also better prepared for faster and sustained development -- because they have longer established and more experienced national institutions for development; on average they are bigger geographically and in population and are therefore potentially more viable than most African countries; they are already relatively more developed and therefore more "attractive" to foreign producers and investors; their high-level and middle-level manpower resources are bigger; etc.

On the other hand, the situation facing African countries is very different. A number of aspects of this situation are well-known: for example, most African countries are very small (13 have a population of one million or less; a further 12 have populations of about 5 million or less; while only Nigeria, Egypt, Zaire and Ethiopia have populations exceeding 30 million); there is a severe shortage of trained manpower; a number of African countries have yet to achieve satisfactory levels of national consolidation or unity (e.g. in about one quarter of African countries there are internal conflicts of one sort or another either because of ethnic differences, border conflicts or general political and economic collapse); in almost all African countries infrastructural facilities, especially for transport and communications purposes, are exceedingly inadequate, etc. Another factor now also becoming known is the fragility of the continent's environment and the rapid rate of degradation -- two examples of such damage being the "southward march" of the Sahara desert, and the accelerating loss of soil in virtually all these countries. Some of these environmental losses are almost irreplaceable.

A significant factor in the African development situation, a factor which is not often recognized or given sufficient weight even by such organizations as the World Bank and the IMF, is a phenomenon of which development experts have little experience. This is the high speed with which various forces affecting Africa's development are interacting with each other. Changes, often unplanned, are taking place at a pace never witnessed before. The main force behind this phenomenon is the high rate of increase in population. When the population of a country doubles in 18 to 20 years, and given the fact that the country in question is already poor and does not have the necessary manpower, foreign exchange, technological and other resources for managing that increase, then enormous economic, social and political consequences can be expected. The interactions between the high rates of population growth, the resources available, the environment and the expectations of the people for food, employment and better living conditions in general create major challenges in terms of knowledge (planning), the magnitude of the action needed, and the severely short period of time within which such action should be undertaken. For example, what challenges in the area of food supply are created by the population's doubling in 20 years when food production per capita has already been considerably and consistently below the rate of increase in population and in some countries has even been negative? How are the required job opportunities to be created, especially when about 70 per cent of the population is under 25? What about provision of education, health and other services? Will it be possible to maintain law and order, especially in the furiously expanding urban centres which are doubling in population every 10 years or so?

These interactions present a development challenge of a nature which has not been encountered before. The situation contains many conceptual and intellectual challenges in addition to the practical ones. In particular, the orthodox standard approach of using per capita incomes and their growth rates as targets for development performance must be regarded as inadequate -- and perhaps even misleading and dangerous. What, for example, would be the rate of growth of per capita income needed to achieve satisfactory levels of employment if all other things remained unequal? In other words would it not be unrealistic in Africa to see employment creation as something which will result from per capita income growth rates in an automatic fashion? It appears to me a kind of "new economics", certainly in planning terms, is needed in which the major considerations would be basic human requirements such as food supply, employment, education, health, water supply and other such physical material needs instead of per capita incomes. Planning targets should be for such physical requirements, not per capita income (2). Moreover and very importantly, strategies for pursuing such targets should be reviewed. For example efforts to create enough jobs should include expansion of smallholder production in agriculture and here land reforms may be necessary;   encouragement of the informal sector in the urban and rural areas; greater public support through credit and extension services for smallholder production and informal sector activities; necessary changes in education and training programmes in order to emphasize skills for ready and self-employment; industrial location policies which would ensure expansion of rural towns; family planning measures, etc. To assume that an increase in per capita income would somehow generate the required job opportunities and therefore concentrate on that strategy would, in the case of Africa at any rate, be a prescription for more unemployment.

Unfortunately the proposed approach in both target-setting and implementation strategies does not have ready-made theoretical planning tools and systems. This is a challenge not only to development economists but also to experts in political science, sociology, business management and to natural scientists. All such experts must be involved because the development problematic in Africa calls for a truly multi-disciplinary approach to design new tools and strategies for dealing with it. Past experiences are certainly useful; but for Africa they are not "sufficient" for the job.

This intellectual challenge is a most urgent matter because of the prevailing tendency or pressure to prescribe programmes and strategies that will not work -- at times could make matters worse. In that connection and as we have seen in recent years, the response of the World Bank, the IMF, and the donors in general to the situation facing the African countries has been to urge reliance on more or less market-based economic analysis and prescriptions. In the process African countries have been urged (at times forced!) to liberalize their markets; reduce protection to their industries; devalue their currencies; reduce or abolish subsidies; increase agricultural producer prices; raise rates of interest; all but eliminate budgetary deficits, etc. Further, they are asked to undertake such measures within very short periods of time e.g. the IMF Standby arrangements. It should be pointed out none the less that some of the policy measures advocated by the World Bank and the IMF are often necessary in dealing with the development crisis. For example low agricultural producer prices, rates of interest and exchange rates, and expansion of the budgetary deficit, etc. in many cases call for firm corrective action. Therefore what is said here should not be seen as condemning such policy measures wholesale. The main points being made are that:

i) On their own such measures are not sufficient for the job;

ii) The measures proposed are often expected to be implemented within entirely unrealistic time frames;

iii) Some of the measures ignore social and human consequences which then hinder further development;

iv) Some of the measures, such as those which lead to less growth and more unemployment in countries which cannot afford social security arrangements, are inappropriate;

v) Some results are unexpected and probably perverse e.g. frequent falls in real producer food prices and destruction of small-scale low import/high labour intensity manufacturing enterprises; and

vi) Very fundamentally, action is also necessary at the international level (3).

It is to the credit of African countries that many of them have carried out so-called "structural adjustment programmes" of types which require rare political courage -- kinds of programmes which, it should be noted, leaders in many industrial countries would not dare apply to their own economies. Unfortunately, the results of these efforts have not been successful in many cases: in some the result has not been the renewed growth which had been hoped for but increased hardship on the already poor people, social upheavals, and at times the overthrow of the government itself. Such results could be expected because the prescriptions given to those countries were never sufficient to deal with the problem. In particular, the World Bank, the IMF and the donors have consistently ignored or under rated the enormous importance of external factors in the creation of the economic and social crisis facing the African countries. For example to ignore these countries' dependence on commodities and the enormous collapse in commodity prices in recent years (to the extent that for sub-Saharan Africa the real prices are now lower than 50 years ago) (4); to ignore the obstacles created by high interest rates in financial markets and the growing inaccessibility to those markets by African countries; and to underestimate the necessity of concessionary resources and the consequences of the substantial reduction in such resources in recent years etc. is to engage in partial analysis to say the least. Further, for the World Bank, IMF and the donor countries to urge African countries to adopt more open and export-oriented development strategies while the industrial countries maintain severe tariff and non-tariff barriers against the products of African countries (e.g. meat, sugar, horticultural commodities) could be regarded as rather hypocritical. I am aware that both the World Bank and IMF have argued for freer export access for, and larger resource transfers to Africa, but they do not in any operational sense link these exhortations to the world to programme imposition in Africa. One other point: to ask African countries to undertake many important measures, including severe reduction in the already low living standards, more or less overnight is to treat these countries as mechanical constructions in which changes could be taken without regard to social and political consequences -- even if such measures were the right ones.

These are some of the realities which must be taken into account in designing programmes for enabling the African countries to embark upon the task of reversing the prevailing trends in their development. Development in Africa is most certainly possible. First, the continent has the natural resources to do better in development than has been the case so far. In particular the continent is extremely rich in natural resources. For example, Africa also has 97 per cent of the world's chrome; 85 per cent of its platinum; about 70 to 80 per cent of its gold and diamonds; and about 64 per cent of its manganese. Africa has plenty of other minerals such as copper, uranium and cobalt. In addition, and in spite of limited exploration which has taken place in the continent, Africa has substantial oil and natural gas resources and tremendous hydroelectricity potential (estimated to be at least 25 per cent of the world potential). Furthermore, and in spite of the fragility of the African soil, the continent has the capacity to produce much more food than it actually requires, especially given better water management, greater use of irrigation, and application of new technologies including the use of fertilizers and chemicals. Incidentally the application of fertilizer per hectare in Africa is only a small fraction of the amount used in Asia.

However, in the area of high-level manpower the situation is not favourable. In Africa this problem is twofold. First, there are severe shortages in many countries. Secondly and also very worrying is the growing "brain drain" now taking place in the continent. For example there are four times as many Ghanaian doctors abroad than in Ghana itself (5). The causes of this brain drain include poor economic circumstances (often caused or started by external factors) and internal social upheavals. Obviously Africa cannot afford to lose any of its trained high-level manpower resources. Therefore, urgent efforts are needed to deal with the "push" factors behind the brain drain. The "pull" factors must also be recognized. These also call for deliberate and active measures, which should include ensuring that education programmes contain elements for promoting nationalism and patriotism. High-level and middle-level manpower is a key issue because almost all the development efforts now needed call for more properly trained manpower (6). Indeed in many cases technical assistance is still needed. In the area of unskilled workers the situation is, of course very different -- there is serious and growing oversupply. Indeed the challenge which now looks impossible is to create enough job opportunities for the rapidly growing labour force.

POLITICS AND DEVELOPMENT IN AFRICA

Before making a few specific suggestions on what Africa itself can do to deal with its development challenge, a word or two on the social and political consequences of the economic situation now facing African countries might be in order. In that connection there are major challenges in the area of social and political management posed by the development crisis now prevailing in a framework of high and rising expectations for better living conditions from the rapidly increasing numbers of people. In these situations some will be tempted to think that only authoritarian regimes can contain emerging pressures and enforce the necessary measures for development. Certainly, democracy as understood in the West, will face a major challenge in the next 20 years or so in Africa. In fact that challenge already exists, and many African countries are now looking for ways of ensuring that the challenge of development can be met through strategies which remain essentially democratic. That is the way I interpret the increasing attractiveness of the "one political party democracy" experiments in Africa. Given the multi-ethnic make-up of these countries (and therefore the risk that multiparty systems would be ethnically based), and given the need for national unity and consolidation (one of the basic necessary conditions for development), then the one party political system makes eminent political sense today. Unfortunately, those commenting on the matter appear to be disinterested in establishing the justification for such experiments and consideration of how those experiments could be made more democratic where weaknesses might exist. Instead, there appear to be, at least in the West, preconceived convictions against such experiments. Consequently the one-party experiments have been condemned "before hearing". It cannot be stressed too strongly that African countries must devise their own administrative, social and political systems for dealing with the unprecedented crises facing them. In doing so, they should be ready to learn from the experiences of other countries; but it would be entirely unwise for them to copy traditions and systems in a blind fashion.

However and as already stated, democratic principles will be under serious pressure in Africa -- even within the single political party systems. In that connection it should be stressed that it would be a tragedy for the African countries if the notion (held by some) that democracy could be put in cold storage for the time being and pulled out in years to come were to prevail. Authoritarianism has never been able to promote economic development as effectively as those democratic systems which guarantee mass participation in all aspects of development. Even in the brief experience of Africa it is clear that democratic civilian administrations have achieved more in the way of development than military dictatorships. Therefore the development pressures facing African countries must not be used as excuses for suppressing democracy. Indeed upholding of democratic principles is one of the requirements for better development performance in Africa in the years to come.

Another likely temptation in Africa will be to think that economic and social problems can be overcome reasonably quickly through left-wing oriented management systems. Such temptations must not be underestimated. In fact, though the socialist countries of Eastern Europe -- also China -- are modifying their ideological and economic management practices away from rigid socialism, one can expect that in Africa temptations to think that socialism will be the short-cut solution to the prevailing and intensifying economic and social crisis will increase. The attractiveness of such temptations will be increased in those countries in which development patterns lead to unacceptable inequalities in income distribution and in which corrupt practices and tendencies are not vigorously suppressed.

Socialism will not produce short-cut solutions to the African economic crisis. Indeed, those African countries which have attempted reasonably serious socialist experiments in the past have fared badly compared with those which have encouraged personal initiatives within mixed-economy type of systems. In any case no system of economic management will work unless it is based on developing the capacity of the people so that they can work for their own development: discipline, hard work, and courage to take the difficult decisions when they are needed.

Another temptation which is likely to spread in Africa is to think that military administrations would do better in dealing with the development crisis and its attendant economic and social pressures. In many African countries military administrations have already been imposed, on the argument that the politicians have failed the people and their countries, and that military intervention is necessary to clean up the mess and establish better conditions for economic growth. However, experience so far shows that military intervention leads to greater instability of the political and social systems. Experience also shows that military governments are not as effective as civilian administrations in promoting development. Military interventions must therefore be resisted as strongly as possible. This will not be an easy exercise, especially now that most African countries have armed forces far larger than they really need for their own internal requirements while economic and social pressures continue to intensify. The most effective ways of preventing military interventions, in addition to appropriate education and training for the soldiers, include the following:

i) Getting the people to participate fully in all economic and political programmes, including the process of decision making;

ii) Ensuring that the thrust of public development efforts is the welfare of the people in all parts of the country;

iii) Firm suppression of antisocial activities, especially of corruption and negative tribalism;

iv) Education of the people about all development problems, including the relationships between short-run and long-term aspects, and possible solutions to those problems; and

v) Maintenance of democratic principles, including properly conducted and regular elections.

THE NECESSITY OF CO-OPERATION BETWEEN AFRICAN COUNTRIES

Much more can be said about the implications of the development situation facing African countries in the area of social and political management in the years to come. However, I shall now come back to the main theme of the Symposium and to ask specifically the following questions: given the internal and external realities facing the African countries, what can they do to safeguard their survival and political independence (7)? Should African countries wait until the powerful external forces discussed earlier and which continue to affect their development adversely have been dealt with internationally? Is there anything they can do on their own and which they are not now doing, at least sufficiently, to tackle their economic and social crisis?

Complete answers to these questions require more space than we have available. The following is a brief summary to add to and strengthen the policy recommendations implied in the foregoing discussion on the internal and external factors in Africa's development crisis. First, Africa must not wait for international reforms to take place. Depending on one's interpretation of the situation and prognosis of political developments in the industrialised countries, one can be fairly or very pessimistic about early agreement on such changes or reforms. However, Africa and other developing regions must never give up hope in their struggle for more equitable economic relations between themselves and the industrial countries. This is a struggle which must be pursued continuously and through all forums such as the Uruguay Round of Multilateral Trade Negotiations; the meetings of the UN General Assembly and its various bodies; the negotiations for the next Lomé Convention; the meetings of the World Bank and IMF, etc. To the extent that all the

138

developing regions can work together, their "bargaining strength" will be increased and possibilities of some success assured.

With regard to African countries' de-linking themselves from the rest of the world, the answer is straightforward: they cannot manage to do so, and nor should they try to. African countries are much too dependent on the rest of the world to be able to "de-link" themselves from it (8). As noted above, many African countries are much too small to be able to deal with their development requirements entirely on their own. That has been one of the experiences learnt since these countries achieved political independence. That reality has been strengthened by what has happened over the last ten years or so. During that period most African countries have undertaken structural adjustment programmes and economic reforms of very fundamental nature, but because of their internal weaknesses and the unfavourable external environment these efforts have not achieved much. In fact it can be argued that in most African countries what is lacking is not national policies for development; what is missing is external support to enable those policies to produce the desired results.

Even if the external environment were to improve, it would still be necessary for African countries to co-operate with each other if they are to achieve significant results from their development efforts. The fact that the needed changes in the external environment are unlikely to be realized in the near future makes such co-operation that much more imperative. In fact co-operation among African countries is one of the necessary conditions for their development. In this sense the concept of de-linking, in a modified form, makes sense. What is now needed in Africa is a concerted, comprehensive and politically pursued effort to increase the continent's capacity for self-generated development. In that regard my analysis of the situation convinces me that a deliberate programme of collective self-reliance amongst African countries, essentially through production-sharing and arrangements to increase intra-African trade to facilitate such production, is now the only viable alternative open to these countries to do something about the overall economic crisis they are facing (9). The kinds of programmes these countries have been following so far and which have largely been based on the advice of the World Bank, the IMF, the donors and on inherited approaches to economic planning have simply not worked, and their continuation will mean perpetuation of Africa's poverty, vulnerability to changes in prices of the few commodities which these countries export, and dependence -- economic and political.

African countries must simply actively co-operate with each other and thus establish better conditions for their growth. In that co-operation intra-African trade is the most important element. Promotion of that trade will require *deliberate economic and political action* to re-orient these countries' trade. That "trade diversion" will not mean economic inefficiency: indeed if there is evidence of economic inefficiency being pursued for narrowly selfish purposes it is protectionism and export dumping in the industrial countries -- for example the EEC is now the second largest exporter of sugar and beef. African countries are now importing large quantities of food items (wheat, maize, rice, vegetable oils and dairy products) and simple manufactures which they could easily produce on their own given production-sharing and the necessary trade arrangements. Therefore, while these countries should do all they can to secure agreement on the necessary international supportive measures for the commodities they export, for the external capital they need, etc., they must embark on self-generated strategies based on economic co-operation on the broadest front possible. Such an approach is not only viable and feasible; it is also absolutely essential given the internal and external circumstances facing these countries now and in the foreseeable future.

If the World Bank and the donors wish to support co-operation in Africa one of the things they could do is assist in the development of infrastructural facilities in the continent. Transport, communications and other basic services are so inadequate that they seriously inhibit internal development and economic transactions with neighbouring countries. Indeed, as far as trade is concerned, lack of transportation facilities is a much bigger barrier than tariffs, exchange controls, and lack of satisfactory payments arrangements. The urgent need to improve Africa's roads, railways, harbours, etc. cannot really be exaggerated.

PEOPLE'S PARTICIPATION IN DEVELOPMENT EFFORTS

One other measure which African countries must undertake urgently and with determination is to base all their development efforts more on the people's participation and involvement and to do so to the fullest extent possible. People are the main beneficiaries of development; but people are also the main instrument for that development. Wherever governments have tried to promote development for the people the results have always been disappointing, and at times disastrous. On the other hand where development efforts have been based on the people themselves the results have been consistently better. Moreover and as argued earlier,the risks ahead against democracy, and the need to avoid ideological confusions, demand people's involvement in all economic and political programmes. In other words, people's involvement and participation as advocated here are essential for better and equitable development performance and maintenance of democratic principles.

WHO SPEAKS FOR THE WORLD?

I would like to conclude by discussing briefly the issue of the management of the international economy. At the beginning of this paper I made a number of observations about the world in which we live. Most of those observations showed that, in my view, our world is not a happy or attractive place. However, I also believe that this must not be regarded as the predestined order of things. Our world can be a better world, especially in the relations between North and South, through planned efforts instead of leaving the world to evolve on its own through forces of nature and the so-called market forces. Further I believe a realistically and sensibly "managed" world is possible, and that such management can be undertaken without introduction of rigidities in the functioning on the international economy.

As I think about these matters a question which keeps on coming up and for which I have no answer is *"Who speaks for the world?"*. The world consists of rich developed countries and poor nations struggling to survive. In the past two decades or so the rich countries have tended to ignore the poor countries or to assume that their own success will also help the poor countries. This approach of lack of concern for the poor, an approach which for image purposes is often referred to as the "trickling down" strategy by the industrial countries, has led to a more divided world between the rich and the poor; a world of food surpluses in the industrial countries while hundreds of millions in the Third World are undergoing severe hunger and malnutrition; a world threatened by environmental disasters from pollution and the consequences of growing mass poverty in the poor nations; and in a world in which vast financial and high-level manpower are spent on defence instead of productive programmes for human development and welfare. In this situation who speaks for the world? At present no one. Do we have to wait until there is a major breakdown in the international economy like that of the Great Depression, or a major international disaster like the Second World War, to agree on a better and equitably managed world economy? Who speaks for the world? This Symposium is essentially asking that question; and it is hoped that the OECD group of countries will make it their business in the next decade and beyond to promote "a one-world and one-destiny" concept. Such an initiative would be welcomed by all.

NOTES AND REFERENCES

1. I am aware that the Cairns Group includes some poor agricultural exporters, but it is marginal relative to the United States and the EEC.

2. The basic argument here is also strengthened by the empirical evidence that in some cases, average per capita incomes could increase with the poor becoming poorer.

3. Some of these points are discussed in the IDS Bulletin Vol. 19, No. 1, *Stabilisation -- For Growth or Decay?*, IDS, Sussex, January 1988.

4. See CULPEPER, Roy, *Forced Adjustment,* the North-South Institute, Ottawa, 1987, p.2

5. The brain drain in Africa has actually accelerated in recent years. For example, it is estimated that over the last three years or so Nigeria has lost more than 200 specialist medical doctors to foreign countries and universities.

6. The term "properly trained" is used because there is the danger that, for certain reasons including short-run political considerations, more university graduates with general liberal arts degrees will be produced than the numbers required. It is in the areas of natural sciences, agriculture, engineering, health and *trained* teachers, administrators and managers that should be given emphasis.

7. Political independence is, in my view, a very important issue since presumably no country would wish to be economically "linked" while being politically dependent on other countries.

8. Actually, and as argued earlier, the problem is that global political and economic trends are de-linking these countries even though they do not desire that result.

9. For a detailed analysis of this argument and related issues, see my book, NDEGWA, Philip, *The African Challenge: In Search of Appropriate Development Strategies,* Heinemann Kenya, Nairobi, 1986.

DISCUSSANTS CONTRIBUTION

by

Bashir BAKRI

I agree with Philip Ndegwa when he says that Africa must not wait for international reforms to take place and our presence here must be perceived as participation in the struggle for more equitable relations between North and South. Despite the fact that in the end my presentation expresses my personal viewpoint, it has drawn considerably on trends of thinking which characterise the Sudanese scholarly and academic community as well as that community in Africa as a whole. Specifically, I would like to convey the University of Khartoum's intention to follow up the debates which will be generated in this symposium and the recommendations which will be reached.

All the above must be seen in relation to my personal experience with the OECD Development Centre since the early 1960s, a time when I was Sudanese Ambassador to France.

First, I would like to commend the authors of the papers before us on their admirable efforts and the high calibre of their contributions. However, I would stress that the papers should not be seen as representing a view from the North that is in opposition to that from the South, rather each should be seen as complementary to the other.

1. Both authors clearly place great emphasis on the issue of governance and the specific political system to be adopted if we are to overcome the current problems of managing the crisis in Africa.

   Nonetheless, I find myself in disagreement with some of the specific alternatives offered by the authors. First, as far as the one-political-party democracy suggested by Ndegwa is concerned, my view is that in the past the success of such a system has largely depended on the existence of a charismatic leader (Nyerere in Tanzania, Nasser in Egypt and Nkrumah in Ghana, are cases in point). Therefore, we must question the viability of such experiments in the absence of such leaders and more specifically whether the historical milieu, which was vital to their coming to power can be reproduced in the contemporary situation.

Recognizing the many dangers of adopting a western-style liberal democracy in Africa, nevertheless I feel it is the least harmful system and the safest in terms of reducing the possibility of involuntary de-linking. Both authors have also neglected to mention the problems of governance in the countries of the North. Clearly De Gaulle and Palme in the North for example, with their interest in problems of Africa, have made a lot of difference in the past and might have had a similar impact in the future, had they lived.

2. I feel that both authors have underplayed the cultural dimension in the development process. In the case of Africa, in particular, when the OAU came into existence it recognized the political boundaries established by the colonial powers. These boundaries had been drawn up without regard to issues of cultural identity, a fact which has complicated processes of nation-building and led to numerous cases of armed conflict (Biafra and Southern Sudan are cases in point). This problem can only finally be overcome through the creation of new multi-state federations which could treat issues of cultural identity with more suppleness (an example might be a Union of the States of the Nile valley including Egypt, Sudan, Ethopia, Kenya and Uganda). Such unions can better face and deal with similar big entities in the North such as the European common market, United States/Canada and South East Asia.

3. This leads me to the crucial theme of this Symposium: issues of linking and de-linking. Both authors have concentrated on ways to prevent the process of de-linking. Though I agree to a large extent with their analysis, my own suggestions are, in contrast, more geared towards how to further the process of linking, since I am more concerned with how to negotiate linking on conditions set by and favourable to countries of the South. This could more easily be achieved if we face the North from a strong and unified position as groups of nations rather than individually.

As far as structural adjustment programmes are concerned, they should be designed in such a way as to mitigate their adverse socioeconomic effects, ensure that the human dimension is taken into account, further improve the well being of the poor and disadvantaged in African societies -- notably through redirecting social and development expenditures -- and make short-term stabilization and adjustment measures compatible with -- indeed part of -- long-term structural transformation.

Finally, we have discussed the debt burden as an obstacle to development in developing countries for a long time. In Sudan, with the agreement of that country's government, UNICEF purchased the debt owed to the Midland Bank, a sum of $800 000. The Sudan government paid a discount sum in local currency equivalent to this debt which was then used by UNICEF in drilling water for the region of Kordopan. This operation was executed very successfully by UNICEF.

144

If a part of the debt of the world were given to international organizations to execute development projects in the Third World, this would represent a solution of repaying debts through development. We prefer development rather than relief as an answer to disasters. Disasters, natural or man-made, have become one of the features of our world in developing countries. In Sudan, we are preparing a symposium on disaster management.

DISCUSSANT'S CONTRIBUTION

by

G. Arthur BROWN

Although the subject to be discussed refers to poor countries throughout the world, both Philip Ndegwa and Goran Hyden have sought to limit their analysis to sub-Saharan Africa. This is probably a good proxy for poor countries and in my comments I will not seek to extend the coverage. There is so much in these two excellent papers on which one should concentrate, that to widen the coverage would detract from the important issues they have raised.

Both see involuntary de-linking as more than likely if present trends continue. Indeed Ndegwa feels that for many African countries, depending on the definition used, involuntary de-linking may already have taken place. One could argue that where the countries of the developed and developing world are so diametrically apart in standards of living, in available food and nutrition, in housing and water, medical care and education, that notwithstanding some minimal commercial links, these countries are not in the same league. The only common thread is the existence of human beings and the fact that we all inhabit the same planet, but all else is different in both degree to an exaggerated extent, and in many cases in kind also.

Both authors look back to the colonial era for the roots of these differences, with Ndegwa blaming the OECD countries specifically. He would attach more importance to the external environment than would Hyden. The relative share of responsibilities of blame on both external factors and internal are, however, not that great when both analysis are compared and what is striking are the similarities of diagnosis and remedies coming from persons looking at Africa through different eyes.

Everyone would accept that the external environment has been a hostile one for the poor countries. Developed countries, since the oil crisis, have certainly been more concerned about their own economic health and prosperity than in devising a concerned policy to help the poor countries. Certainly, charity and hopes of dampening social upheavals have been the leading forces motivating aid, rather than policies to help with the achievement of self-sustaining growth. Ndegwa longs for, and believes that an objectively managed world economy in which the interests and concerns of poorer countries are safeguarded is possible. Skeptics will point to the abortive attempts to establish the NIEO, the New International

Economic Order. Euphoria was high in the 1960s and 1970s that a sort of just society redressing the extremes between rich and poor countries was possible of achievement. Thousands of man hours of negotiations went into global negotiations to achieve the NIEO and the objectives of the various development decades. There was no lack of time devoted by the international communities in various forums to bring about this better managed world economy but even the staunchest stalwarts gave up. Is there room for believing that this is one of those ideas which were good but whose time had not yet come? Is there a basis for assuming that if not a full-fledged NIEO but some positive movement towards it is now possible?

Hyden particularly points out the tremendous shifts which have occurred in the political and economic arenas. President Bush recently banished the use of the words "cold war". The resolution of tensions between the super powers and the settlement of regional conflicts provide a totally different setting than even five years ago. The shifts in economic power are even more striking. In this environment, could one actively revive the idea of diverting the funds which would be saved on military expenditure to development? Would the huge surpluses accruing to some countries be recycled in a way in which petro dollars were not -- be recycled on a grant or soft loan basis?

Hyden makes the startling statement that foreign aid to Africa needs to be reduced, and Ndegwa feels that the World Bank should confine itself to funding infrastructures like roads, railways, or telecommunications. I agree with many of the criticisms of foreign aid. But I see a need not for a reduction, but a change in the way aid is provided. With increased aid funding, there could be a one-time write off of all external debts in the very poorest countries some fifty or so -- public, private, and multilateral, with the private debt redeemed at the existing heavy discount. Many African countries are not paying debt charges due on their loans, but the overhang of this debt and continuing pressures it exerts result in an excessive preoccupation in decision-making and economic planning. African countries would be able to start with a clean sheet, with no negative balances. The sums involved are not large. To prevent lapses, a concerted policy of integrating adequate aid to support a development programme would be needed. Structural adjustment has become a dirty word and I have avoided it, because if structural adjustment means nothing more than pursuing those economic policies which will engender growth, why refer to structural adjustment at all? Why not speak of growth policies or economic development policies?

Even with the debt wiped out, poor countries will require financing to meet the gap between immediate minimum consumption and investment requirements on the one hand, and available resources on the other. The world should accept that no viable policy can be based on cutbacks in standards of living which are already abysmally low. Further, the ability to save for investment is curtailed by the unavailability of resources to meet even these minimum consumption needs. We sometimes tend to be mesmerised by percentages. A growth rate of 5 per cent per annum is considered outstanding but if the country has a per capita income of $200, 5 per cent will give $10 per annum, 20 cents per week, 3 cents per day. What can be made of this? No matter how expertly poor countries manage, they will not escape the poverty trap if there is not both a generous and sensible approach to meeting the gap between a gradual improvement in unacceptable low standards and some minimum standards.

And what is meant by sensible? It means donors ceasing to play God, ceasing to enforce their priorities as a condition of aid on the grounds that recipients either do not know better or cannot be trusted. Everyone pays lip service to the sovereignty argument. Countries must be free to determine their priorities -- but this is not put into practice. It is true that what we need are rationally determined priorities based on knowledge and understanding of how the economy works, and the ability to manage the implementation of the policies needed to achieve the agreed goals. This must be distinguished from irrational policies based on conflicting and unachievable goals. My conclusion, therefore, is that one of the highest priorities of technical assistance must be the helping of countries to get the capacity to set up data bases, collect and analyse information, know the advantages and disadvantages of various alternative policies, so that they can make the best use of both internal and external resources. On this basis, donor governments and multilateral institutions could then make sector or programme grants and loans unconditionally leaving countries to determine their best use.

But both Ndegwa and Hyden have reminded us of the reality of African politics. Hyden claims that politics is at the root of the African crisis. Not only is there cruelty and inhumanity between ruler and ruled but the economic resources of the state are regarded in many cases as indistinct from the personal fortunes of the ruler. As an African, Ndegwa invites us not to condemn without analysis what he calls a one-party democracy. Many would say the term itself is inconsistent. It ill becomes an outsider to intervene in these issues and make the mistake of proposing what is best for Africa. Suffice it to say, no matter how favourable the external environment and enlightened the provision of aid, the gloom in the forecast of both authors will undoubtedly be realized if there is not some form of governance acceptable to the African people which is put in place.

One obvious point here is that unless western concepts of improved standards of living -- health, housing, nutrition, etc. -- are abandoned, no matter how much natural resources are available and how much foreign aid, there will not be sustainable development if the human resources are not available. There is a direct link between inhuman and dictatorial government and absence of human resources. It is the best brains who leave. Such capital as is accumulated leaves the country to build a nest egg when the owners have to run from tyranny.

I believe that if good governance comes to Africa, much else would follow. Hyden has set out some of the necessary conditions. If I understand Ndegwa, his conclusion seems to be that even with good governance, he would see some form of de-linking as making sense. He sees the future of Africa as coming from collective self-reliance based on regional co-operation. To quote him, this is the only viable alternative open to African countries.

I wish I could share his optimism. The history of regional co-operation in both the political and economic spheres has not been good. It is not as if it had not been tried. The regional economic body which really flowered into true regional economic co-operation was the East African Community but as we know it died. There is now a veritable "alphabet soup" of regional bodies in Africa, but apart from numerous meetings, it is difficult to see concrete achievements other than an output of paper. The single exception is the Regional Banks and it is possible that in the field of financial co-operation, there are benefits to be achieved if properly pursued.

Chapter V

INTERNATIONAL POLICIES FOR ASSISTING THE POOR COUNTRIES IN ATTAINING BALANCED AND SUSTAINABLE DEVELOPMENT

HUMAN GOALS IN RETROSPECT AND PROSPECT

by

Richard JOLLY

The theme adopted for the 25th anniversary symposium of the OECD Development Centre is to define the contours of a "world development strategy based on growth and solidarity" which would reverse the trend towards two-track development and, in the case of this paper, explore international policies for assisting poor countries in attaining balanced and sustainable development. At first sight, this may seem an idealistic endeavour in a world where dominant economic powers are still wedded to free market philosophies, small government and limited national and international interventions. The problems of successful economic intervention at the international level are considered much more difficult today than when the Development Centre was founded in 1963 -- a time when international trade and finance were still within governmental control and the OECD countries, led by the United States, were more closely united around activist Keynesian approaches.

Yet the pendulum may be about to swing again -- back from the extremes of non-interventionist philosophy to the realisation that governments need to do more than simply assure national defence and the efficient working of markets. For example, the environmental threats of global warming and ozone depletion, deforestation and desertification all require a macro analysis to guide national and international action. In another arena, 1988 has seen dramatic demonstrations of how super-power leadership can ease military conflict and provide a climate for peace and disarmament initiatives. The American Economic Association has captured the current economic mood. Based on the preoccupation of a recent AEA meeting, the *New York Times* commented that "this appears to be becoming a less caustic, possibly a gentler, kinder age", it added: "If economic growth and a free market place are the all-purpose solutions to poverty, economists are starting to ask, why has American poverty worsened in the last two decades (1)?

In an effort to explore the direction of international development policies during the coming decades, this paper will address three topics:

i) The changes in social conditions in developing countries over the last four decades;

ii) Some of the longer term trends in international and social policies over the last two centuries; and

iii)   Development policies for the 1990s: human goals as a central and feasible focus of assistance to poor countries for attaining balanced and sustainable development.

The presentation will draw heavily on the recent experiences of UNICEF, not to promote the organisation but in an attempt to make a more practical contribution. In putting forward these thoughts, I must first acknowledge my debt to many friends and colleagues both inside and outside of UNICEF. No organisation, nor any individual, is an island unto itself. The interactions and provocations, inspirations and often absurdities of day-to-day international life require external friendships and involvements to maintain a sense of proportion.

SOCIAL PROGRESS SINCE WORLD WAR II

Notwithstanding the severe economic and human setbacks in Africa and Latin America during the 1980s, Mahesh Patel comments in a forthcoming paper that:

"The social image of the Third World has altered vastly since 1950. Its social progress has in so many ways been much superior to its economic advance. The widespread concern with eliminating this or that pressing social evil -- malaria, smallpox, high IMRs (infant mortality rates), illiteracy -- has obscured a fuller perception of how immensely different are the social snapshots of the 1950s and that of the South of the 1980s" (2).

In death rates, infant mortality rates, life expectancy, literacy rates and school enrolments, developing countries as a whole and in their different groupings have not only made rapid progress since 1950 but traversed in three decades or so "a social distance" which took most of the industrial countries a century or more to cover. With infant mortality, for instance, Patel notes that:

"The average IMR for the developed market countries was 30 in 1960, with a range from 17 (Sweden) to 46 (Spain). By 1986, 18 countries, classified as developing countries, with a total population of 1.2 billion, about a third of the total population of all developing countries, had reached this range of infant mortality rates".

In 1950, the low income countries had infant mortality rates equivalent to those of the new industrial countries of Europe in 1850, or about 200 deaths in the first year of life per 1 000 live births. They were literally a century behind in terms of this social indicator. In 1985, only some 35 years later, infant mortality rates in these low income economies had fallen to about 70 per thousand. This is equivalent to the average IMR for the developed market economies of Europe in 1940.

Mahesh Patel concludes:

"In absolute levels, it took almost 100 years for the IMR of the new developed market economies to fall from 200 to 70. This achievement was replicated by the low income countries in just 35 years".

Reduction in infant and child mortality is by no means the only impressive social advance in recent years. Indicators for life expectancy, literacy rate, and school enrolments also reflect progress. However, during the 1980s, progress ground to a halt and in some cases retreated in many African and Latin American countries -- a tragic and unnecessary reversal in light of the tremendous gains during the previous three decades.

Moreover, such "social progress" already has considerable economic significance, in improving the basic human capital on which future economic and social development can be built. In addition, the social progress outlined, especially the advances in female literacy and the reductions in IMR should help to provide the conditions for fertility rates to fall. Lower population growth rates in turn hold promise of easing the economic cost of sustaining this social progress and making some acceleration of long-run economic growth easier to achieve.

THE EVOLUTION OF INTERNATIONAL AND SOCIAL POLICIES FROM THE 1800s

To set the current situation in historical context, it may be instructive to go back even further in reviewing social progress. Table 1 illustrates the evolution of social policy and the changes in morality in relation to children over the last two centuries, both at the national and international levels. The left column traces the evolution of international developments and the right column reviews national developments in social policy and action for children, primarily using the case of England. Four important trends can be observed:

i) Broadened perspectives and preoccupations in economic development from the national to the international, and even to the global level;

ii) A shift from emphasizing improvements in personal morality and the ethical beliefs of individuals as the means of social advance, to a strengthening of law and formalised obligations, at first nationally but in this century, internationally;

iii) Broadened legal and administrative concern with human and social issues in the course of industrialisation and economic development, at first nationally, but in this century spreading to the international level; and

iv) A trend from personal and casual perceptions of human needs towards analyses based on systematic information, statistics and formal reporting.

Looking back over 200 years highlights the significant and generally positive changes which have occurred in national and later, in international social policies. Arguably, the interaction between morality, legislation, economic advance and internationalism has been a significant force behind social progress. The following sections will review some historical trends, which owe much to the vision and leadership of outstanding individuals, as well as to important social movements. At the very least, such a review may inspire us as to where we may go in the future.

Growing internationalism

Let us first remind ourselves how far we have come along the trend towards growing internationalism. As F.P. Walters's *History of the League of Nations* makes clear, "Before the League, it was held both in theory and practice, that every State was the sole and sovereign judge of its own acts, owing no allegiance to any higher authority, entitled to resent criticism or even questioning by other States. Such conceptions have disappeared for ever; it is not doubted, and can never again be doubted, that the community of nations has the moral and legal right to discuss and judge the international conduct of each of its members" (3).

Walters notes several distinct lines of thought and influence leading to 20th century internationalism. There were the 17th and 18th century contributions of the radical moralists and the radical philosophers, the Quakers who dreamed of peace, and the lawyers who called for international law, pre-eminently Grotius, whose book on the Law of War and Peace was published in 1625. By the 19th century, their ideas had been given strength by the imperatives of practical co-operation to cope with the increase in trade, communications and other international economic relationships.

In parallel, there was a growing political awareness of the benefits of consultation and arbitration rather than belligerence and war. Walters comments that "between 1815 and 1914 situations critical for peace led on numerous occasions to meetings of the great powers and that their deliberations were able on some of these occasions to avert the danger. Between 1815 and 1900 disputes and differences between States were submitted to arbitration on some 200 occasions, and in the vast majority of these cases the arbitrators' award was duly carried out by both parties". Yet, as Walters notes, the Concert of Europe "rested on no formal instrument: its members were not bound to meet, and when they did meet, their proceedings were governed by no constitutional obligations".

The creation of the League of Nations in 1919, its death and the rebirth of internationalism with the United Nations in 1946, is familiar to all of us. But perhaps too often, in our preoccupation with the weaknesses, biases and partial nature of internationalism as it has developed, we overlook the dramatic change from the international anarchy of ideas and total lack of organisation which existed before.

The struggle for social progress at the national level: The example of Britain

Against the backdrop of a growing internationalisation, Britain offers a national example of the struggle to give greater importance to human and social issues. During the course of industrialisation and economic development, some of the earliest experiments in state intervention for the welfare of children took place in Britain. Before drawing some international parallels, I will identify a few of the policy landmarks in the history of children's development.

The early English labour laws reflected the popular view that poverty was the result of shiftlessness. Indeed, a statute in 1575 provided for the use of public funds to employ children in order to "accustom them to labour" and "afford a prophylactic against vagabonds and paupers" (4). Opposition to child labour reform endured until the 1800s, when committed individuals mounted a moral crusade against the harmful consequences of relying solely on the "free exercise" of capital. By the 1830s, a changing society began to bring pressure upon the political system. In the name of promoting their physical, moral and religious welfare, children became the prime objects of statutory intervention.

The Factory Act of 1833 was the first in a series of legislative measures to set a minimum age for children employed in factories and coal mines, and to control the number of working hours per day. The Act set the minimum age of employment in textile mills at nine years and limited children aged 9 to 13 to an eight-hour day. In 1856, 6:00 am to 6:00 pm was established as the limit within which children could work. By the 1870s, the working conditions of children had become a responsibility of the state: legislation for adults was to follow. As noted by one observer, "The child labour movement has in every country supplied the stock-troops in the struggle for decent working conditions" (5).

As further limitations on the use of child labour were introduced, so was legislation to promote the education and health of children. By 1880, education was made compulsory for 5- to 10-year-olds, regardless of whether parents were in agreement. In 1908, the neglect of a child's health by a parent was made a legal offence. The introduction of a broader range of welfare legislation during the early 1990s not only recognised the hopeless inadequacy of the earlier Poor Laws, but also the need for systematic state social policy and support. After the crisis of the 1930s, and spurred by the Second World War, a more comprehensive approach to employment, health, education and the other dimensions of social policy was established with the creation of the welfare state in Britain, paralleled by other developments, sometimes more comprehensive, elsewhere in Europe. Once the political commitment had been made to embark on measures of social reform, legislation followed rapidly, as did more strident efforts at enforcement.

Some international parallels

At this point, let me return to international policy developments. Let me simply note the enormous contrasts between the limited early economic initiatives of the League and the ILO (not to mention the ill-fated World Economic Conference of 1932-33) and, a generation and a World War later, the comprehensive international attempts to support and co-ordinate national economic policies represented by the establishment of the Bretton Woods organisations in 1944, the IMF and the World Bank (then, the IBRD). Soon afterwards came the enormous international transfers of resources from the United States to Europe under the Marshall Plan during 1948-51, in Churchill's phrase, "the most unsordid act in history". The Marshall Plan provided support for the postwar reconstruction of the European economies, thereby recognizing the need for support from one nation to others, based on international co-operation in economic planning. Later this principle was extended in aid to developing countries, though almost always with resource transfers less by an order of magnitude than those of the Marshall Plan and with much more of the planning done or heavily influenced by the donor party. In 1964 came UNCTAD, the creation of Prebisch (and others) which not only recognised the need for positive resource transfers, but for action to *offset* the unequal bargaining powers in economic matters between developing and developed countries. Slightly before came the First Development Decade, introduced by President Kennedy's personal call for a United Nations frame of action to accelerate economic development within the developing countries.

The main point to be drawn from this overview is that, initially, the major international institutions and developments primarily had an economic focus, suggesting a parallel with the initial focus of 19th century *national* policies on economic issues. Although the ILO in its early years had brought social concerns to internationalism, the dominant preoccupations of the League, as of the United Nations, was with the political and economic, notwithstanding the important emphasis on human rights in the basic charter of the United Nations. Even the UN resolution on the First Development Decade was essentially an economic document. It was left to Hans Singer, in elaborating the three page resolution into a solid, 100 page action document for the UN Secretariat, to introduce the human dimensions in a highly percipient statement written in 1962:

"The problem of the underdeveloped countries is not just growth, but development. Development is growth *plus* change; change in turn is social and cultural as well as economic, and qualitative as well as quantitative. It should no longer be necessary to speak of 'economic and social development', since development -- as distinct from growth -- should automatically include both".

It was not that human and social issues were forgotten, but, unlike the economic policies, they were considered to be matters of national rather than international concern. The main shift in focus came in the 1970s. A succession of world conferences drew attention to the neglected dimensions of development, the international ramifications, and the need for international stimulus and support for broader national action: the Stockholm Environment Conference in 1972, the World Food Conference in 1974, the World Population Conference in 1975, the World Employment Conference in 1976 and the Habitat Conference on Shelter in 1978. Over the same period, the World Bank, under the leadership of McNamara began to emphasize the eradication of poverty as a key objective of international aid and development.

Recent advances for children

Narrowing the focus to children, there have also been some important developments at the international level. First, the international effort to eradicate smallpox, particularly from 1966 to 1978 has resulted in 2 million *fewer* deaths per year at a total cost of less than $300 million (equivalent to the cost of three fighter-bombers). For technical reasons the eradication of smallpox could only have succeeded as an international effort; it depended on an international perception of the problem and its solution. Encouraged by this dramatic international achievement, proposals came forward for accelerating immunisation against other diseases, eventually leading to the Alma Ata Declaration on primary health care and the international call for Health for All by the year 2000.

The WHO/UNICEF immunisation efforts during the 1980s, and UNICEF's call for a Child Survival and Development Revolution form part of this trend. UNICEF gives these actions high priority toward the general goal of halving infant and child mortality rates by the year 2000. They are also having an impact. In spite of the economic setbacks of the 1980s, the number of children under 5 years of age dying each from readily preventible causes had fallen by an estimated 2.25 million by 1988.

There are also parallels between the emergence of "Adjustment with a Human Face" and the earlier experience of broadening national economic policy-making to take account of its social implications for children. Only five years ago the IMF viewed its contribution to adjustment programmes as limited to economic issues and consequences. However, reflected in the forthright statements of the IMF Managing Director in 1986 (and later the IMF), now clearly recognises that adjustment programme must take into account the human implications.

Nevertheless, as UNICEF's *State of the World's Children Report 1989* makes clear, the economic crises of the 1980s -- increasing debt, declining commodity prices, limited export markets, and high interest rates -- have had a tragic impact on children and women in developing countries. To a considerable extent, this is also the result of neglect and weaknesses in national policy-making. Yet, it is also a consequence of international weaknesses and of limited perceptions and mandates. That the latter is in part responsible for the human consequences is still disputed in some quarters -- although there is more agreement than three years ago.

159

In this, there are parallels, as mentioned earlier, between 19th century national attempts to separate economic policy-making from its social consequences with these latter-day attempts to separate international economic policy-making from its social consequences.

In terms of legislation, national movements for institutionalising and codifying legal concerns for children have their direct international parallels. At the international level, the process of codifying children's rights began with the Geneva Declaration on the Rights of the Child, adopted by the League of Nations in 1924. The next step in the process was the adoption in 1959 of the United Nations Declaration on the Rights of the Child, which plays an "advisory" role. Being put to the UN General Assembly for ratification in Autumn 1989 is the Convention on the rights of the Child, which goes one step further toward defining universally acceptable minimum standards. As a legal treaty which will be binding on the states that ratify it, the new Convention has a broader significance which is obvious when set in the context of the above-mentioned international trends concerning children.

Finally, it is worth mentioning what many see as a small technical detail but which is of much more fundamental importance: international support for establishing better statistical and information systems on social issues. The System of National Accounts (SNA) has been widely promoted by the United Nations since the late 1940s. It emerged from national concerns with unemployment during the 1930s: to tackle unemployment using Keynesian techniques, national policy required national accounts, constructed to identify investment, consumption, government expenditure, exports, imports, etc. Spurred by these needs, and supported by numerous UN conferences and technical assistance missions, the SNA has now led to a global system of national economic accounting. This has not merely provided a basic statistical system, but has greatly influenced the way in which we perceive and even think of international economic issues and development. The challenge is now to establish broader statistical systems and information flows that will more adequately reflect the broader dimensions of progress in an internationally comparable way.

The above historical trends should form part of our thinking about future international policy: not only the broadening of economic policies from the national to the international level, but also the growing concerns with the social dimensions of development in legal, institutional and statistical matters. None of these trends proceed independently. They remind us that development is not merely a technical issue, but is ultimately a matter of ethics and political action. They remind us that morality marches in step with capacity, and that capacity is not just a matter of technical and economic feasibility but of public awareness and political will. Finally, it shows us that although human and social progress are influenced by economic advance, there is also a heavy role for leadership and action, driven less by the finer balancings of economic calculus than by the broader visions of political commitment and enlightened international self-interest.

Against this backdrop, I will sketch a framework for international development policy in the years to come. The emphasis will be on international support for substantive and measurable progress toward enhancing human capacities, with the international agencies playing a catalytic role. In this context, their main function is to stimulate and support countries in setting goals and together with governments and donor agencies, to work directly on the realisation of these goals in poorer countries.

The rationale for this focus on basic human needs is political, humanitarian and strategic for future economic growth. Amartya Sen put forward the concept of human capabilities as a basic focus for development efforts ensuring better nutrition and universal access to health, education, water, sanitation and shelter (7). These are all priorities for ensuring that a country's population realise their human potential with the physical and intellectual preparation needed to be productive -- and needed to participate in a democratic society.

In stressing basic human needs as a necessary condition for ensuring human capabilities, it is important to avoid the political sensitivities created by the emphasis on basic needs at the end of the 1970s. Basic human needs must never be put forward as the *only* development goal, let alone as an alternative to the national and international structural reforms needed to limit the inequalities of power and economic influence which exist today, particularly between the rich, middle-income and poor countries. Having occurred in many industrialised countries in the past, structural reforms must eventually be made part of international policy-making.

A call for building up human capabilities is not a call for a unique approach, nor for a single view of the relative roles of government and non-government initiatives. The approaches will continue to vary, country-by-country and over time. But just as international economic policy-making has developed, so it is now necessary for parallel developments to occur in social and human fields.

The social role of international agencies: lessons from experience

Some important lessons can be drawn from UNICEF's experience in promoting progress towards a few of the key human and social goals of the Third Development Decade. Since the early 1980s, UNICEF has focused on the following goals.

To reduce infant and under-5 mortality rates (U5MR): the target is to halve 1980 rates by the year 2000, and in all countries to reduce IMR to a maximum of 50 and U5MR to a maximum of 70 by the same year.

To accelerate immunisation against the six main preventable diseases: the aim is to achieve universal coverage for tuberculosis, whooping cough, diptheria, tetanus, polio, and measles for children under one year by 1990.

To promote oral rehydration therapy to reduce deaths from diarrhoeal dehydration: the aim is to ensure 100 per cent access to and 50 per cent use of ORT by 1989 (although in practice, UNICEF is aiming for 1990).

The last two goals derive directly from resolutions by Ministers of Health meeting in the World Health Assembly by the immunisation goals were also made part of the Third Development Decade.

The main lessons learned by UNICEF have come from using these goals as catalysts for mobilising greater action for children in developing countries and from applying the principle of "management by objectives" within the organisation. Below are some of the possibilities for future application which emerge from UNICEF's experience.

International support for country-level action

Without a doubt, the most important factor for achieving set goals is action at the country level. None of UNICEF's past achievements would have been possible without the decision by governments to act and without the commitment of the relevant national ministries. In turn, recent experience shows that this rarely occurs at the national level when there is an international "vacuum". The accelerated action for child health witnessed in many countries during the 1980s can usually be attributed to co-operation between governments and the international community. Sometimes it has been technical support from WHO which has provided the stimulus for change, sometimes intense UNICEF advocacy, and sometimes the example provided by other countries in similar circumstances. In Africa, it has often been the provision of additional financial support which has acted as a spur. The nature of the world today, with its vast communications network and abundance of technical knowledge, is such that few countries can make decisions on these matters totally in isolation.

Regional or sub-regional initiatives are also important, as exemplified in 1986 by the South Asian Association for Regional Co-operation (SAARC). For the first time, it took substantive decisions on co-operative action toward human-focused goals, covering most of the areas listed in Table 2. The role of non-governmental agencies in generating demand and mobilising for action has also been significant. Churches and mosques, womens' movements, Rotarian, Boy Scouts and Girl Guides have all worked to generate an awareness of the possibilities and a commitment to action. In addition to raising funds, this has attracted millions of volunteers.

Collaboration

Collaboration is essential, if only because many national and international actors are already involved in the areas of action. As regards the Child Survival and Development efforts in the 1980s, major support has come from working groups formed by representatives from governments, donor countries, and international agencies. One reason for the success of many of these groups is that they have managed to avoid the deadening formalities of formal co-ordination, instead forming a more focused and operational grouping of individuals with vision, knowledge and resources behind them.

"Management by objectives"

"Management by objectives" has perhaps been of greater significant than even now is realised. By adopting targets that were measurable and could be monitored, country by country, a focus on targets and performance was introduced which has been of the greatest importance for accelerating towards human needs objectives into the field operations of UNICEF.

An illustration of this is the adoption of targets for immunisation. Initially there was a considerable amount of rhetoric. Gradually, however, as more countries developed a system for monitoring immunisation coverage, it became possible in 1986 to obtain regular data. By 1988, a system was in place to monitor a country's achievements at quarterly intervals, as well as its probability of achieving universal immunisation by 1990. We have now reached a point where, region by region, we can identify the countries where progress is satisfactory and those which require additional support.

Statistics for monitoring

As every planning manual makes clear, monitoring is essential. Yet, experience has revealed many practical lessons on the role of statistics for monitoring, which many manuals omit. First, detailed monitoring is not required to get programmes underway -- indeed, the demand for monitoring only grows as progress accelerates. For UNICEF, it was only after measurable progress was being made toward its immunisation and oral rehydration therapy (ORT) goals that serious questions were asked about the impact on national rates of infant and child mortality. Until then, we relied mainly on local studies to assess impact and to advocate the practical effectiveness of immunisation and ORT.

As the interventions grew in scale, it became critical to develop measures of national progress toward reducing IMR and U5MR. At this point, UNICEF realised that most international data on child mortality was not based on recent first-hand evidence from countries, but were estimates calculated by the UN Population Division in New York. (Although serious effort is put into these statistical constructs, their base is usually an extrapolation from a census of 5, 10 or 15 years earlier.) Hence, attention was shifted to the annual collection of data on infant and child mortality rates based on sample surveys. This is still at an experimental stage, not for reasons of technical feasibility but for reasons of cost. (By using students as enumerators, it may be possible to produce estimates of IMR within five percentage points at a cost of $20 000 per survey -- and for the results to be available within three months.)

IMPLICATIONS FOR THE GOALS OF THE FOURTH DEVELOPMENT DECADE

The above examples have been recounted, not to suggest that UNICEF has any monopoly on such experience, but to stimulate thinking on how similar approaches might be developed to achieve the basic goals of a more human-focused development decade. The basic approach is straightforward: the various agencies within the international system should take sole or collaborative responsibility for the specific goals agreed upon for DD4. At present, UNDP, WHO, UNICEF and the World Bank are working together in support of the International Drinking Water Supply and Sanitation Decade goals, which have been extended until the year 2000. This offers a reminder that agencies *can* work effectively together and that collaborative approaches are often appropriate. (Some basic goals in the areas of health, education, nutrition, and the environment, are set out in Table 2.)

There are, however, some issues which need to be resolved. For example, is it possible to mobilise the same degree of effort and attention for a range of human goals as was achieved for immunisation, ORT and the reduction of infant and child mortality? If so, will the political process of agreeing on goals by countries or even agencies permit sufficient selectivity (and phasing) to make mobilisation possible? The "political" experience of preparing for earlier decades is not very encouraging -- even UNICEF's early attempts to focus on CSDR goals were at times divisive within the organisation, with many arguing that we were becoming too narrow in focus and including too much.

Another vital area is country-level co-ordination by international organisations. Although some parts of the UN have strong field representation and others are growing stronger, international agencies are still too centralised to effectively tailor their programmes and elicit the local involvement which is essential to make progress towards human goals. Sustained action over the longer run requires community participation and the support of local institutions.

One of the strongest arguments for making sustainable policies for alleviating poverty and meeting basic human needs, the *dominant* objective of aid, is that most voters think that this is what aid should be about. This view comes through strongly from a number of public surveys in industrialised countries. If this is the case, there is a clear basis for maintaining the political interest and support needed to continue aid over the long term.

As with all policy matters, public opinion is only one of the factors behind continuing development assistance. At the risk of further oversimplification, three additional factors can be identified which are necessary to mobilise and sustain support: political leadership; clear goals for development assistance; and demonstrated effectiveness in achieving them. In emphasizing these factors, I am not ignoring the economic interests within donor countries, which can be very influential in determining the amount of direction of aid. However, there is sometimes a tendency to overestimate the importance of economic interests and to underestimate the importance of public opinion. Even in the most committed countries, development assistance forms hardly 1 per cent of GNP and only some 3 to 4 per cent of government expenditure. Many surveys have shown that to a considerable extent, aid is supported by a public opinion which arises in part from a sense of solidarity and a humanitarian concern for poverty.

It may therefore be time to return to a policy of "real aid" -- aid which is strictly allocated and used for development objectives. If the new ethos referred to earlier in this paper is to come about, if political and public commitment to the changes now needed to put development back on the rails is ever to be mobilised into sustained pressure for an internationally co-operative development effort, then development itself will have to be redefined to give priority to meeting the essential needs of all human beings. This is the kind of development which the majority of people in the poor world seek, and this is the kind of development which the majority of people in the industrialised world would support.

NOTES AND REFERENCES

1. *New York Times*, 30th December 1988, p.D2.

2. PATEL, M.S. *Towards Eliminating the Social Distance Between the North and the South: Main Directions for the Fourth Development Decade*, UNICEF, New York (forthcoming).

3. WALTERS, F.P. *A History of the League of Nations,* Vol. 1, Oxford University Press, Oxford, 1952, p.2.

4. TRATTNER, Walter *Crusade for Children*, Quadrangle Books, Chicago, 1970, p.23.

5. ABBOTT, Grace *The Child and the State*, Vol. 1, University of Chicago Press, Chicago, 1938, p.79.

6. Report of the Secretary General, *The United Nations Development Decade: Proposals for Action*, United Nations, New York 1962, E/3613.

7. SEN, Amartya "Development: Which Way Now?" *The Economic Journal,* 93, December 1983, pp.745-62.

Table 1

THE INFLUENCE ON SOCIAL POLICY:
AN EVOLUTION FROM ETHOS/MORALITY TO
LEGISLATION/ORGANISATION

International	**National**
	18th century
"Peaceful" Quakers Radical moralists and philosophers	Children as the responsibility of parents **1789** "Universal" declaration on the Rights of Man (France)
	19th century
	1830s-40s Legislation to restrict the ages & hours of working children (Britain)
1850 Concert of Nations	**1848** First in a series of public health acts (Britain)
	1876 Legislation towards compulsory education for children (Britain)
	20th century
	1908 Parents legally responsible for neglect of child's health (Britain)
1919 ILO established; sets minimum working age for children **1919** League of Nations	**1919** Founding of International Save the Children Fund (Britain)
	1920s Welfare legislation covering health, old age & unemployment (Britain)
1930s "New Deal" **1944** Bretton Woods (IMF/World Bank)	**1944** Legislation for national education system (Britain)

International	National
1946 United Nations Marshall Plan	**1946** Legislation for universal health service (Britain)
	1946 Legislation for accident insurance at work (Britain)
1948 First UN peacekeeping force	
1959 UN Declaration on the Rights of the Child	
1961 First UN Development Decade	
1964 UNCTAD	
1971 Second UN Development Decade	
1972 Stockholm Environment Conference	
1975 World Population Conference	
UN Women's Decade (1975-85)	
1976 World Employment Conference	
1978 Global eradication of smallpox	
1978 Habitat Conference on Shelter	
1981 Third Development Decade	
1988 UN's Programme of Action for Africa's Economic Recovery & Development (1986-90)	
1989 UN Convention on Child Rights	

Table 2

WHO/UNICEF COMMON GOALS FOR HEALTH DEVELOPMENT OF WOMEN AND CHILDREN BY THE YEAR 2000

1.   Reduction of mortality

1.1   Reduction by 50 per cent of maternal mortality rates from 1980 levels

1.2   Reduction of 1980 infant mortality rates by at least half or to 50 per 1 000 live births, whichever achieves the greater reduction

1.3   Reduction of 1980 under-5 mortality rates by at least half or to 70 per 1 000 live births, whichever achieves the greater reduction

2.   Womens' education and health

2.1   Achievement of universal primary education and 80 per cent female literacy (1)

2.2   Access by all couples to information and services for child spacing

3.   Better nutrition

3.1   Reduction of the rate of low birth weight (2.5 kg) to less than 10 per cent

3.2   Enable all women exclusively to breast-feed their children for four to six months and to continue breast-feeding with complementary food well into the second year

3.3   Virtual elimination of severe malnutrition among under-5 children and reduction by half of moderate malnutrition

3.4   Virtual elimination of iodine deficiency disorders

3.5   Virtual elimination of the blindness and other consequences of vit-amine A deficiency

---

1. Each country to define the age group

4. **Control of childhood diseases**

4.1 Global eradication of polio

4.2 Elimination of neonatal tetanus by 1995

4.3 Reduction by 95 per cent in measles deaths and reduction by 90 per cent of measles cases, compared to pre-immunisation levels as a major step to the global eradication of measles in the longer run

4.4 Reduction by 70 per cent in the deaths due to diarrhoea in children under the age of 5 years; and 25 per cent reduction in the diarrhoea incident rate

4.5 Reduction by 25 per cent in the deaths due to acute respiratory infections in children under 5 years of age

5. **Control of the environment**

5.1 Universal access to safe drinking water

5.2 Universal access to sanitary means of excreta disposal

5.3 Eradication of guinea-worm disease by 1995

5.4 Achievement of the safer and more sanitary environment, with significant reductions in radioactive, chemical and other microbiological pollutants

A VIEW FROM THE SOUTH

by

Manmohan SINGH

THE ROLE OF INTERNATIONAL POLICIES IN DEVELOPMENT

Sustained development is a process of structural transformation requiring effective institutional, social and economic reforms designed to promote and reward risk-taking, thriftiness, innovation and productivity growth. Thus understood, development cannot simply be imported. In the final analysis, the pace of development depends crucially on the willingness and ability of the ruling elite to implement a viable package of domestic reforms which are needed for a successful structural transformation. Naturally, the precise content of any such package has to be country-specific.

Thus, international policy measures in support of development are no substitute for an efficient framework of domestic policies. Nevertheless, the international economic environment as represented by the international arrangements governing the flows of capital, trade and technology can heavily influence the effectiveness of domestic programmes for achieving development objectives. A favourable environment can help to soften very considerably the harsh edges of the process of structural transformation of a developing country. On the other hand, an unfavourable international economic environment increases the social and economic costs associated with the transition and it can also affect the realization of the full developmental potential of an economy.

From a purely technical angle, it can be argued that almost every economy has a hidden surplus potential to achieve a savings rate of 15 to 20 per cent of its national income, the level which is often considered to be of strategic significance for the realization of sustained growth. Yet the process of converting the potential surplus into productive savings can have significant social and economic costs, particularly if the whole process is to be compressed and completed in a relatively short period of time. It may involve a degree of political, social and economic regimentation which is undesirable. The availability of external assistance on reasonable terms can help to avoid these costs.

In a similar way, a favourable international trading environment can also have a beneficial impact on the pace and intensity of development. The import needs of an economy inevitably rise in the process of development, for few countries are so richly endowed as to plan voluntarily for a regime of autarchy. Thus an international trading environment which provides expanding opportunities for exports helps to bend the balance of payments constraint. It also enables a country to improve its growth prospects by taking due advantage of economies of specialisation and of scale made possible by participation in the international division of labour.

The build-up of export capacity, particularly in the case of manufactured goods, is linked in an important manner to the state of international arrangements which regulate the flows of technology. If technology can be imported liberally and on reasonable terms and conditions, a determined developing economy has a chance to leapfrog and to shorten significantly its period of transition to the state of the mature economy.

THE CLIMATE FOR DEVELOPMENT CO-OPERATION

In the postwar years, there has been a good deal of discussion of the need for a truly global strategy of international co-operation for development. Nevertheless, one has to admit that what is now in place in the catalogue of entries under international co-operation for development is a series of *ad hoc* measures, many of which had their origin and justification in the context of geo-political, strategic considerations evolved during the cold war phase of postwar history of the world. The market-oriented ideology, which has gained ascendancy among the major Western powers in the 1980s, has already greatly weakened the fabric of development co-operation evolved in the previous three decades. As the cold war recedes in importance, the entire structure looks most fragile. Clearly, a new basis has to be found for building a more durable and vibrant structure of international co-operation for development.

The humanitarian sentiment and an appeal to human solidarity have not been altogether absent from the considerations which have influenced thus far the climate for North-South co-operation for development. The aid performance of the countries of Scandinavia and of the Netherlands can be explained only by reference to these noble considerations. However, such considerations have not been a dominant influence on the aggregate of international economic relations evolved in the context of development co-operation. The fate of the well-reasoned Brandt Commission report is a testimony to the dismal state of affairs. International economic relations are fundamentally power relations and co-operation for development has been no exception to this general rule.

What then are the prospects for North-South development co-operation in the 1990s? There are certainly reasons for cautious optimism. First of all, the disastrous social and economic consequences of the massive retrogression in development co-operation which took place in the 1980s are now well documented. While governments of developed countries have been largely unresponsive, the devastation of the social and economic fabric of a large number of developing countries seems to have made a visible impact on important segments of public opinion in developed countries. The activities of non-governmental agencies, youth organizations and various church groups point to the growing awareness of the conditions of destitution to which several developing countries have been reduced in the wake of the world economic crisis of the 1980s. It is now recognized that the severe import compression forced on the developing countries in the 1980s by the combined incidence of debt burden and a steep fall in commodity prices has had a significant adverse effect on the export growth of a number of developed countries, notably the United States. Recent developments in the technology of mass communication have also helped to gain wider acceptability of the world being viewed as one global village.

In particular, the looming global environmental crisis has created fresh awareness of the need for global partnership for a sensible use and management of the vital life-support system of our biosphere. Deforestation, loss of tropical forests and soil and water degradation in developing countries have consequences extending far beyond their borders. In many ways, the environmental crisis is the direct outcome of the persistence of mass poverty in developing countries. Thus, there is scope for building new coalitions of international interests in favour of a more durable and broad-based strategy of development co-operation.

Nevertheless, one must not underestimate the magnitude of the roadblocks on the approach to a more hopeful era. After all, an appeal to human solidarity has still not been able to overcome to any significant degree the formidable resistance in the developed countries to the scaling-down of the developing countries' burden of indebtedness, the servicing of which is known to have imposed such heavy social and economic costs on the indebted countries. Similarly, developed countries have shown great hesitation in removing discriminatory trade restrictions on developing countries' exports, maintained often in violation of GATT principles and obligations, even though it is realized that such restrictions add to the pool of unemployed and those living on the borderline of starvation in the exporting developing countries. Humanitarian concerns have often produced valuable results in tackling international emergencies such as famines or floods. But they have not succeeded so far in breaking the hold of powerful vested interests on the legislative and administrative processes of developed countries which continue to block the reform process for accommodating essential developing countries' interests.

The environmental concerns can no doubt provide a powerful new ground for a concerted attack on global poverty. However, politicians in most democratic countries have a short-term horizon of four to five years. As a result, governments often lack adequate inducements to take due account of longer-term concerns, even though these are recognized to be of more fundamental importance than matters of the moment.

For all these reasons, one cannot readily assume that a more hopeful era of development co-operation is on the horizon. The ideology of the 1980s has been such a powerful influence on dominant thinking in the major developed countries that it will take quite some time to shake off its legacy. In the meantime, all those who believe in revitalizing development co-operation have their task well cut out. They have to co-operate to evolve a more lasting structure of development co-operation which will appeal to public opinion in both developed and developing countries.

AREAS OF IMMEDIATE CONCERN

The essential contours of the new long-term structure of international co-operation for development will no doubt take considerable time to evolve. In the background of the experience of the 1980s, only a highly selective approach can be the basis of a new promising start. In the meanwhile, there are some obvious areas where urgent international action is called for if the development tempo is to be revived and sustained at a reasonable pace in the next few years. For want of time and space, I can do no more than list these areas and flag the essential issues.

The debt burden

There is now a growing awareness that the debt crisis, which affects a large number of developing countries, both middle-income and low-income countries, is a crisis of solvency. Without a removal of the overhang of debt, the development prospects of the indebted countries will remain highly uncertain. In view of the continued uncertainty of fresh flows on a large scale, a reduction of debt and debt-service is the only practical means to deal with the perverse and inequitable phenomenon of persistent negative transfer of real resources from developed to a large number of developing countries. There has been some movement in the case of low-income countries. However, even in their case, the pace of action has been far too slow and the promised action is also grossly inadequate.

The continued need for concessional flows and the role of multilateral institutions

One has to recognize that aid weariness in developed countries is a fact of life. As such, continued legislative support for larger aid flows cannot be taken for granted. With the exception of countries like Japan, bilateral aid programmes currently do not offer the prospect of a significant growth potential. Similarly, replenishment of resources of institutions like the IDA (which provide assistance on highly concessional terms), which require approval of national legislatures at short intervals of three years, might face greater difficulties. Yet the need for concessional assistance, particularly in the case of Sub-Saharan Africa and the poorest countries of South Asia, is still very substantial. For example, the rather short-sighted policy of drastically reducing the access of countries like India to the resources of the IDA, is beginning to show up a profile of debt service which can potentially be very disruptive of India's development in the future. Thus, providing a growing volume of financial resources to institutions like the IDA and concessional windows of the regional development banks is a task of the highest priority.

In this context, it is necessary to review the processes and procedures of replenishment of concessional aid funds. A replenishment exercise which has to be repeated every three years (as in the case of the IDA) places too severe a strain on the negotiating process and capabilities. Perhaps a beginning could be made to increase the length of the replenishment period to five years.

One should also think of new ways of providing additional resources to these institutions by devising mechanisms which do not require frequent appropriations by national legislatures. An agreement to allocate a modest amount of SDRs on a regular basis in favour of the IDA could provide valuable supplementary support to its operations. Of course, since interest on SDRs is now close to short-term interest rates prevailing in the major financial centres of the world, there will be need for interest subsidy to enable the IDA to lend on concessional terms. This technical problem is not insurmountable, provided the necessary political will exists to sustain the operations of institutions such as the IDA at a reasonable level.

Obviously, what I have in mind is a revival of the interest in the famous link proposal which has been extensively discussed in the past. There are clearly no serious technical arguments against the link proposal. Basically, the objections have been political in the sense that donor countries do not wish to give up their control over the distribution of aid flows. At a time when bilateral aid flows seem to have exhausted their growth potential, this argument loses much of its force. Indeed, the implementation of the link may be the only means of ensuring a moderate growth in overall concessional aid flows in the face of stagnant bilateral aid and the growing aid fatigue.

Tapping the capital markets

International capital markets have a significant potential for meeting the requirements of development capital in the Third World. However, as long as real interest rates remain as high as 8-10 per cent per annum (as has been the case in recent years when nominal interest rates are deflated by the export price index of developing countries), there are severe constraints on the developing countries' ability to absorb such flows. There is clearly need to have a fresh look at the old Horowitz proposal for interest subsidies which was discussed extensively in the 1960s. Now that bilateral aid budgets are not expected to grow very significantly, a much better use of these aid funds would be to provide interest subsidies in suitable cases on loans provided by international financing institutions. In the context of recycling Japanese surplus savings, Saburo Okita and Lal Jayawardena of WIDER have offered an imaginative proposal which seeks to tap the Japanese capital markets for providing assistance to developing countries. This proposal deserves support.

Protection against exogenous shock

The progressive integration of major Western economies and the removal of restrictions on capital flows have not been accompanied by adequate efforts on the part of their governments to co-ordinate their macroeconomic policies. As a result, the uncertainty and instability in the world economy seems to have increased very considerably in the last fifteen years. The international price of oil also affects macroeconomic performance in a large number of countries, both for producers and consumers of oil. The failure of international attempts to impart a measure of stability to the oil price has accentuated this uncertainty and instability. While developed countries have succeeded in devising effective mechanisms to reduce the effects of great environmental uncertainty on their economic performance, developing countries' ability to do so is limited by the structural and institutional domestic rigidities of their economies. Besides, very often developed countries' attempts to deal with problems of macroeconomic instability have increased the uncertainty and instability faced by developing countries. For example, their success in controlling inflation in the 1980s has been to a considerable degree at the cost of depressed commodity prices and terms of trade of developing countries. Thus, the continued volatility of international interest rates, exchange rates and of commodity prices greatly affects the ability of developing countries to ensure orderly implementation of their medium-term development programmes.

In the mid 1960s, the World Bank, in response to an Anglo-Swedish resolution passed at the First Session of UNCTAD, had formulated a scheme of Supplementary Financial Measures designed specifically to protect the integrity of sound development programmes in the face of an unexpected deterioration in the international economic environment. However, the rapid expansion of world trade in the 1960s reduced the urgency of action in this matter. With the increased uncertainty and unpredictability of international economic environment in the 1980s, and its unsettling effect on the economies of developing countries, it is necessary to revive interest in a proposal like supplementary financial measures.

In this context, it is also necessary to reassess and expand the scope of schemes like the IMF's Compensatory Financing Facility and the EEC's STABEX. The Compensatory Financing Facility was originally designed as a quasi-automatic facility with very low conditionality. In the 1980s, under the ideological pressure of some developed countries, the IMF had to increase very substantially the conditionality associated with the drawings under this Facility. Access limits were also reduced. As a result, the stabilizing role of the Facility in the face of unexpected shortfalls in export earnings was greatly reduced.

176

Recently, the IMF has decided to create a new Compensatory and Contingency Financing Facility (CCFF), which combines the erstwhile Compensatory Financing Facility with a new External Contingency Mechanism. The new facility will have an overall access limit of 105 per cent of quotas, with limits of 40 per cent each, applying both to the compensatory and contingency elements, and an optional tranche of 25 per cent available to supplement either of these, at the choice of the recipient. However, the low access limits and the high degree of conditionality attaching to the use of the new facility greatly reduce its effectiveness in dealing with the disruptive consequences of unforeseen developments beyond a country's control.

Reform of the international trading system

The Punta del Este Declaration of the GATT Ministerial Meeting held in September 1986 which launched the Uruguay Round of Trade Negotiations spells out the minimum action which ought to be taken in the interest of trade and development needs of the Third World. Thus, definite commitments have been made regarding standstill and roll-back of protectionism inconsistent with the provisions of GATT, removal of restrictions on tropical products, reduction of protective levies which discourage processing of primary products in developing countries and the return of trade in textiles to the normal disciplines of GATT. Judging by the trend of negotiations, not much progress seems to have been made in translating these promises into a concrete action plan. On the ground, discriminatory protectionism seems to be on the increase. Major developed countries are increasingly using the trade policy instrumentalities to secure concessions from the developing countries in wide-ranging fields including the legislation relating to protection of intellectual property rights and regulation of foreign investment. Events thus seem to be overtaking the Uruguay Round.

The United States and the European Community constitute the two largest trading blocs in the world. In both of them, the protectionist sentiments are on the increase. In the United States, the new Trade Act has strong protectionist overtones, though much will depend on the manner in which the new United States' Administration might choose to apply its various provisions. There is a danger that bilateral approaches for dealing with trade issues such as through the recently concluded US-Canada Free Trade Agreement may be used more aggressively to include countries such as Japan and Mexico. In Europe, the sentiment of building a "fortress Europe" has considerable appeal and this temptation may increase as the Community approaches 1992, when all remaining intra-EEC barriers to the movement of goods and factors in production will be removed. A fragmentation of the world trading system will be particularly harmful for the poor countries whose bargaining power *vis-a-vis* powerful trading blocs is extremely weak.

A period of slow overall growth of world trade which is now clearly on the horizon make it all the more necessary that every possible opportunity should be

177

provided to developing countries to enable them to increase their share in world trade in areas where they have a competitive edge. An open nondiscriminatory trading system with effective provisions for nondiscriminatory safeguard action and an even-handed trade dispute settlement mechanism -- which protects the interests of the strong as well as of the weak -- are essential conditions for meeting the trade needs of developing countries.

Transfer of technology

Taking into account the growing influence of technology on development processes, a new international consensus needs to be evolved in which development needs of the poor countries would figure prominently on the global agenda for research and development. New frontier technologies, such as genetic engineering and bio-technology can have a revolutionary impact not only on production levels but also in promoting an ecologically sound and sustainable use of such scarce resources as land, water and energy. There is thus a need for innovative collaborative mechanisms to integrate science and technology effectively into the development processes of the Third World. Developing countries need active international assistance to enhance their technological capacities.

SOUTH-SOUTH CO-OPERATION

Given the importance of the North as a source of capital, markets and technology for the developing countries, the Third World cannot give up its struggle for a restructuring of North-South relations. Yet the South cannot realize its full development potential by putting all its eggs in the Northern basket.

There are several objective factors which suggest that the North cannot play the role of the South's engine of economic growth, and that the South must look for new dynamic growth promoting impulses within its own economies.

It is now accepted by all concerned that the exceptionally high-growth rates realized by the OECD countries during the period 1950-1973 -- which is often described as the golden age of modern capitalism -- are a thing of the distant past. Most available projections of OECD growth point to an average growth rate of 2.5 to 3.0 per cent per annum during the next ten to twelve years. As a result, the rate of growth of world trade is bound to be much less than that realised during 1950-1973 (7 to 8 per cent growth in volume terms). The persistence of this trend would imply a much slower growth of Northern import demand. Moreover, the protectionist sentiment is also likely to remain strong under these conditions, particularly in countries with high rates of unemployment. As regards capital, there is no assurance that surplus savings of countries like Japan and West Germany will necessarily flow in the direction of developing countries. Indeed, the present arrangements whereby structural surpluses of countries like Japan and West Germany are invested in a structurally deficit country like the United States may prove to be more durable than is often assumed. The United States, being the world's largest economy as well as the greatest debtor, enjoys an unusual degree of bargaining power in dealing with its creditors. Thus, creditors may have no alternative but to finance US deficits for quite some time to come. Moreover, one has also to recognize that with the integration of European capital markets, the scope for surplus European and Japanese capital in the less developed countries members of the enlarged European Community will increase very considerably. Finally, the opening up of the Soviet economy to international capital will provide yet another avenue for absorbing surplus Japanese and European savings.

Similarly, recent developments in the area of technology transfer to developing countries are also not very encouraging. The acceleration of the pace of innovations in the major developed countries has led to an intensification of pressures on developing countries to open up their markets to exporters of technology. Thus, intense pressures are being brought to bear on developing countries to bring their domestic legislation on protection of intellectual property in conformity with the perceived interests of technology exporters. If this trend gathers momentum, technological transformation of developing countries by importing, adapting and absorbing foreign technologies will receive a setback.

For all these reasons, countries of the Third World are in danger of being marginalised if they do not fully exploit the vast latent potential of South-South co-operation in trade, investment, technology development and numerous other fields through viable bilateral subregional, regional and inter-regional arrangements. Effective South-South co-operation can be a powerful instrument for widening the development options of the South.

It is often argued that the potential of South-South co-operation is limited because most of the economies have a similar factor endowment and are thus more competitive than complementary to each other. This statement has some validity but much less today than it had 30 years ago. Since then, a number of countries in the South have achieved a fair degree of industrialisation and this has given rise to a new set of complementarities among developed countries. For example, the four newly industrialised countries (Hong Kong, South Korea, Singapore and Taiwan) have now the fastest rate of growth of imports of primary products.

In the same way, the growth of Third World multinationals in the last ten to fifteen years has highlighted the new opportunities that now exist for the flow of technology and capital on mutually beneficial terms.

Developing countries are generally short of savings. OPEC surpluses have now largely disappeared. Nevertheless, there is still considerable scope for increased OPEC investments in other developing countries as part of the inevitable process of portfolio diversification.

179

Thus, today's Third World has a combination of markets, a reservoir of technical skills and investable resources which can provide a powerful push to the process of South-South co-operation.

It is sometimes argued that South-South co-operation is an inferior strategy as compared to one seeking integration in the world market as a whole. However, this is unlikely to be the case if the world market is either closed to the developing countries or is likely to grow at a very slow pace. New entry into the world market under such unfavourable conditions might involve a severe loss on terms of trade and it might even give rise to immiserization.

Moreover, there are several areas where regional or subregional co-operation is the only effective route to exploitation of some common resources or to deal with some common problems. One instance is the control of floods in the Indian subcontinent and exploitation of the vast latent hydroelectricity potential of the Himalayan rivers. Without effective control of deforestation in Nepal and other countries of the region, the flood menace can never be brought under control. Similarly, in the African context, an effective control of the phenomenon of desertification is inconceivable, except in the framework of arrangements for regional and subregional co-operation for the control of overgrazing and deforestation. The development of inter-state river basins and scientific use of scarce water resources for food security are also feasible propositions only in the context of viable regional and subregional arrangements. Organization of scientific and technical research and setting up of centres of excellence in selected branches of higher learning are also eminently suitable cases for South-South co-operation.

With regard to trade in manufactures, it is conceivable that there may be a possible trade off between regional and subregional arrangements on the one hand, and participation in the world market as a whole on the other. However, in actual practice, there may be no real trade off. Thanks to rapid advances in science and technology -- particularly in microelectronics, computer numerically controlled (CNC) machines and computer-aided design -- the old fashioned division of products into labour-intensive and capital intensive is increasingly losing its relevance. Thus, several developed countries have been able to enhance the competitiveness of their textile industry through a process of capital deepening. Thus, availability of cheap labour may not be a material factor in achieving a breakthrough on the export front.

Economies of scale remain a significant influence on world trade in manufactures. Moreover, in a world increasingly dominated by science and technology, competitiveness in the international markets is dependent on a country's ability to devote large expenditures to research and development. Under these conditions, it may not be possible for many developing countries to enter the world market straight away. Regional arrangements may be the only viable route to overcome the initial handicap of a small domestic market and inability to invest adequately in research and development.

Indeed, even if the intention is eventually to integrate into the world market, regional, subregional and inter-regional arrangements may hasten the transition

180

to the realization of this goal. An analysis of trade among developing countries suggests that expansion of this segment of trade can confer important benefits by way of learning which can facilitate penetration into the wider world market at a subsequent stage.

For all these reasons, South-South co-operation provides an important new dimension to international policies for promoting development of poor countries. It certainly will help to accelerate the tempo of development of the South. If it is successful, it will have a favourable impact on North-South trade and on the growth prospects of developed countries as well.

It is a well-known proposition in economic theory that in a situation where trade and payments restrictions cannot be removed, pursuit of a nondiscriminatory approach in the application of these restrictions does not necessarily promote world welfare, and that under these conditions a discriminatory approach relying on selective liberalization and expansion may well be a superior alternative. In the history of postwar Europe, one can recall the historic role played by the European Payments Union (EPU), a discriminatory arrangement for liberalization of intra-European trade which discriminated against the United States in the revival of Europe's economy. It also provides an instance when the United States, in recognition of its longer-term interests, not only permitted this discrimination, but also provided the initial resources for financing the operations of EPU.

In the same spirit, countries of the North and the international financial institutions they control need to take a more supportive interest in arrangements seeking to liberalize and expand trade and other relations among developing countries on a preferential basis. Many of these arrangements are languishing today for want of adequate financial support. It is high time international financial institutions regarded liberalization of trade and promotion of economic co-operation among developing countries as an important aspect of international co-operation for promoting sustained development in the Third World and in the economy as a whole.

In the emerging world economy, the North cannot be expected to play the role of the engine of Southern growth, but the North can and should supply some fuel and lubricants to propel the growth process in the South.

DISCUSSANT'S CONTRIBUTION

by

Elliot BERG

The papers by Manmohan Singh and Richard Jolly raise numerous issues. I will discuss several that seem to me especially provocative.

The first has to do with the future of policy-based lending, market-oriented reforms, conditionality, the role of the World Bank and the IMF -- in short, the whole intellectual and institutional apparatus associated with formal structural adjustment programmes. Neither paper has much to say about these matters. Dr. Singh observes that "the market-oriented ideology" of the 1980s has "greatly weakened the fabric of development co-operation", and asserts that something new has to become the basis of international co-operation for development. His policy proposals, however, do not deal directly with the larger issues involved. Richard Jolly's paper makes one reference to "international weaknesses and ... limitations in perceptions and mandates ..."; he implicitly calls for a shift in the focus of aid towards direct poverty reduction programmes and the satisfaction of basic needs. It is not clear whether this is to supplement or replace policy-based lending and the push for market-oriented reforms. Judging from the recommended changes in aid strategies put forward in the 1989 UNICEF *Report on the State of the World's Children,* replacement seems to be what he has in mind.

Both writers may perceive the aid relationship of the 1990s as being free of these concerns, which have been so central in the 1980s. From their interventions, it is clear that this is so because formal structural adjustment and market-oriented policy lending programmes have to be judged a failed experiment and abandoned by the international financial institutions.

Despite the lack of growth in the 1980s, even in many countries that have adopted adjustment programmes, it is too soon to call the overall adjustment effort a failure. Most adjustment programmes, after all, are very recent. In the main theatre of structural adjustment, Sub-Saharan Africa, it was not until 1985 that one could see general turnarounds in such indicators as real exchange rates and real producer prices. Moreover, most reform programmes are partial and hesitant; institutional changes, from public expenditure systems to deregulated markets are still embryonic. Before these changes can have much impact they have to change strongly rooted regulatory arrangements that prevent effective functioning of markets.

Despite their recent and partial character, finally, the 1988 *World Development Report* presents some evidence that African countries with "strong" adjustment programmes have had significantly better economic performance than others.

All of this suggests we will not be "beyond adjustment" in the 1990s. The issue will be how to do it better. This will involve more than dropping the name "structural adjustment", and more than taking account of "social costs". It will require the development of more appropriate conditionality, better vehicles of policy dialogue, more effective donor co-ordination and a better balance between project and policy loans. These are by no means simple issues.

Take the conditionality issue. Conditionality arises not from the irascibility of the international financial institutions or those who finance their operations. It arises for three reasons. First, all governments have some propensity to allocate public expenditures for activities that are not economically optimal. This is so because all governments have non-economic objectives. Some of these we like (targeted subsidies for the poor, for example). Some we may be uncertain about (regional equity). Some we don't like (presidential airlines, agricultural or industrial white elephants, larger armies). In addition to non-economic objectives, there is the factor of leaky decision-making structures for public investment.

A second source of need for conditionality is the likelihood of an inverse relationship between availability of finance and pressure for reform. And a third reason is that donor legislators and others want to know that policy loans are doing something to promote development.

For these reasons, conditionality is essential in some form, but the present arrangements are clearly unsatisfactory. There is too much conditionality (to institutional reforms for example, or to policies on which there is technical disagreement). It is ineffective and it is counterproductive. It does not address the major obstacle to reform -- lack of agreement by LDC leaders and intellectuals that market-oriented reforms will work. Instead of encouraging a joint search for real solutions to real problems, game-playing prevails -- getting agreement on a document that will satisfy everybody, then keeping it on track in the face of uncertain compliance records.

A further issue has to do with aid volumes, and intrusiveness. It is an issue particularly for heavily aided countries. Beyond a certain level, aid inflows become extremely disruptive of local economies. This is the case, much commented on, in many heavily aided states in Africa. In recent years, aid has amounted to 10 per cent or more of GDP in between fifteen and twenty African countries. Foreign assistance is providing virtually all public sector investment in most of these countries, and a large share of total public spending. Payment of salary supplements is now common. There are of course positive effects from these aid inflows, but they also bring many negative consequences. Investment decision-making systems are disrupted. As many practitioners in heavily aided countries know, there's no project so bad that it cannot usually find some donor to finance it. Food aid and non-project loans create local currency counterpart funds that are often used by donors to support "their" projects and programmes, a practice that accentuates tendencies towards reduced budgetary discipline. Donors come to be arbiters of institutional life and death; programmes or agencies that find favour among donors survive, those that do not often die. The results are hardly in line with natural institutional selection.

In no other continent has foreign assistance been so large a share of GDP, investment and public spending as it has in Africa. It would be surprising if this fact were entirely unrelated to the inefficiency in resource use and the slow growth of indigenous institutional capacity that characterizes so much of Africa's recent history.

There clearly is a dilemma here. Additional assistance is needed in the poorest countries, many of them already heavily aided. They have very limited access to private capital markets, and the commodity exports they rely on face gloomy price prospects. But few can absorb more aid without exacerbating the kinds of disruptive effects outlined above. The world community will have to find less disruptive ways of transferring resources to these least-developed countries -- in such ways as shifting to more project lending and using more fully the laboratories, universities and other institutions of the industrial world to address the problem of the poorest. Meanwhile, the inevitably slow process of building institutional capacity has to be speeded up so these disruptions can be contained in the future.

DISCUSSANT'S CONTRIBUTION

by

Lal JAYAWARDENA

We have two fascinating papers dealing with the kinds of international policies needed to support developing countries, to which it would be difficult to do justice in the time I have available. Each author has understandably chosen to project an institutional viewpoint -- Richard Jolly, that of UNICEF, and Manmohan Singh, that of the South Commission. I feel entitled, therefore, in commenting, to project some of the emphases which have characterised the work of WIDER (World Institute for Development Economics Research of the United Nations University) since it commenced functioning in the spring of 1985. I propose in what follows briefly to summarise what I see as being the main theme of each paper, bringing in the relevance of WIDER's work to that theme sequentially.

Richard Jolly's paper sees international policy in the 1990s as emphasizing the basic human needs dimension in development policy. First, measurable international goals need to be set and most international agencies should encourage developing countries to set and plan for the realisation of these goals. What I find fascinating is the way in which WIDER's own work programme is working towards this identical goal, and I propose therefore to illustrate this.

In the first place, there is conceptual work. Richard Jolly has already identified the contribution of WIDER Research Adviser, Amartya Sen, in putting forward the concept of enhancing human capabilities as the basic focus for development efforts through better nutrition, universal access to health, education, water, sanitation, and shelter. A WIDER Research Conference last summer, planned with Professor Sen's help, brought together economists and philosophers to develop this conceptual framework further by investigating the meaning of the "Quality of Life and Living Standards". In addition, a WIDER programme in which Professor Sen is also involved seeks to appraise specific social security programmes that low-income countries might seek to integrate into their own plans, ranging from more general studies of the experience of China, Costa Rica, Jamaica, Cape Verde and Cuba, to the more specific case of the free school meal programmes in Madras, the food subsidy programme in Sri Lanka, and now I would imagine the kind of minimum income programme which Sri Lanka's own political imperatives have surfaced at the recent Presidential election, and to which the new President is firmly committed.

As always, the issue is about the relative contribution of domestic and international resources to any of these basic needs-oriented endeavours. If total resource availabilities fall short of requirements, and if political imperatives imply little trimming back of stated goals, then the inevitable resolution of the problem is through a cumulative inflationary process with its attendant social upheavals and costs. This consideration becomes relevant because traditional development policy has always viewed external support to a country as being complementary to domestic economic policy reform. This latter has hitherto been assumed to involve two components: i) an improved management and incentive structure through appropriate decentralization and exchange rate and pricing reforms; and ii) an enhanced domestic public savings effort through increased taxation and the trimming of subsidies and welfare expenditures.

It is this latter aspect of conventional policy which both Richard Jolly's and -- I may add -- Philip Ndegwa's framework, imply examining particularly closely. As Philip Ndegwa puts it, "To ask African countries to undertake many important measures including severe reduction in the already low living standards more or less overnight is to treat these countries as mechanical constructions in which changes could be taken without regard to social and political consequences -- even if such measures are the right ones".

In addition to the work being done on human capabilities questions, another programme in this area has sought to focus on the issue at the level of individual country studies of adjustment and development policies in association with Professors Gerry Helleiner and Lance Taylor. It has proceeded in two phases. The first -- which could be called "the what might have been" phase -- has been completed. This asked whether countries might have implemented in the past decade alternative adjustment policy mixes that could have produced the expected positive results of adjustment policies in terms of GNP growth and improved balance-of-payments performance at a lower social cost than was in fact incurred by maintaining, for example, social service and welfare expenditures that had to be curtailed. The 17 country studies conducted within WIDER have shown that alternative policy packages were indeed available and that had they been implemented, the social costs of past programmes might have been avoided while preserving the gains.

The second phase of WIDER's programme now underway may be described as the "what ought to be" phase. The idea is for each country to set, first, minimum development goals in the area of basic needs for the year 2000, second, minimum employment goals that would involve the absorption by then of the backlog of unemployment and of additions to the labour force, and third, associated improved income distribution objectives. These development goals would be translated into the more conventional SNA National Accounting framework involving associated GDP growth targets and investment requirements to be financed by a reasonable split between domestic and foreign savings.

It is at this point that the exercise may well run counter to the traditional approach which seeks to reward domestic resource mobilization efforts by providing supplementary external capital inflows. If current living standards set a floor, as argued by Philip Ndegwa, to the domestic savings that can be extracted at the commencement of a fresh development effort, then domestic savings can only be expected to grow out of incremental income. In so far as some reasonable proportion of this has to be appropriated to basic needs-oriented expenditures whether of a consumption or investment kind, then it may well be that a substantial proportion of a country's infrastructure and productive investment efforts will require foreign savings. In other words, in any development policy framework for the 1990s which respects basic needs considerations, additional external inflows will have to be thought of not so much as rewarding a domestic *resource* mobilization effort as complementing what Dr. Manmohan Singh has so well described, namely the other elements in a "process of structural transformation requiring effective institutional, social and economic reforms designed to promote and reward risk taking, thriftiness, innovation and productivity growth.

In brief, development in the 1990s will require a far larger draft on foreign savings in support of consumption, broadly defined, given the impoverishment that has occurred in the 1980s adjustment decade, than it was customary to think of in the past. The aggregate significance of this exercise is that there may well be no major foreign savings constraints if substantial developed-country surpluses are likely to persist well into the 1990s. Indeed, what the WIDER "Year 2000 Project" seeks to do on the basis of the 17 country studies in hand is to try to project a needs-oriented external resources gap for the developing countries as a whole that is consistent with a minimum socially necessary growth rate of GNP, taking basic needs, employment, and income distribution considerations into account. On a quick census around the table of country study authors at a meeting in Helsinki this summer, minimum socially necessary GNP growth rates of around 6.5 per cent to 7 per cent were thought of as being required during the 1990s. This is to be contrasted with the experience for all developing countries in the period 1973-80 of real GNP growth of 5.4 per cent and during 1980-87, the "lost" development decade, of 3.9 per cent.

It should be realized that growth rates of the required magnitude were in fact reached by the low-income countries and the exporters of manufactures during the period 1980-87 where their respective growth rates average 7.4. per cent and 6.3 per cent. If the global adjustment effort centred around the needed correction of the United States deficit is managed without throwing the world into recession, then it may well turn out that persisting developed-country surpluses may be adequate to finance growth rates of this order. Indeed, one of the objectives of macroeconomic work being planned in WIDER is to examine under what circumstances such an outcome would be feasible. In general, this would require that the United States adjustment be accompanied by measures necessary to maintain world activity at a sufficiently high level. A consideration of the issues in this area bring me to the territory of Dr. Manmohan Singh's paper to which I now turn.

The main thrust of that paper is one of cautious optimism about the future prospects of North-South Co-operation veering towards pessimism as I hope to show. Having flagged several essential areas where international action is needed, Dr. Manmohan Singh goes on to place a considerable degree of emphasis on the potential of South-South co-operation for "dynamising" southern economies. This is based primarily upon the consideration that growth in the North is bound in the future to be moderate and that, with the demise of the golden age of modern capitalism, there is no prospect of a revival of a major growth impulse from the OECD countries towards developing countries. Similarly, he argues that there is no guarantee that the surplus savings of Japan and Germany will necessarily flow in the direction of developing countries. They are more likely to continue to be absorbed in financing the United States deficit and to move towards new frontiers in the socialist world, towards the Soviet Union for example.

The Third World, therefore, has no choice but to exploit its vast latent potential for mutual co-operation. The North can help in this through providing financial support for a variety of possible regional co-operation arrangements in the South on the analogy of the support extended to the European Payments Union by the United States in the 1950s.

This is a view of the world which I tend very much to share in the large, so to speak. There is, in my view, no long-term alternative to building up institutions in support of South-South co-operation. But I do think that there are many opportunities presented by the current international situation that would enable North-South co-operation to take place to a far greater degrees than at present, if the enlightened self-interest of the North is enlisted in this endeavour. It is this aspect of the matter which Dr. Manmohan Singh's presentation does not, in my view, adequately emphasize, and which I shall seek to elaborate.

Let me illustrate this from Dr. Manmohan Singh's account of the climate for development co-operation. He locates, quite rightly, the steps taken so far towards North-South co-operation in the geo-political-strategic considerations of the cold war. As the cold war recedes, so does this rationale for support for the Third World. Similarly, traditional appeals to human solidarity which have also influenced aid have had to take second place to the ascendancy of a market-oriented ideology. The plight of debt-ridden countries, and indeed the destitution resulting from severe import compression, has not yet forced itself upon the world's conscience despite the activities of humanitarian groups. While environmental concerns provide a new ground for North-South co-operation, the priority likely to be given to them is limited by the short-term horizons of politicians. In the end, though he does not say it in so many words, Dr. Manmohan Singh is pessimistic rather than even cautiously optimistic. To quote his conclusion, "all those who believe in revitalising development co-operation have their task *well cut out*" (emphasis added)

The particular nuance I would wish to add to Dr. Manmohan Singh's argument is, as mentioned, that this task will be rendered significantly easier if a concerted attempt is made to enlist the enlightened self-interest of the North in supporting development.

There is first the opportunity of marrying together the resolution of the world's twin debt problem -- that of the United States and of the developing countries -- in mutually reinforcing ways that would promote world growth. It is wide-

190

ly accepted that improved macroeconomic management of the world economy requires a correction of the United States current account external deficit by an amount in the range of $150 to $200 billion. Since this is equivalent to 8 to 10 per cent of world exports, a correction of this order of magnitude is expected to have major deflationary consequences on export markets unless offset by corresponding expansion elsewhere. The conventional view on this question asserts that the necessary expansion should come from the major surplus countries, like Japan and Germany and from surplus developing countries, such as Korea. An alternative view asserts that this is unlikely to happen to the extent required to offset the deflationary bias of the required US adjustment and is, in any case, unnecessary to the extent that surpluses no longer required to finance a US deficit can be usefully absorbed in supporting Third World development. This requires both policy changes in the United States to relieve its own indebtedness, and policy reform especially in debtor countries to make them attractive as recipients of, say, Japan's and Germany's surpluses.

Recycling need not always be an euphemism for taking from the prudent to give to the profligate, for transfer in turn to the irresponsible -- an accusation levelled against the private banking community who lent so boldly to developing countries in the 1970s. In the WIDER Study Group design for recycling, evolved by Dr. Saburo Okita, Dr. Arjun Sengupta and myself, which Dr. Manmohan Singh has supported, the profligate would be appropriately disciplined, and the irresponsible penalized to a degree. The design involves an international debt reconstruction facility, which passed on the discounts on debt in secondary markets to developing countries in exchange for domestic policy reform packages and looks to Japan to take an initiative in support of this process. The conditionality would be of a *long range* character, and elaborate by a Policy Co-ordination Committee meeting annually with the developing country concerned in ways which imply the kind of long-term Development Contract Minister Stoltenberg has advocated at this Symposium (1).

Our own proposal was quite modest in regard to the scale of recycling. We assumed that Japan might adopt a current account surplus target of $50 billion, equivalent to 2 per cent of its then GNP, in which form it eventually also became Japan's official target, and suggested that half that amount -- namely $25 billion -- could be recycled annually to developing countries over a five-year period. The Japanese current account surplus has, however, turned out to be much more resilient than anyone expected when we wrote our report almost two years ago. According to the OECD's latest World Economic Outlook (2), it is expected still to be around $80 billion in 1988. The surplus has held up despite the implementation in Japan of $40 billion domestic expansion package which was broadly consistent with the current account target of $50 billion, and current projections show that the surplus is expected to fall modestly to $70 billion in 1990 and stabilize at least at these levels in the following decade. In that event, there would be scope for considerably more recycling to developing countries through deliberate policy action than we had proposed.

The crucial question, however, is the *manner* of bringing about the switch in the flow of world savings from financing the US deficit to financing Third World development. Unless policies are properly framed and co-ordinated, there is a real risk of precipitating a recession in the United States with possible repercussions elsewhere. The favourite candidate nowadays for policy action is a consumption recession in the United States induced, among other things, by a rise in the gasoline tax by 25 per cent to raise tax revenues by $25 billion, and by the introduction of a nationwide consumption tax. The path of a consumption recession may run the risk of triggering a generalised global recession by affecting United States imports quite sharply and by virtue of its internal reverse multiplier effects, so that putting the American house in order may well end up bringing the world house down. In other words, world income as a whole could fall, including that of Japan, so that Japan's excess savings today would just not be there to be lent to developing countries tomorrow.

It is at this point that thought needs to be given to alternative ways of reducing the US deficit which do not court the same risk of bringing about a world recession but will release Japan's savings to flow to developing countries. One obvious question is whether the relaxation of the cold war does not permit the United States to grasp a disarmament option for reducing its budget deficit which has, until now, been regarded as foreclosed. Dr. Manmohan Singh, in his paper, has expressed the fear that the easing of the cold war will remove past politico-strategic incentives to support Third World development. The alternative scenario is that it would represent an unparalleled opportunity for propelling OECD economies into a second Golden Age, especially if there is a positive United States response to President Mikhail Gorbachev's recent unilateral disarmament initiative announced at the United Nations.

A paper by Sam Nakagama (3), Chairman of Nakagama and Wallace Inc. of New York, addressed the issue in an interesting way last June and deserves to be better known. Nakagama is a well-known Wall Street economic forecaster with an amazing track record of accuracy including the prediction of the October 1987 stock market crash, and his audience largely comprised his blue-ribboned clients. He talked of three magic magnitudes plaguing the US economy, each of $150 billion. Two of these are readily recognisable -- the US current account deficits, respectively, in the balance of payments and in the budget. The third, invisible up to now in public debate -- at least until President Gorbachev spoke in the United Nations -- Nakagama reckoned to be the cost of maintaining the US defence commitment to Europe. He wondered whether in the current climate of *glasnost, perestroika* and *détente* and European insouciance about any threat from the East, reducing this commitment might not offer a relatively painless solution to the US budget deficit conundrum. This struck me as being relevant radicalism -- less far-reaching than most conventional disarmament nostrums, and within the realm of the possible for a new US administration seeking a bold initiative. As I listened in the company of hard-bitten Wall Street bankers who had previously heard an appeal from a former United States Navy Secretary for Japan to step up her defence role to the evident puzzlement of several Japanese present, I had a dream.

A phased reduction in the US deficit through relaxing its commitment to Europe would free Japanese savings to flow to developing countries in ample and hitherto unprecedented volume. A debt reconstruction facility, set up on a Japanese initiative, would be allied to what I can only describe as self-reliant conditionality -- i.e. reform packages that *countries* could design for *themselves* in consultation with the international financial institutions -- or for that matter a Japanese Trust fund -- for the first time, in recent memory, on a basis of sufficient finance. I expect this is what Mr. Stoltenberg has in mind in advocating the notion of Development Contracts between individual countries and the donor community. This would help defuse the tensions that currently exist between developing countries and the international financial institutions, which in large part stem from the use of conditionality to ration today's grossly inadequate volume of finance. Policy reform, accompanied by substantial programme lending and the resulting dynamism in the Third World, would create both project development and private investment opportunities on a scale that could usher in for the developing countries during the 1990s, the kind of Golden Age that Europe enjoyed in the 1950s and 1960s in the wake of the Marshall Plan. The Golden Age could extend to the OECD economies as well if structural change in the US economy and in Europe following *détente*, could re-orient industrial capacities in the advanced economies in a manner that would meet the vast unmet needs of the Third World, and reduce if not eliminate today's substantial levels of European unemployment. In short, a virtuous circle could be set in motion by thinking what until recently has been the politically unthinkable.

In the cold light of day after Nakagama's presentation, I tried to do the homework needed to test out this intuition. The $150 billion magnitude for NATO mentioned by Nakagama turns out to be about half the nearly $300 billion appropriated for all US defence expenditures in 1989, according to the report presented by the Secretary of Defense to the Secretary of Congress on 11th February 1988 (4). Two categories within this $300 billion expenditure -- for Procurement, and Research and Development, Test and Evaluation -- distinguished in the report, total around $120 billion and provide a rough measure of the weapons production capacity of the United States. Assuming that half this amount *pro rata* represents the capacity of the US arms industry attributable to NATO-related purposes, then the Nakagama proposal can be expected to release something like $60 billion of US industrial capacity to meet the Third World's unmet needs.

The industrial capacity so released amounts precisely to half the combined surplus of Japan and West Germany expected for 1989, of $120 billion. Since even the most ambitious proposal so far made public for recycling the Japanese surplus -- the WIDER Plan -- also envisages that no more than half its expected surplus should be recycled through deliberate policy action for Third World purposes, the proportions revealed by this piece of homework do not appear implausible.

Nevertheless, recycling to developing countries even of the dimensions of $60 billion annually is clearly inadequate to offset the deflationary impact of the needed correction of the US deficit if this is set at $150 billion. While some part of the slack will have to be taken up by domestic expansion in the surplus economies, there will still remain a significant lee-way for additional flows to developing countries. Countering the deflationary gap resulting from the correction of the US deficit, given the constraints to domestic expansion in the surplus economies, requires additional flows to developing countries and this would take the form of project finance, both in the public and private sectors. There would appear to be a particular need for refurbishing run-down infrastructure in debtor developing countries as a result of the import compression of recent years. There is, indeed, evidence -- and the case of Thailand has been cited -- that infrastructure constraints have become a major obstacle to absorbing increased foreign private investment flows from Japan, even where all other conditions are favourable.

What needs to be examined in parallel, therefore, are ways of promoting private flows to developing countries to counter the residual deflationary gap. In addition to relaxing infrastructure constraints, any comprehensive approach to the problem of redirecting private capital flows would need to address at least three audiences. First, there is an audience in the surplus economies where attention needs to be drawn to current domestic policy constraints in expanding foreign investment posed by limitations, for example, in investment insurance arrangements. There is, second, an audience that needs to be addressed within the wider international community as regards the limitations of the current mechanisms for multilateral investment insurance; the World Bank's Multilateral Investment Guarantee Authority (MIGA) may turn out to be too meagre in relation to the potential volume of investment that would need to be supported. There is, third, an audience in host developing countries which needs to be addressed concerning the policy and other obstacles that inhibit the inflows of foreign private investment.

All proposals for international action for resource transfers or on other aspects of reform in the areas of trade and international monetary arrangements require, however, an appropriate institutional framework for their implementation. The recent past has witnessed a major erosion of the authority of the key multilateral institutions charged with the governance of the world economy. Key decisions, whether on the debt problem, the setting of international exchange rates or global macroeconomic policy co-ordination, are taken within a limited group of developed countries, an inner core of which consists of the G5 the G7.

Potential initiatives for imaginative international action, as for example those available to Japan, often tend to be stifled and muted in their public expression by the concerns of other members of this limited group. This, as has been recently argued, has been the fate of Japan's initiative on developing country debt presented at the June 1988 Toronto Summit as the Miyazawa Plan. "Although the Miyazawa Plan was presented as complementary to the Baker Plan, it was not welcomed by the US Government. In Toronto it was ignored while at the September annual meetings of the IMF and the World Bank in Berlin it was openly attacked by US Treasury Secretary Brady. The general interpretation was that the US wants Japanese money but does not want the plan to usurp its leadership role" (5).

Experience has shown, however, that when a significant group of countries is able to speak on key issues with a single voice, their viewpoint has of necessity to be taken into account. This has been the case so far with the Group of 77 comprising the developing countries in general, the Group of 24 which has represented the G77 in the Bretton Woods institutions, and the so-called Cairns Group of both developing and developed countries with interests in primary commodities who have coalesced in the preparation for the Uruguay Round of trade negotiations.

By extrapolation it becomes plausible to argue that the creation of a group comprising all countries other than the Summit 5 -- the Non-Five -- on a basis where decision-making within the group is entrusted to a small governing body not exceeding 10 to 11 members, could facilitate the development of a single viewpoint on key international economic management issues. A notable example could be that of an approach to the debt problem where a unified position by the Group of the Non-Five could provide a constituency, so to speak, for thinking going on currently within Japan. Another example is the development of a viewpoint on approaches to a more durable set of international monetary and financial arrangements.

The first order of business of the Group of the Non-Five would be to seek through its Governing Board annual meetings with the five key Summit countries. These annual meetings could constitute an Interim World Economic Council depending on the subjects that would be assigned to it. Such a mechanism is no more than an institutionalisation of a "Cancun type" world Summit with the difference that the selection of countries taking part would be determined on the basis of objective criteria, reflecting a country's share in world trade, GNP and population.

The Governing Board of the Group of the Non-Five would allow illustratively, for three members each from Europe, and Asia and Oceania, two from the Western hemisphere including Canada, and one each from Africa and the Middle East. Illustratively again, in Europe, there could be two European Community constituencies, and another primarily made of Eastern European and neutral countries. In Asia and Oceania, there might be two constituencies formed under the leadership of India and China, and a third Pacific Rim constituency including Australia and New Zealand. In the Western Hemisphere, Canada might join in a constituency including Central America and the Caribbean, as is indeed partly the case today in the IMF, with a second South American constituency. There would be provision for the Soviet Union to join as an observer from the outset with full membership resulting from a further decision to join either GATT or any of the Bretton Woods institutions.

The objectives of the Group in seeking an Interim World Economic Council would be as follows:

1.   To lobby loudly and persistently for representation in the G5 Summit. The new Group would announce from the outset that, if invited, it would be prepared to designate one or more of its members to participate in the Group of Five and Summit meetings.

2. To develop joint positions on all the main issues pertaining to the management of the world economy -- exchange rates, interest rates, finance, debt, trade, etc.

3. To demonstrate, by its own mode of operation, the possibility of developing an efficient (i.e. small) but representative vehicle for discussion and negotiation on the major issues of international economic co-operation.

4. To resist, by all possible means, further erosion of the multilateral institutions resulting from the increasing tendency of the Group of Five and the Summit to take key decisions outside the existing multilateral framework. This would include using the considerable influence that the Group would have within these organisations to try to ensure that relations between them and the Group of Five and the Summit were not just a one-way street, as is to a large extent the case today.

5. To develop proposals for a major reform of the existing international institutional framework. Proposals for monetary reform would, I imagine, command a very high priority in this context. What is needed is a new international monetary system designed and developed in order to avoid unduly large swings of exchange rates over the medium-run which distort international resource allocation and strengthen protectionism in the countries with overvalued currencies.

Above all, the Group's mandate would lay out very clearly its essentially *political* objective of providing a counterweight to the Group of Five. In doing so, however, it should be stressed that the aim is not to create a new division between "them" and "us", but rather to mobilize pressures to narrow and eventually bridge the gap. Thus, the ultimate aim of the new Group would be to make itself redundant. For what the Group would be dedicated to is establishing a truly international mode of governance for the international institutions of the 21st century.

To summarise, therefore, there are several reasons for being somewhat more optimistic than Dr. Manmohan Singh has been about the prospects for North-South co-operation, and in particular, for bringing about the substantial recycling of surpluses in developing countries that would be entailed in pursuing Dr. Richard Jolly's basic needs-oriented development strategy. First, there seems to be a viable adjustment path for the United States to take in correcting its deficit that courts the least risk of world recession, if this were to focus on disarmament rather than on inducing a consumption recession through a consumption tax. Secondly, there is an opportunity for recycling to take up the resulting slack in the world economy, provided it proceeds *pari passu* with the US adjustment, given the reluctance of surplus economies to expand. Thirdly, there is an opportunity for recycling to occur under a regime of alternative conditionality in support of improved economic management in the Third World, especially if a system of *long-term* Development Contracts is put in place as advocated by Mr. Stoltenberg. Fourthly, there is a unique opportunity for marrying OECD industrial capacity released through disarmament with the unmet needs of the Third World and of restoring a second Golden

Age. Fifthly, this process would involve the provision of external finance to developing countries not only in the form of programme lending but of project lending and private foreign investment for the promotion of which both national and international mechanisms would have to be developed. Finally, there is an opportunity for developing a mechanism for monitoring this process of economic revitalization by reviving annual World Summit countries to organise themselves effectively for such a process by delegating authority in a structured fashion to a small representative Governing Board chosen from among its membership.

NOTES AND REFERENCES

1. STOLTENBERG, Thorvald "Towards a World Development Strategy", in this volume.

2. *OECD Economic Outlook*, Number 44, December 1988.

3. NAKAGAMA, Sam "Mathematics of a Falling Dollar: $150 Billion Budget Deficit, $150 Billion Trade Deficit, $150 Billion a Year for Nato", Nakagama & Wallace Pacific Basin Seminar, New York, 29th June 1988.

4. I am grateful to Professor Emma Rothschild for her very valuable assistance in looking further into these magnitudes.

5. STALLINGS, Barbara "An Increased Japanese Role in Third World Development", *Overseas Development Council Policy Focus* 1988 No. 6.

DISCUSSANT'S CONTRIBUTION

by

F.A. MALJERS

I feel honoured that a distinguished group like you is interested in a few comments from a representative of industry, or to put it differently, the shop floor.

For a long time multinationals have been the favourite scapegoat of a large number of politicians and academics, but I was rather happy to hear the confirmation here that this is changing now. Though we realize that everybody needs a scapegoat -- after all major religions are based on the scapegoat principle -- I admit that it is much more pleasant to be appreciated and respected.

My company has a turnover in developing countries of about $5 billion (out of a total of $30 billion) in 1987, an investment of about $2 million and we employ about 120 000 people. My personal perspective is probably rather influenced by the fact that I have been responsible or operations inter alia in two developing countries, namely Colombia and Turkey. What I would really like to try in the short time allocated, is to give a few comments from micro experience, which you will hopefully find useful in your macroeconomic considerations.

I don't think there is much that I have heard here with which I would really disagree, though I might put a different emphasis on a number of issues. My comments derived therefore are intended to broaden the discussion and not to be controversial, though some may find a few of my remarks mildly iconoclastic.

The first phenomenon which I consider to be somewhat overestimated in the discussion is the role of governments and related to that, of international institutions. Now I realize that I may, in turn, underestimate the role of international institutions -- and certainly in this particular meeting that would not be received well. Still, I would like to submit to you that governments and international institutions, important though they may be, are not enough to stimulate economic development.

The second issue I want to mention is that there is an enormous diversity in Third World countries which, I think, sometimes disappears when we talk about the "average" developing country. In my company we refer to the average developing country as Begonia when we discuss our strategic plans, but we realize that there is no actual country which is like Begonia in all respects. In each case we have to be more specific and we have to know, for instance, what is the capacity --

199

in your terms -- to absorb help from outside. When we make major investments decisions, we try to look at much more details than what Begonia is and where Begonia can go. I will come back to this subject.

As a third point, I would like to mention with special emphasis, the role of the development of the private entrepreneur. He can be a local farmer, a local trader or the owner/manager of a large company. Let me remind you that all large companies started as small local traders or local industries. In many developing countries centralised control, excessive bureaucracy and regulation discourage the local entrepreneur and thus stifle the growth of local enterprise. This is a problem which is not always sufficiently understood in the Third World. From my preference for the entrepreneur, you will have deduced that ideologically I am supporter of the market mechanism. I realize that this has its imperfections and that governments will have to set rules. I also realize that there are instances where the market is held responsible for many evils. Having said that, I can only repeat what Jean-Claude Paye said in his introductory remarks, namely that the market mechanism may not be perfect, but so far it seems to be the best we have found. I believe that even Mr. Gorbatchev is now a somewhat late and probably rather hesitant convert to this particular idea. So, if you do not believe in the advantages of the market mechanism, I would be interested to know what alternative you prefer and where this particular alternative is used. Personally I have not been able to think of anything better yet.

Apart from these introductory remarks, there are two specific issues I want to raise with you: the role of foreign private capital investment; and some aspects of the transfer of technology.

What are the major aspects of private foreign investment which differentiate it from aid or debt? The most obvious difference is that private foreign investment provides mostly equity -- a form of capital to be repaid if profits are generated providing money to pay dividends. In this particular respeect it has a considerable advantage over debt. Much more important, foreign investment comes combined with know-how. It provides skills on an ongoing basis. It is therefore much more than just capital. It may be interesting in this context to look briefly at the major elements on which a company like my own bases its investment decisions.

Firstly, there has to be a market above a minimum size and with a certain growth potential. Whilst we operate in large markets and in small markets, a company like Unilever which sells rather pedestrian products such as tooth paste, table oils, tea and soap, likes countries where there are many mouths to be fed and teeth to be brushed. If there is no market for our products then there is obviously no reason to invest.

This brings me to an important problem. In a number of countries, for instance some of the African countries, markets are too small to make efficient production feasible and I support the idea of regionalisation. As suggested by Mr. Jolles -- as a possible solution for this problem. After all it is almost im-

200

possible to see adequate economies of scale even for relatively simple products in a country with less than a million inhabitants.

A second condition for investment is that a company needs assurance that it can operate under the same conditions as local businesses. Or, as the British say it so elegantly, there has to be a level playing field. That sounds as a simple and fairly reasonable request, but it is often difficult to realize. It has been already said by a number of people in this conference that many countries have grey sectors in the economy, sometimes very substantial in size, where the rules are different. A company like ours has a principle of sticking to the rules. An example of the problem to be faced is the way in which an overvalued currency can stimulate illegal imports -- or smuggling in the vernacular -- whilst the authorities are not very effective in stopping this, for whatever reason.

The third condition for investment is that the country should be sufficiently stable -- and I mean here especially political stability, though economic stability also is important -- but operating in turbulent economic conditions is something one can learn and since in many countries we have been present for about 100 years now, we have learned something about operating in turbulent economic conditions. Even so, sudden changes, for instance in import regulations, can be disastrous for an individual company and for industry as a whole. Similarly, extreme forms of price control have at times wrecked the industrial structure. If a government regularly takes such measures, it will have a serious effect on its ability to attract foreign investors.

The fourth major consideration in deciding on investment is that we like to remit profits if we are successful in our venture. Of course there again both the government and the investor have to adopt a reasonable attitude. In addition we like to receive payments for our technological inputs. The stopping of dividend payments, of course, happens from time to time, and under extreme conditions a foreign investor may have some understanding for a limited period. If it happens abruptly and its main objective is clearly to help a local political situation, however, it is very difficult to see how a country could indeed be attractive for investment in the longer term.

It may be useful to add that companies have long memories when they feel wronged by the government of a host country. It may be appropriate to remind you of the book of Genesis, where it says "the inadequacies of the fathers are visited upon the sons until the third and fourth generation".

There are of course many other important elements in taking investment decisions in general but I have concentrated here on the ones which I thought particularly relevant.

The second issue I want to raise, is a popular one: transfer of technology. I was interested to read in Manmohan Singh's paper that he feels the gap between developed and developing countries is widening. He suggests that it is important to enhance the technological capacities of the Third World countries to "leap-frog", I quote now, and shorten its period of transition to the state of a mature economy.

I think that it is true, but I was rather disappointed to see that Mr. Singh does not pay more attention to the relationship between direct investment and transfer of technology. Private foreign investment can, and usually does, also imply the transfer of technology as well as with capital investment. In this connection I was interested to see a very interesting book by Dimitrios Germidis, of the OECD Development Centre, in your book exhibition in the hall, on the transfer of technology. I have asked him to send it to me, but a footnote in the catalogue indicated that it is only available to developing countries. I am not quite sure whether that means the book is very good or very bad. But if I were to receive it, I will certainly study it with interest.

I quote Mr. Singh again, and with approval, that "there is a need for innovative collaborative mechanisms to integrate science and technology effectively into the development processes of the Third World". Let us think about the problem of how to do this. Technology is only useful to a developing country in the form of applied knowledge. It is not, as is sometimes suggested, enough to transfer a scientific concept of the description of a production process from one place to another. To benefit from technology more is required than the reading of scientific magazines or manuals. Even listening to learned speakers in conferences may not be enough. Technology, like swimming, only works if learned in practice. Therefore, at the end of the day, the main way -- perhaps even the only way -- to transfer technology is through people.

Transfer of technology is thus more complex than it sounds. The word technology is often used in the narrow sense of the skills needed in manufacturing, but there is much more to industry than only manufacturing. There are also the skills required in marketing, selling, quality control, purchasing, finance, accounting, logistics and distribution and in personnel management. None of these techniques can be applied in isolation, they need to be used together. They have to be integrated in one package of technology, adapted to the special needs of each country and transferred as one system.

A related question, raised a number of times, is that of appropriate technology. Listening to the various remarks here, I began to wonder whether we all mean the same with the word "appropriate". Appropriate in my interpretation means you compare something with something else. We consider technology appropriate if it can work successfully in the country where we want to apply it. A very difficult issue in that respect is the effect of various technologies on the employment situation in a country. I listened with interest to earlier remarks on this issue. It is far from easy to find the right balance between the desirability to optimise employment now and the need to be competitive in the longer term. Looking back we may have made more mistakes by giving in to the short term employment point, than the other way around.

Now, briefly, how do we transfer technology? First, we do it through people. We have a very extensive programme to develop managers and employees. This is a continuous effort of which we are very proud. The second point here is that we lose quite a number of the people we train. That seems inevitable and we have learned to accept that. We lose these people to local companies or to governments. That in a way may be both good news and bad news. It is good news because it gives the country and the industry more well-trained managers. It is bad news for us, because we have to replace so many of our good people on an almost continuous basis.

In addition to that, of course, we are also involved "willy-nilly" in training third parties. This includes teaching retailers how to control stocks, helping transporters with logistic systems, assisting warehouse operators with layout planning, and many similar subjects. Of course, I could also talk about the 120 000 people we employ in developing countries and how on things like safety at work, environmental aspects, and secondary labour conditions we try to improve standards, which we hope that many other companies will sooner or later follow.

I would like to say a few words about agriculture, particularly because some provocative remarks were made earlier. The role of a multinational working in agribusiness -- and especially in agriculture -- is often criticised, though often on widely different grounds. It seems to be almost impossible to do the right thing here and the situation reminds me of the anecdote of the soviet worker who had a new job.

The first day, underestimating the problems of public transport in the Soviet Union, he arrived rather late and, taken to the workers committee, was accused of sabotage. The second day he took an earlier bus and arrived 10 minutes before factory opening time. To his surprise, again he was taken to the workers committee, now accused of industrial espionage. The third day he decided to do it absolutely correct, waited outside the gate and entered precisely at the right moment. Again, the poor man was brought to the workers committee this time accused of bourgeois conformism.

This is the feeling I sometimes get when I read about the perceived benefits and disadvantages of multinationals in agribusiness. We have palm oil plantations, amongst them some of the most productive in the world, and we are rather proud of that. We are also in prawn farming in the Ivory Coast, salmon fishing in Chile, in tea plantations in Kenya, and palm oil and rubber plantations in Malaysia, Nigeria and Colombia. Is that bad or good for these countries? I think on the whole it is good, but of course I cannot give a definite answer. When I hear about the worries that bio-technology R&D is done mostly by multinationals, as Mr. Singh mentioned, I am not clear what alternative he has in mind. Should we give it perhaps to an international institute, and if so, how are they going to pay for it and what are they going to do with it? I feel that if there is a problem -- and I am not sure that there is, I, for one, don't have the answer.

I support Mr. Singh's rejection of increasing tariffs and the raising of barriers in international trade. The EEC's Antonio Costa assures us that protectionism could be right as long as it was applied to the right product . He has that endearing form of selective loss of memory which one so often encounters in Brussels, when one hears how senior officials try to wish the EEC agricultural problem away. Here is a political entity, the European community, with a budget of which well over half is spent on agriculture, and they hardly talk about it. I must say, speaking to Mr. Costa that he has authorised me to say that he felt, like me, that agriculture protection went much too far in the Community. Reciprocating his goodwill, I admit that progress has certainly been made, though in my view not nearly enough.

I would also like to remind you that the EEC agriculture policy can create considerable problems for agricultural exports from the developing countries. As an example I mention the proposals to put a levy on vegetable oils. This is just one aspect of the problem of commodity prices, which would merit a full conference in itself. Virtually everybody would like a much more stable level of commodity prices, but many countries act differently from the principles they claim to believe in. For instance, the United States -- and I mention that because of remarks by a previous speaker -- has stopped the import of orange juice from Brazil to please the orange growers in Florida. The justification for that looks probably different to a senator from Florida, than to an orange grower in Brazil. These tendencies can be very dangerous.

This form of protectionism makes the repayment of the debt, so often mentioned here, even more difficult than it already is. If indeed we are accepting the often-used arguments in favour of some protectionism, the barriers for international trade will increase further and this will almost certainly increase the problems of many developing countries. A related issue is the protectionism between the developing countries, or in the "South" as mentioned by some speakers. That would also make me rather worried; I can see that a case can be made occasionally for a short period but protectionism on a poor country with a small market, may result in an economic system, described in "Alice in Wonderland" where there is an island where people try to make a living by taking in one another's laundry.

Reading through the interesting papers produced for this conference I began to wonder whether I am an optimist or a pessimist on the prospects for the developing world. I think at the end of the day I am predominantly an optimist. I realize however, that he dividing line between optimists and pessimists is very thin. It may be useful to keep in mind that a pessimist is often an optimist with experience. Let me leave it at that.

Chapter VI

TOWARDS A WORLD DEVELOPMENT STRATEGY BASED ON GROWTH, SUSTAINABILITY AND SOLIDARITY: POLICY OPTIONS FOR THE 1990s

ON CULTURAL AND SOCIAL SUSTAINABILITY

by

Lourdes ARIZPE

To examine the issue of interdependence in a multipolar and globalised, yet dualistic world economy, we must start by clarifying the frame of reference in which it is to be analysed. As a starting point, all we have learned through historical and anthropological research indicates that the world today is facing not only a rearrangement of economic polarities, but a full-scale civilisational change.

Such change, as in previous historical instances, is being driven by technological advances that will alter the mechanics of everyday life, as well as the social structure based on forms of production organised on the raw materials-factory-assembly line pattern of 19th century industry. Policy changes stressing the market economy and economic globalisation of the economy are also bringing about a political reordering of capitalist and socialist industrialism. The changing role of the State and the challenge of ethnic and cultural minorities, in the context of trends towards global interdependence, will require a redefinition of the political structure of Nation-States. Biotechnology, in a few years, will change the nature of agriculture, which is still the basis of the livelihood of the majority of the world population, especially in countries of the South. At the same time, human biogenetics and demographic trends have already impinged on the most private of domains, that of the family and of biological and social reproduction. Post-industrial culture, which is surely a misnomer, in the North is fostering a fragmented sense of self and of social place. In developing countries, people perceive their traditional cultures and identities as alarmingly imperilled by the new possibilities of electronic communication and audiovisual culture. There have been only two previous instances in history in which such overall social change has taken place; that is, in which *all areas of human and social life are being affected*. It is, however, the first time in history that *the whole of the world is being affected almost simultaneously*. However, as Soedjatmoko perceptively states, the Third Technological Revolution is already underway before the first and the second technological revolutions have reached to the whole globe.

In spite of these two clearly defined characteristics of today's global change, discussion of world trends has not been holistic in analysing and in proposing policy actions. It has concentrated on finding solutions to economic problems, and on beginning to create an awareness as to the ecological sustainability of development actions. This paper will stress that both the economic and the ecological challenges are interwoven to issues related to the social and cultural sustainability of world development.

Secondly, discussion of world trends has not been global in the sense of trying to create a world citizenship, instead of trying to accommodate as far as possible national, corporate and conglomerate economic interests. We are still global citizens with a tribal mind.

If we are facing a major civilisational change, should we then concentrate on creating a "grand design" for the future? This is neither possible nor desirable. History shows that all great social transformations have happened without a blueprint -- or most of them, at least. Changes today are so varied and so inextricably linked that uni-disciplinary predictions are hardly worth the effort. However, it is certainly true that human goals and shared perceptions have guided such transformations and, especially, have given people a sense of purpose and of solidarity without which changes can become dangerously violent. Thus, we must at least begin to think of policy guidelines that can be propitious actions for a new world society.

A FIRST STEP: GLOBAL ACCOUNTABILITY

While we cannot predict *where* change is leading us, steps must be taken to ensure greater accountability of national governments and multinational conglomerates to the global citizenship, to stop corporate and national virtues from turning into global vices. As Mahbub Ul Haq has correctly pointed out, just when we require international institutions and internationalism, the United States, World Bank, IMF and GATT have declined in world economic management. On way of doing this would be to develop international law into a global juridical system and to have multilateral institutions slowly evolve towards institutions of a world government. This, of course, will be fiercely opposed by the hegemonic powers but, faced with the globalization of issues and the threat of collective survival, it will have to be done sooner or later. Surely some leaders, many thinkers and many global citizens are already willing to break the gridlock of parochial interests to build a new world.

Perhaps this process would be made easier in a one-world approach, that entails more direct negotiations which would allow checks and balances to be introduced and means found to make them effective. In a multipolar scheme of greater autonomy of regions, global negotiations may be more balanced but would regions internally have a pluralistic scheme of negotiation? As many speakers pointed out in the seminar, the North-South divide can also be found within countries, both in the North and in the South.

What should be obvious from previous historical experience is that economic polarisation into a two-track system tends to create political, social and cultural tensions that make it unsustainable in the long term.

The Latin American experience with dualistic economies showed them to be inherently unstable. Economic growth in the region since the 1950s created such disparities in income distribution that, among other things, guerrilla warfare became widespread in the 1960s. Dictatorial or authoritarian regimes further exacerbated political militancy and had to give way either to military regimes and "dirty wars", or to costly populist policies. The "miracles" for the few turned into nightmares for all.

Dualistic economies will be even more unstable internally in the 1990s. First, a higher educational level of most of the population in most developing countries will make economic polarisation politically more untenable. Secondly, the mass media, unless it is totally reality-washed, will make economic disparities constantly known and thus spark off more frustration. Thirdly, at least two of the major religions in the South, Catholicism and Islam, are doctrinally opposed to extremes of wealth and poverty; a dualistic economy will strengthen fundamentalisms, or irrational pseudo-religions, or, in the best of cases, politically conscious theologies such as the Theology of Liberation in Latin America. Religious conflict will then fuel political and social strife.

A SECOND STEP: TAKING SOCIAL SUSTAINABILITY INTO ACCOUNT

Since the 1950s, development policies have either ignored or taken the social and cultural dimensions of development for granted. There was an implicit assumption that these dimensions would fall into step with whatever new economic realities arose. This was indeed the case until the 1960s, because in the North, as well as in the South, the private sphere of family, reproduction and personal relationships was as stable as the rock of Gibraltar. In the South, geographical mobility was running a slow, manageable course. In both hemispheres, cultural identities were secure and ethnicity dormant, while in the hegemonic cultural and artistic world in the North, the *avant-garde* was busy voluntarily de-linking itself into an "art for art's sake" solipsistic spiral. Thus, the train of economic growth was able to run smoothly along the two taken-for-granted rails of social and cultural stability until the early 1970s when in both hemispheres, for different reasons, the train started derailing.

The inertia of the private sphere exploded: some attribute this to the State's wanting to control the last autonomous frontier in society; others to the fact that women finally rebelled. It has been argued that the demise of religious belief undermined psychological and moral certainties and created "homeless minds" or "hedonistic values" in the North and messianic -- political or religious -- movements in the South; that the weakening of traditional religious, community and family institutions left individuals alienated and alone; that the need to control population growth and the invention of the "pill" and of other contraceptives catapulted the whole process of biological and social reproduction into the public sphere; and that feminism turned this ongoing process into a visible ideological and political movement. In fact, the feminist slogan of "the personal is political" is to date the most succinct description of this historical development. At present, research has shown, though, that this overall change was due to the historical combination of profound and simultaneous changes in religion, reproduction, and womens' roles.

Previously, industrialism, both in its capitalist and socialist forms, had found a balance in keeping the private sphere of reproduction on a different logic from that of economic production. Now this sphere -- both in its biological and social dimensions -- is posing fundamental and unexpected problems for economic growth. Just to mention the main ones: i) the decline of population in countries of the North; ii) overpopulation -- as related to economic capacity to sustain a given population -- in many regions of the South, linked to rapid ecological depletion; iii) continuous South-North labour migrations; iv) the changing gender dimensions of the structure of employment; v) womens' expanding leadership of urban and rural movements of the poor; and vi) growing "matrifocality" of families, which has also been termed the "feminisation of poverty".

To our dismay, such issues are most often absent from economic development plans, or are mentioned alongside as "social problems". This represents both a theoretical and a methodological challenge for economic development models. This challenge becomes even more important if the problems of blatantly "anti-social" phenomena are added to the picture. If one puts together a few "hard" data such as the fact that US prisons are now insufficient to hold the swelling criminal population, that suicides continue to be one of the major causes of deaths in the North, that drug addiction and production is alarmingly on the increase, that religious or sectarian fanaticisms are growing everywhere, that alcoholism, prostitution and criminality (including military-sanctioned criminality) are also on the rise globally and that a surprising number of urban people are really believing that, as the Apocalypse says, we are on the verge of millenary destruction, a mentally and socially unbalanced world comes blatantly into view. In strictly economic terms, one could say that the world economy is becoming blacker by the day. Has this been taken into account in development models? Or is this the part that everyone will try to leave out and throw into the hands of the police and the military? This could bring us to a very sober thought: if part of political sovereignty is being handed to the market, and an increasing part is being handed to the police and the military, how much civil political sovereignty will there be left for development to continue to be a rationally driven activity?

The above has been described in some detail because the whole point of this paper is to stress that, together with ecological sustainability, priority attention must be given to the *social sustainability* of economic growth. It should be clear by now that in some vital areas social and cultural factors, such as the ones mentioned above, are already altering the patterns of economic growth.

In this dimension of "social problems", one must add, in the South, the most massive and disruptive transfer of people from rural areas to urban centres in human history. The social and cultural dislocation which has ensued is unparalleled, although I for one am convinced that human creativity and sociability could rebuild cultural ties in a few generations. *If conditions are given that allow it.* This should be one of the most crucial areas for policy action in the coming decade.

For, in speaking about the population which is in danger of being involuntarily de-linked or marginalised in a two-speed world economy, let us be very clear whom we are speaking about. Without doubt we are referring mainly to rural peoples, farming families mostly, and the urban poor which, in the South, are overwhelmingly migrant farmers. Indeed, farming families will probably be the most victimised social group in the globe in the coming decades, whichever model of world economy is taken because they are caught between three advancing forces. The first, biotechnology, is about to change a form of production which is 15 000 years old into an unrecognisable new way of life. In this new way of life, farmers will not be able to farm without the high technology inputs controlled by the few. Never has a power of such extraordinary implications been held by so few. The second is linked to the crash of agricultural commodities in the world market which is making farmers all over the planet go bankrupt. Those in the North, however, have rich governments who subsidize, regulate, give social security, turn farms into hotels or otherwise find ways of minimizing the blows to farmers. In the South, farmers are blown away like the sand in the desert, thus creating a social desertification of rural areas just as damaging as the soil desertification. The third force is hitting harder in the South as well, and this is ecological depletion. The combination of economic, biotechnological and political factors are taking their livelihoods away from millions of farming families, aggravated, in some cases, by demographic trends, who are now edged towards depleting ecological resources. Surely this must be a high priority area for policy action in the coming decades, but not by way of providing only immediate relief; the challenge is to rethink the economy of the future in terms of a unified territorial distribution in which the rural forms of production can be linked to the high speed on. Further research and creative thinking, as well as political will, are needed to achieve this.

A THIRD STEP: CULTURAL SUSTAINABILITY

In spite of superficial trends towards cultural homogenisation, or, more likely, because of it, never has cultural diversity been so often, and so belligerently, defended in the modern era. As centripetal forces at the global level pull towards a transnationalisation of the economy and of culture the reverse seems to be happening at the microsocial level as centrifugal forces atomise national identities into ever smaller units. The main issue here for development is how a two-speed world economy or a one-world model would interact with the boundaries of national, ethnic or communal identities.

On this issue it is important to be aware of the following analytically different processes:

1.   In many countries, some groups, consciously and willingly, will want to stay out of a modernising development, for the time cycles in which they live are circular, and, in fact, timeless. Their wishes must be respected. This will be the case of some religious sects and some ethnic groups, both in the North and in the South. The decision should be left to them, with a clear understanding that they will then not desire the goods and services of a modernising economy. Their problem may be, then, that many of their younger generations will constantly be slipping out to the consumer society, but this will be their problem, just as their standard of living will be their choice.

If, instead, they are forcibly or charitably handed out a Western way of life, their psychological and symbolic structures will be destroyed as has happened with indigenous peoples all over the world. What they do need is State protection against those who covet their lands, or who want to exploit their labour. New schemes to do this are now being explored in different countries: in Canada, the Inuit are negotiating that a separate province be created for them in the Arctic lands; in Nicaragua, a statute of regional autonomy was granted to the Atlantic coastal area where most Indian and black minorities live.

The main point is that these groups are fighting because they don't want to change, but what will happen if the basis of their livelihood is changed, even indirectly, by biotechnology, by environmental concerns or by telecommunications? They may then fall into a second category.

2.   The first group, who are defending an ancient form life and culture, must be distinguished from those who are retrenching into traditional customs or religions because they are being marginalised. That is, they lose their livelihood, or they foresee that the new economic context will be barren land for them, and this may be quite factual since in a dualistic economy they would most likely be left in the stationary side. This would be the large majority of the population in rural areas in the South, as well as unskilled workers in the cities, both in the South and in the North. It is this perception of their increasing exclusion from the high-speed economy, usually accompanied by political marginalisation as well that leads them to take up sectarian identities, be they religious, esoteric, political or ethnic. Because they are closer to the high-speed economy in Northern cities, such phenomena are more prevalent there. In the South, centuries old identities still provide this shelter. The first group is fighting because they don't want to change; the second is reacting because they have been left out of change. If the first group is offered a place in economic growth, they will refuse it; the second will accept it because they have nothing else to fall back on. From a policy perspective, it is this very diverse group which requires actions to stimulate their own de-

212

velopment but with some way of linking it to the high-speed economy to avoid its involuntary de-linking from the latter.

3. The third factor creating centrifugal tendencies is political advantage. Cultural identities have been and are being used to mobilise for liberation purposes, or to gain power in national politics, or to rally macroregional political forces. Nationalism -- both in nation-states, or in "nationalities" in socialist systems -- and ethnicism are now being taken up as banners in this struggle. In some cases, groups are demanding greater political autonomy in a most varied range of movements -- which it would be too long to go into here -- i.e., the Irish, the Basques, the Armenians, the Sikhs or the Kanaks. In other cases, they are combining religious defence with regional influence as in the case of Iran and Libya. Cultural identity is not an end in itself, but a means towards achieving some political purpose.

4. Finally, centrifugal tendencies are also put into play when cultural identity is used to defend national markets. When the British government launched its "Buy British" campaign at the end of the 1960s, it opened the way for a wide range of protectionist campaigns in commercial warfare among rival economies.

These four different trends must be kept in mind, then, when asking whether plurality and diversity will be part of the new world organisation. It certainly will be. Against those who argue that more development and more mass media automatically mean more cultural homogenisation, the best contradicting example is that of Europe itself: in spite of its advanced industrial development and wide-ranging communications, 3 000 languages are still spoken there, and the voices of cultural minorities are very much alive.

In the near future, these four processes will most likely continue to influence social and political events, both as an action as well as a reaction to macroeconomic centripetal tendencies. A two-speed economy, though, would certainly exacerbate such conflicts because marginalisation will most probably run along pre-existing national and ethnic boundaries, thereby deepening disparities of development. This, then, would be a formula for chronic political instability and social strife in all countries.

From the policy perspective, the priority in this cultural dimension would be to change legislation or to create it, especially in countries of the South, to ensure a balanced political participation of all ethnic groups, and to give autonomy, as far as possible, to regions and groups who demand it. However, some minority leaders are even demanding that the organisation of nation-states be dismantled; and this is echoed by those who see the new geo-economic blocs as the major political actors on the world scene. This is both unrealistic and undesirable. All scientific studies have shown that social and cultural diversity is an inherent trait in the human species -- in animal species as well -- and that only a few generations of relative isolation are necessary for a new culture and social organisation to be formed. Demographic growth patterns, inventiveness and aggressiveness, to name a few traits, of human groups, vary greatly and thus rules of political organisation of a medium-range geographical span are necessary to attenuate and solve conflicts. This is what nation-states in fact try to do, but this means that the state must be responsive to the demands of cultural minorities. Also, macroeconomies in a multipolar world would not be able to deal effectively with a myriad of minority groups, nor would the latter have any leverage for defence or negotiation in global developments.

A SPECIAL ISSUE: KNOWLEDGE TO SUSTAIN DEVELOPMENT

Another area which is vital for development, especially in the South, but which routinely gets lost in the interstices between technology and ethnicity, is that of knowledge, specifically that knowledge variously called traditional, local, empirical or ethno-scientific, but which is vital to development.

In this respect, it is important to emphasize that the present conditions of the international system are making people in countries of the South poorer in economic resources, but they are also making them poorer in knowledge, and, what is perhaps even worse, poorer in the confidence with which they could continue to create knowledge. This trend will foster an historically unprecedented skewness in cognitive and intellectual wealth in a world which has had a multipolar intellectual and scientific history: Egypt, Mesopotamia, India, the Inca, Mesoamerica, China, Benin, the Arabs, Greece, Europe; never in history has any region been the only perpetual creator of knowledge.

For although economic multipolarity is envisaged for the future, is not scientific and technological monopolarity insidiously building up? It is not a question of refusing to recognise the extraordinary achievements of Western science and culture? There is no doubt that the West, through rationalism, created the intellectual conditions to sustain scientific progress, but it is a question of putting this into focus: its great "age of discovery" -- which everyone is anxious to celebrate in its 500th anniversary in 1992 -- was also the "age of appropriating" the world's resources. Everyone immediately thinks of economic resources, rarely do they consider the enormous intellectual resources which Europe also took from the East, the South and everywhere.

For, ever since the Elizabethan Age -- and some even believe this was one of the crucial inventions in the advent of science and capitalism -- European scientists and intellectuals have been scrupulously protected in their creative rights and rewarded for their time-consuming efforts. Compare that to the fact that never have the "folk" discoverers and intellectuals of the South had the least recognition of their rights or efforts, and this continues right up to the present day.

Corporations and scientists in the North rightly demand that patents be respected in countries of the South, but where are all the patents for all the man/woman-made products, and ideas taken by the North from the South in the

214

last five centuries? What do patents mean when, for example, a plant patent of a corporation in the North is made with germplasm taken from the South, perhaps also making use of botanical "folk" knowledge also taken from the South, and through the brain drain, perhaps employing the best minds born, fed, and educated in the South?

The main point is that the world distribution of the capacity to continue to create knowledge is becoming dangerously skewed and would deteriorate even more in a two-track world model. For the North not only concentrates all the financial, institutional and intellectual resources for research, but it continues to accumulate the physical and intellectual resources from the South.

True, governments in countries of the South are also at fault. Ecological destruction, cultural discrimination, government insensitivity and public disregard for local and traditional knowledge is destroying a wealth that has taken millennia to be built up.

It is hard to exaggerate what this loss of knowledge will mean in terms of human civilisation. Biologists are urgently warning, in the words of E. Wilson, that "the worst that can happen is not the depletion of energy, or economic collapse, war or the expansion of a totalitarian government. These catastrophes would be terrible for human beings but could be repaired in a few generations. The only ongoing process that will take millions of years to redress is the loss of genetic diversity and of species due to the destruction of natural habitats". Precisely the counterpart of this loss of genetic diversity and of species in the realm of cultures is the loss of the diversity of human knowledge and of cultural traditions.

Granted, human beings also have the capacity to adapt to rapidly changing environments, and so room must be left for new knowledge. Yet this gift of adaptation is based on the one single ability that people have over plants, and still over computers, and that is the ability to learn from experience. If this experience, in varied forms of local or traditional knowledge related to pharmacopoeia, ecology, botany, zoology, agronomy, hunting, fishing and collecting, physiological and psychological therapy, and symbolic systems, is erased from the book of human history, this will mean an impoverishment, not only in absolute terms, but in possibilities to learn from experience for scientific and social advancement.

It is not only a question of folk or ethno-science giving important leads which are then developed in sophisticated laboratories (and, by the way, patented). It is equally true that however refined the products of scientific laboratories or seminar rooms, all technology, administrative models or economic policies have to be adapted, moulded and combined with local knowledge if they are to be successful in different geo-ecological, political and social environments. Indeed, some of the worst examples of development failures can be traced to the lack of attention to local conditions.

Policy actions, especially in the 1990s, should give attention to preserving this diversity of knowledge actively. This can be done by, among other things, using the sophistication of information technology to record, classify and dissemi-

215

nate such knowledge bases, and by creating awareness and supporting projects among local populations so they themselves are able to treasure and to preserve such knowledge for their own advancement.

SUMMING UP POLICY PROPOSALS

If the working framework in which we deal with the new world trends is global and holistic, the search for shared goals becomes important. The shape that political ideologies took in the 20th century has now become obsolete; this does not mean that the principles which guided many of them are obsolete. The best of these principles -- equity, democracy, freedom of choice, human and civil rights -- must be given a new shape in the forthcoming decades. The challenge is to shape something which is not yet born but which, in the process of being tried out, will be born.

How to induce this birth? By supporting interdisciplinary research and policy groups, including both North and South participants, to rethink political, social and cultural goals and institutions on a global basis. Of course, as so many participants in the Symposium proposed, new financial and economic managements, as well as environmental institutions have immediate priority.

Just as important is the need to create greater public awareness through the mass media, both in the North and in the South as to the need for a global approach in which shared responsibility and benefits are negotiated for a sustainable world development.

As to social sustainability concerns, research efforts should be directed at incorporating the economic costs of social malaise into economic development models. This is partly a methodological problem, whose solution should be geared, firstly, to creating hard data on such phenomena.

On the policy side, as long as economic dualism persists, the need for some form of social welfare for those excluded from the high-speed economy will continue. Right beside aid or social security, policy should encourage what could be termed "freedom of inventiveness". That is, the ability to create new means of livelihood. How? Among other things, by providing credit for micro-industries, especially for women heads of households, and for environmentally sound agricultural and fisheries micro-projects; by promoting new organisational schemes in high-technology agriculture that will foster negotiated interdependence rather than vertical control; by accelerating and broadening the dissemination of the knowledge base of new technologies and of market movements; by enhancing renewed ties of family, kinship and social solidarity which will continue to give people a sense of belonging without being oppressive to women; by supporting peoples' initiatives to create a new "sense of place" in a global society.

In terms of cultural sustainability, there must be greater awareness that, ultimately, a sense of meaning and of purpose are the two rails on which any train of

216

development must travel, and, therefore, these two concerns must have a place on political agendas. Can Western culture alone provide the answers for globally shared goals? This is no longer possible in a global context. The answers must come out of a constant dialogue between cultures and through science. Such an end can be pursued through mass media programmes, many kinds of research, scientific and educational programmes, and especially art, which explores and enhances such a dialogue.

It would be desirable that special research and policy actions be focused on the multi-ethnic dimension of national societies: will negotiations among such groups be handled at the level of national governments or of macro-regions? What will the patterns of ethnic migration be from less-developed countries left out of macro-regions to the latter? The knowledge base on this topic amassed by anthropological research during many decades should be tapped in this respect. Comparative studies of recent legislation and political agreements with indigenous and national minorities should be pursued.

Finally, a massive effort should be made, the world over, to record local and traditional knowledge, especially in regions where both bulldozers and televisions are doing away with legacies of observation evolved during centuries. This can be done rapidly using computers and ethnographic methods. Ideally, projects by the communities themselves -- especially the young and the elderly -- to record their legacies of wisdom should be stressed.

A TIME OF HARD CHOICES

In general terms, avoiding a global and national two-tiered economy of the rich and the poor means breaking down judicial, political, scientific and cultural barriers that polarize the use of resources. In concrete actions, it means expanding educational services, preserving, acknowledging and adapting local knowledge, promoting democracy, eliminating ethnic discrimination, and opening the mass media to local participation, among other things. Importantly, it does not mean giving handouts, it means rebuilding livelihoods.

As James Grant, Executive Director of UNICEF has recently stressed, it is a time for hard choices. At this moment, there is still time to choose between an apartheid pattern for global development with all its instability, poverty and suffering, or one where the process may be an end in itself for the time being, a participatory path towards the future. This seems to me our only option: not knowing where we are going, we can still decide how to move forward

THE COMPELLING REASONS FOR A ONE-WORLD APPROACH

by

SOEDJATMOKO

It is well nigh impossible, on this occasion of the 25th anniversary of the OECD Development Centre, not to realize how much the world has changed in the past 25 years, and how much more rapid and profound these changes have become in the last decade.

What has radically changed the human condition and will increasingly make its impact felt as we move into the 21st century, is the cumulative impact of interconnected changes in three independent systems. These are changes in the world strategic and political situation, changes in the workings of the international economy, and changes in the global ecology. The impact of these changes forces us from now on to think in terms of sustainable world development, rather than in the conventional terms of national development and North-South relations.

In the strategic area the two superpowers have begun to review their overall military posture and their worldwide strategic commitments in light of their excessive costs, with the purpose of bringing them in line with the limits of their basic economic strengths, and to enable them to address the social and economic problems besetting the domestic base of their military and economic power.

The INF agreement, though covering less than 5 per cent of the superpowers' nuclear weapons arsenal, started a new period of general détente and raised the hope of deep, 50 per cent cuts in their strategic nuclear weapons. Whether that process will continue is not certain; it is still possible that the reduction in numbers will be offset by a race to improve the quality of nuclear weapons. It is also possible that a further deepening of détente will be swarthed by failure to reach agreement on reductions in conventional arms.

If agreements on these cuts could be reached, the United Kingdom and France together would command a number equal to 20 per cent of the number of warheads of the Soviet Union, and China 17 per cent, thus bringing the situation closer to strategic multipolarity. The possession or near possession of nuclear weapons by a number of other countries, and the chances of further proliferation, adds to the diffusion of explosive power in the world. At the same time, a number of persistent conflicts and political processes in the world have shown the limits of coercive power, and proved the fact that a large number of problems do not lend themselves to a military solution. Perhaps most important of all, in terms of the purposes of this paper, is the fact that with the present arms technology and the militarization of the oceans and outer space, national borders now have very little relevance in ensuring the security of the state. The concepts of front-line or rear-guard have lost all meaning. Consequently, new concepts of security are emerging. Détente and the revision of superpower strategic postures are bound to set in motion processes of political change. They are of two kinds: the emergence of regional powers or groupings, and the surfacing of hitherto hidden political aspirations in various parts of the world, each bringing with it its own problems, conflicts and the seeds of both new instability and of self-organization and co-operation.

These changes at the strategic and political level are matched and sometimes enhanced, in magnitude and significance, by changes in the international economy. We have seen the rise of NIEs in East Asia and Latin America, which has radically changed the pattern of competitiveness between countries, but has also led to serious economic and financial imbalances.

The globalization of national economies, made possible by the communications revolution, has led to the internationalization of financial markets and trade, massive and rapid capital movements, no longer related to trade, but driven by global institutional investors and speculators, and the consequent development of new and global power structures that are only accountable to themselves and are beyond the effective reach of any single government. They are a part of a transnational sphere with a commanding access to capital, skills, technology and markets. The French economist Albert Bressand has stated it graphically, though not without a bit of exaggeration: "The US now has two central banks; the Federal Reserve and the Japanese insurance companies."

The heightened worldwide competition resulting from these changes has created powerful forces towards diversification among developing countries and greater economic nationalism, but has also brought the formation of regional economic groupings. The Canadian-US single market is merely the first step in this direction. The European market that will come into being in 1992 will create the largest single market in the world. Other regional groupings may follow. In the emerging global strategic situation a European market may well increase the likelihood that Europe will also, politically and economically, play a more independent role.

However, integration of regional markets, necessary though it may be, may well be a very traumatic experience for the participating countries. When economic restructuring takes place there will inevitably be a painful shakedown period of fierce competition: weaker companies will fall by the wayside or will have to merge with stronger corporations; companies which have relied in the past on government orders will have to make major readjustments. Inevitably there will be major changes in employment levels, patterns and locations, requiring migration of labour or retraining.

In the European case the burning political and economic questions will be: who will determine the economic structure and political substance of the European community -- the bankers, major corporations and the speculators, or will it be possible to retain, although in possibly different form, some of the essential attributes and values of the welfare state? Will it be possible to speed up the economic integration of Europe's internal "South" through an accelerated development effort, without sacrificing Europe's traditional role in development support to the developing countries in general? A third question is: to what extent will the European community be able to withstand the natural tendency in such a transition temporarily to insulate itself from external competitive pressures, and to remain open to the rest of the world?

The answers to these questions will profoundly influence what happens in other parts of the world, and this will in turn exert its impact on Europe. The point is that, while Europe and any other integrated trading area is, of course, entitled to make its own rules and decisions with regard to its common future, it will have to take its decisions in the context of global economic and strategic interdependence. In that way Europe's social problem, and that of any other regional grouping, is inescapably linked to the world's social problem: international poverty.

The so-called Third Industrial Revolution has made it possible for those countries that could make use of these technologies to increase their productivity significantly, thereby further widening the gap between North and South. At the same time, the communications revolution especially has raised expectations in poor developing countries with access to industrial country television programmes, to the point at which the national economy in no way could hope ever to meet those expectations except at the cost of unacceptable inequalities. The contradiction many populous developing countries now have to contend with is that in order to become or remain competitive in today's world, they have to increase their productivity with sophisticated technology that is most often labour saving, while at the same time they have to contend domestically with their massive unemployment problem. They will need information, which today has become as much a capital asset as financial and physical capital. They will have to find ways to have access to that information without exposing themselves to the dangers of unrealistic expectations which might destroy the kind of social cohesion young nations need to nurture in their nation-building effort.

The poverty gap now has three dimensions: i) the gap between the haves and the have-nots; ii) between the knows and the know-nots; and iii) between those who have work and those who do not.

The changes in the political, strategic and economic spheres have not only affected the international sphere, they have also impacted heavily on political and economic structures within each country, on interpersonal relations, on lifestyles, on social cohesion and the loosening of the bond of primary social groups.

No country, no group of countries anywhere in the world, whatever its ideological orientation, has remained immune from the consequences of these changes and the fragility of the world economic system, its exchange rate fluctuations and the Third World debt problem.

No country, whether North or South, East or West, can achieve its social objectives, or for that matter its strategic and economic objectives on its own steam. Likewise, it has become abundantly clear that it is no longer possible to think of development purely as a national effort. It has turned out to be an effort that has to be conducted as part of a larger, global effort requiring the co-operation of North and South, in development on a global scale and co-operation to stabilize the international economic system and correct its malfunctioning.

There is, however, a third set of changes that impinge on the human situation. These have to do with the global changes in the earth's physical, chemical, and weather systems and the earth's biological diversity, resulting from human action. There is now a consensus among the majority of scientists in the world that the warming of the earth's temperature, primarily although not exclusively as a result of the burning of fossil fuels, is now inevitable. Its impact is already discernible in today's changing and often unpredictable weather patterns.

The question that has to be addressed is not how to prevent it -- for that option is no longer open -- but how to slow down and reduce the warming process to no more than three degrees so as to enable humankind to make the necessary adaptations. Without effective international and national actions we will have to take into account the likelihood of an increase in temperature of 6 degrees Celsius over the next 110 years. In that case it is not impossible that by the middle of the 21st century, i.e. during the lifetime of our grandchildren, the grainbaskets of the American Midwest and the Soviet Ukraine will have turned into scrub deserts. Grain will then have to grow in the much less fertile soils of Canada, while other parts of the world will be plagued by too much rain. Towards the end of the century, it is expected that a number of major coastal cities will be permanently inundated because of rising sea levels resulting from the melting of polar ice.

We will have to take into account that already now China, after the United States and the Soviet Union, is the third largest producer of CO_2. In the long term, China's continued industrialization and the industrialization of the Third World is bound to increase CO_2 emissions by a few factors. Even though industrial countries may embark on major efforts to increase energy efficiency, these efforts will not compensate for the greater fossil fuel utilisation in an industrialising Third World. In addition, we all know how poverty is one of the greatest polluters in the world. It drives millions of people to cut the forests to meet their own energy needs.

The point is that the energy problem, including the technology of its generation and the technology of energy use, but also the lifestyles, expectations and values that lie behind each technological choice, has become a global problem. At the present state of technology there is no hope that at the expected higher levels of energy use the world over, the warming process can be halted or slowed down enough for humankind to make the necessary adaptations. The hope that nuclear energy could provide an alternative has, after Chernobyl and other accidents, lost much of its attraction, especially now that apparently unexpected problems of finding politically and economically acceptable locations for nuclear waste disposal have emerged. A report prepared for publication in the December 1989 issue of the American Journal *Energy Policy* on the implications of the so-called nuclear option in the effort to reduce CO_2 emissions concludes that the transition to nuclear energy will require an investment level that is impossible to achieve either nationally or internationally. Dr. Keepin, one of its authors, recently stated to the press that if the nuclear industry were to commission a new nuclear plant every two days, the CO_2 level in the atmosphere could be kept more or less constant. This would mean a 20- to 30-time enlargement of total nuclear capacity in the whole world, which would cost $587 billion per year.

This means that only nuclear fusion and the soft technologies would most likely be able to mobilize enough financial and political support to provide a feasible alternative. This implies that the research and development for these technologies on the scale they deserve to be undertaken should not be left to blind market forces which determine the prevailing cost of oil. Rather, the costs should be compared with the likely cost of moving major cities from their present locations to higher ground. These calculations should also take account of the unpredictable food supply problems which will result from the general changes in weather patterns and increase in temperature.

It is obvious that the problems of energy needs of the industrial countries and those of developing countries are not separate problems. There are of course quite a number of other environmental problems which require a broad international effort. The hole in the ozone layer is one of them, acid rain and the storage and disposal of toxic waste another. Certainly there is a need for an international energy regime that could regulate the transition of industrial countries and an industrialising Third World towards an ecologically less destructive pattern, and organize the R&D necessary to that end.

The other problem under this rubric is that of international poverty and population growth. It is at the moment quite fashionable to speak about compassion fatigue or aid fatigue when discussing diminished political and financial support for development assistance. The problem, however, is an entirely different one.

Except perhaps for the four Little Dragons -- South Korea, Taiwan, Hong Kong and Singapore -- which have managed to overcome this gap, global economic and social dualism still exists. This gap is now in the process of widening as a result of the complex of problems which manifests itself in the debt burden of the Third World, the net resource flow to the industrial countries, and the stagnation and even regression of the economy, resulting in the destruction of all the progress achieved in the area of health delivery, education and other social services. It is bound eventually to lead to major political convulsions, and in those cases where re-democratisation has occurred, its reversal. According to Saburo Okita, 1980 saw a net inflow of $39.3 billion to the developing countries, while 1985 witnessed a net outflow of $31.0 billion; an enormous shift of $70 billion.

Apart from the debt problem the rapid development of labour-saving technologies has further widened the gap, through rapid increases in productivity of the industrial countries of the North. In the increasingly competitive world of today, this development confronts the latecomers in industrialisation with the dilemma of how to become, or remain, internationally competitive, and still be able to deal effectively with the massive unemployment problem that is beginning to strain the resilience of the political systems in their own countries, whatever their ideological orientation. It should be possible, and necessary, to think of combining high-tech and low-tech, labour-saving and labour-intensive components in the production process. However, not much work has been done in this direction.

The crux of the matter is that if nothing is done, the enormous disparities in standard of living and in birthrates between the industrial and and developing countries will become so great that the pressure to migrate to the industrial countries will turn into an irresistible floodtide. That pressure is now greatest on the border between Mexico and the United States and between the northern and southern riparian states around the Mediterranean Sea. It is quite likely that pressure will grow and will manifest itself in other places on the globe as well. Even in the Third World itself, especially in Africa where because of war, drought, land hunger or land exhaustion, territorial borders are transgressed by huge numbers of people. Similar occurrences take place in South Asia, and even within such large populous countries as Indonesia and China. We can no longer escape the implications of the fact that together we keep on losing arable land every day while populations keep on increasing.

We will all have to choose from three alternatives if we want to prevent such massive and global redistribution of population:

1. To deal with the problem of underdevelopment and international poverty on a scale that does justice to the magnitude of the problem;

2. Accept the free movement of people in the way the free movement of capital across the globe has now by and large been accepted; and

3. A combination of the first two options: a much higher level of international development co-operation, a much higher level of immigration from the Third World, coupled with policies that aim at increasing the absorptive capacity and the necessary tolerance in the receiving country. It means essentially to accept the inevitability of multi-ethnic states in the industrial world.

There is another dimension that irrevocably ties the South and the North together. Despite the unexpectedly favourable rate of economic growth of the OECD countries, it is clear that when the developing countries continue to stagnate, a combination of overproduction in the North and under-consumption in the South may well occur. It is therefore in the interest of the industrial countries to reach a settlement of the Third World debt problem in a manner that will make resumption of economic growth possible, and a much increased resource flow to the Third World.

It will be important to realize that in the long run, demographically speaking, the markets of the industrial countries are bound to shrink, both relatively and in absolute terms, while an accelerated development will turn the growing population in the Third World into potentially new markets.

These two gargantuan problems will make it unlikely that there ever will be a future for the industrial world that is separate from that of the poor countries. That in turn means that to continue thinking of a world with a two-track economy as a permanent feature is not a sustainable proposition. It should now also have become obvious that the two-track concept is nothing else but a reformulation of the familiar "structural dualism" engendered by the impact of the industrial revolution in the metropolitan powers on their colonies, to suit the present much more dynamic processes of technological and social change. Economic, as well as demographic and ecological interdependence will force all of us to find solutions to our own problems in a global context, and within the limits of the earth's carrying capacity. It is in the interest of each and all of us that we articulate our own vision of the future within the context of a simultaneously developed global vision that encompasses human survival, human solidarity and the habitability of our planet. We will have to do so in a world of very rapid and profound social change, that seems to surpass the adjustment capacity of our social and political institutions, with an international system in which no country, no single group of countries, in fact even no governmental organization of any kind is in control, and in which new players at the transnational as well as the sub-national level have made their presence felt in extremely powerful ways. It is no exaggeration to state that the "governability" of the global system as well as of many states is at risk. A great deal will depend on whether it is possible to make the transnational sphere socially accountable. Much of our thought and reaction patterns seem to be hopelessly obsolete. At the same time global economic growth is an essential condition for humankind to be able to make the major adjustments that sustainable development demands, while human solidarity is not only an ethical category but also a condition for common survival.

The problem of development assistance is therefore not a question of charity, but is everybody's problem. It concerns the maintenance of the ecological life support systems for the human species and the governability of the human community. It is therefore no more a utopian vision, but a practical necessity. It is a problem of humankind's general preparation for life in the 21st century -- and as we know, or at least suspect, how unprepared we all are for that future.

What are the rough contours for such a world development strategy? In which general directions should we look? It is impossible to do more at this stage than sketch a very provisional road map for further discussion and reflection.

1.   It is already quite likely that the methods of the decades of the 1960s and 1970s, of global negotiations, may not work for the moment. The prevailing climate in international politics which insists that everything should be left to free, or should one say "blind" market forces, is not conducive to their resumption. It should be said that,

given the complexity of interlocking interdependencies and with considerable scientific uncertainties still remaining on a number of concrete issues, it might be more suitable to improvise within the limits of fairly generally accepted goals, and to look for ways to initiate new thoughts and processes among smaller, strategically selected groups of North and South, in search of new approaches. Even the following very rough suggestions will require further elaboration and precision. Most likely we will develop them as we go along.

We will then have to look in the direction of a much larger transfer of productive resources to the developing countries. The Brandt Commission's now almost-forgotten report mentions a target of 3 per cent of GNP in the form of ODA and private funds, much higher than the 0.7 per cent established by the OECD. It still looks to me the most telling figure. As against this, developing countries will have to commit themselves to bring about the necessary adjustments for the absorption of such a large scale transfer.

2. This process should be preceded by collective steps to stabilise the international economy at a level and in a way that takes full account of the interests of the developing countries.

3. Unrestricted increase of international trade. Protection would be justified only for the most underdeveloped countries. A restructuring of the international division of labour would leave low value-added manufacturing primarily to the Third World, while the industrial countries would concentrate primarily, though not exclusively, on high value-added production. It would be ideal -- and rather utopian -- if the transition of the industrial countries to a post-industrial information society could take place in lockstep with the pace of industrialisation of the Third World. Such a linkage would lead to a major increase in international trade, without the spectre of a regularly recurring debt problem. In any case, all markets should remain open for the exports of developing countries.

4. The Third World debt should not be an obstacle for further economic growth, unless the economic plans are too obviously irrational and unproductive.

5. An international consensus needs to be developed with regard to an international energy regime, which should include the R&D for energy generation and energy efficiency. Such a consensus should also encompass understandings regarding the effective dissemination of these technologies and policies across the globe, as well as arrangements with regard to the protection of the tropical rain forests and to an international system of compensation, and incentives and disincentives for those countries in which these forests are located.

6. There is going to be a need to enhance the scientific and technological capabilities of the Third World. Without a massive and global spread of scientific and technological knowledge and skills, the dependency of the Third World and the gap between North and South are bound to increase, as well as their incapacity to develop their own solutions to their own problems. It would be a major error if fear of competition were to constitute an obstacle to such an international programme. In the long run the consequences are likely to be more costly than co-operating with the industrialisation of the Third World, including the industrialisation of the countryside, something that is still in its infancy.

    An international programme for the dissemination of scientific and technological capabilities in the Third World should also include the enhancement of capabilities in the area of environmental management. Better methodologies will have to be developed towards a more effective integration of development planning and natural resource planning, as well as towards a capacity to participate effectively in global environment regimes that should ensure the sustained habitability of this planet.

7. It will be of the greatest importance that the principles of "fair trade" and "reciprocity" which Europe needs in order to equalize the conditions of competition, not be applied to developing countries in the early phase of their industrialisation.

8. It will be necessary to review the way development assistance is channelled. Channelling through central governments and national bureaucracies has often encouraged concentration of power and even the growth of authoritarianism. It has also led to the bureaucratisation of the countryside, the destruction of traditional village autonomy, local initiative and local accountability. It is very important as much as possible to encourage wherever possible the growth of pluralism and local accountability. NGOs and university centres as well as the media have a major role to play here.

It goes without saying that an effort of this magnitude will be impossible as long as defence expenditures, including R&D in the industrial as well as in the developing countries remain at the present level.

In addition, an approach that so obtrusively deals with matters that conventionally fall within the domestic jurisdiction of sovereign nations, will require much more than critical discussions. It requires profound changes in conceptions of the state and of the international order. It will for instance be necessary, in a kind of second Copernican revolution, to look at the international order not in terms of arbitrary configuration of sovereign states, but as a system in which nation states revolve around a set of shared core values that have to do with human survival and human solidarity. It will be necessary to blunt the sharper edges of the traditional concept of national sovereignty -- something which Europeans now have to get themselves accustomed to -- as well as the expansion of man's moral horizon and of personal loyalties and commitments. These will have to transcend the tribe, the ethnic community, the nation and should encompass the whole of humanity including future generations.

The identification of such a set of irreducible shared values, which aside from those of human survival and human solidarity, should encompass the values of security, justice, liberty, tolerance and human rights, both the individual as well as the more collective social and economic rights, need not in any way lead to the imposition of a single value system on the whole of humankind. Humankind's racial, cultural and religious diversity, like the biological diversity on this planet, ensures rather than reduces the stability of the human race. In this regard, cultural pluralism is based on the fact that these shared core values are imbedded in different value configurations that are specific for each culture and each nation. Judging from the strength of the political, economic and cultural pluralism of which we see so many manifestations at present, this cultural pluralism will most likely continue to exist, despite the powerful homogenising tendencies that can also be observed. The three interdependencies referred to in this paper force us, within the context of a globalised world economy and the likely formation of a number of large trading blocs, to search in each culture for new, culturally specific but globally compatible balances between economic growth, technology, employment, social justice and culture, in an international system that should make a sustainable world development possible.

If this is the direction we should take towards a world development strategy based on growth, sustainability and solidarity, then we should also realize that we are still a long distance away from the point where we could actually begin to move. This was also demonstrated by our discussions in the first two days of this conference. There was little to connect the general optimism that pervaded the discussion of the global economy on the first day with the pessimism of the subsequent discussions about the slow track and about Africa. In the same vein but of much larger significance has been the statement emanating from the most recent meeting of the G-7 to the effect that nothing is wrong with the world economy. This view bespeaks an insensitivity with the economic regression and human suffering that especially the poor and the vulnerable in many countries in the Third World are now experiencing. It suggests, I am quite sure, unconsciously, the beginnings of a spirit of exclusivism, which if unimpeded, may well lead to situations compared to which the cruelty of South African apartheid may simply be child's play. We should stop thinking of the world economy as separate from the rest of the world in which the majority of humankind lives. We should stop thinking that the vagaries of the world economy can be stabilised by treating the problems of the Third World as a residual problem. We cannot afford to keep on trying to fine tune a complex piece of machinery without realising that the machine itself is malfunctioning in a much more fundamental way.

First, the international community is in no mood to take such ideas seriously. The likelihood of a debt settlement policy, rather than debt management, would restore the possibilities for growth in the debtor countries, seem to be quite remote.

By the same token, the likelihood of effective policies that would lead to the resumption of resource transfer to the Third World, will remain very small for a long period. There seems to be no particular desire to stabilize the international exchange markets, nor is there any consensus on what needs to be done, how it should be done, and how quickly.

In fact, there is no analysis of what is happening in the world today, and what is happening to it, that can command international consensus -- the essential condition for international action. There are simply too many contradictory explanations. We are, as Edgard Pisani has said, in a "crisis of intelligibility". Economic theory as well as political philosophy have failed us dismally here. Nevertheless, Europe is engaged in a process of major social transformation, although it is at the same time likely that Europe will remain preoccupied with its own restructuring for a long time before it will be ready to address some of the larger global issues.

We should also be aware of the degree of scientific uncertainty regarding a number of problems at this confluence of different interdependent systems. This of course facilitates justification for delaying decisions. Still, we will have to learn to make decisions in conditions of scientific uncertainty and social instability, most likely by making decisions sequentially, so as not to permanently foreclose any option that might be important later, by committing oneself irrevocably to a single course of action. Apart from stimulating the kind of research that would reduce as much as possible, and as soon as possible, the areas of scientific uncertainty, an effort should be made to develop what could be called a new economics that could relate economic theory to the micro and macro environmental system as well as to new concepts of security, if we want a firmer basis for international consensus and international action. A great deal of new integrative thinking is needed now that the great ideologies that have given shape and direction to the course of history in the first part of this century have exhausted themselves. In more practical terms, more effective tools will also have to be developed that integrate development planning to natural resource planning and environmental management.

Equally important is the need to build into the political process a greater capability and willingness to deal with long-term problems. This will not only involve a greater role for governmental and freestanding research institutions, but also for NGOs, pressure groups, popular movements, linked institutionally through various networks, concerned with such issues. Similarly also for the universities in general. As most of these long-term problems are multi-disciplinary in character, at the interface between different scientific fields, it may be even necessary not only for the universities to make relevant adjustments, but also to review the manner in which governments are conventionally organized in various ministries, with the occasional inter-ministerial task force.

We will, more generally, have to learn to face the inherent complexity of natural and social systems, to accept the fact that we are part of the globe's interaction between natural social systems, and that we are inside it, not outside, and that we cannot control the systems in which we are imbedded. At most we can learn how to influence the probabilities of outcomes within the system. Planning then ceases to be final, but becomes a part of the social learning process, in which both planner, and those affected by plans, learn from each other, and continuously make the necessary adjustments.

It will also be necessary to draw lessons from the earlier grassroots movements: the liberation movements, the labour movement, the women's movement, the peace and environmental movements. These movements did succeed in changing the political agenda of their respective nations. Governments generally reluctantly have followed.

Likewise, it will be important to link national constituencies together into an international network, and begin to persuade the general public and their governments to take international action. Coupled with this should be an effort for government and freestanding research institutions to review the development process and the theories underlying it, in light of the trends towards the globalization of the international economy on the one hand and the political and economic nationalisms in reaction to it as well as the processes of regionalism on the other. For even if there were no political obstacles, the policy instruments that could turn the development effort into a more ecologically sustainable development are still in a rather rudimentary stage. We are still some distance away from the integration of development planning and natural resource planning, from determining what the various points of irreversibility are in processes in ecological damage, from determining the scale of the various international efforts that have to be taken in the field of energy, for instance, pollution abatement, nuclear and other toxic wastes, and from turning the economy to less CO_2-producing energy sources.

In conclusion, it is obvious that the 1990s will most likely not be the decade that will see the enunciation of a clear and coherent world strategy of the kind that our times really demand of us. Rather, we will have to use that decade to prepare ourselves, the general public and our governments, for the evolution of our respective political cultures that is needed.

We should not underestimate the impact of rapid social change on the life and culture of people and their response to these changes. When the rapidity of social change begins to exceed the institutional and individual capacity to adjust to or absorb change, anomic reactions tend to set in, in developing and industrial countries alike. Everywhere now we begin to see such reactions developing. Especially in the face of these powerful homogenizing forces, the concept of a "world without borders" is often seen as a threat to one's own personal and collective identity and interests. Hence the rise of economic nationalism and the retraction of one's sense of self to the primordial solidarity of ethnicity, race, language and religion. The resurgence of religiosity and the deep passions it arouses, almost all over the world, is a phenomenon affecting all religions, in both positive and negative ways. At this juncture in history, not one of us can escape this powerful reality, which is further fuelled by a sense of the spiritual emptiness of much of modern life and by a sense of the essential amorality of the international order as experienced and perceived by many. To this should be added the profound alienation of the young everywhere, irrespective of the ideological orientation of the prevailing political system, as well as the easy availability of arms. No one involved in the efforts and problems of development can afford to ignore them as they profoundly affect the social and political behaviour of individuals, groups and nations.

Nevertheless, there are some very early and tentative signs of hope. At the initiative of Gro Brundtland, the Norwegian Prime Minister and former chairman of the Independent Commission on Environment and Development, a summit meeting of heads of state or government of middle powers is being planned for 11th March 1989 in the Hague that will attempt to set the global agenda on environmental problems. At the informal interministerial meeting of UNEP in Nairobi in January 1989, members of the Soviet delegation, orally and very tentatively, broached the idea of expanding the mandate of the UN Security Council to include environmental crises. If considered too bold, the Security Council could establish a subcommittee from among its members to do so. The suggestion was also made that the Trusteeship Council's mandate be changed to enable it to manage the Global Commons. At that same meeting, other countries suggested for instance that on certain environmental questions, majority votes in the United Nations General Assembly should be binding.

These are timid signals indeed. Nevertheless, they are hopeful signs, even though it is also obvious that no adequate responses can be expected in the coming decade. It is, however, at the same time equally important to realize that at this very moment three major experimentations are going on, the outcome of each of which will greatly affect all of us. These are: i) the experiment in nuclear disarmament and general détente -- it may become an experiment in living with peace, rather than with the constant threat of war; ii) *perestroika* and *glasnost*; and iii) the European Common Market.

All three experiments still face many difficulties and a great many uncertainties and doubts remain. Still the vision and the courage to embark upon them were somehow generated. It is in a sense a manifestation of humankind's continued creative ability. It also encourages us to hope that in the end we will be able to respond in time to the challenges of our common future.

TOWARDS A WORLD DEVELOPMENT STRATEGY

by

Thorvald STOLTENBERG

The OECD Development Centre has described itself as a bridge over one of the more serious divides in the world; the one between the OECD countries and the developing countries. The Centre should be complimented for using the occasion of its 25th anniversary to concentrate on instruments and modalities for further bridge building.

Devising world policy options for sustainable growth in the coming decade and beyond is as difficult as it is urgent. The dangers of great poverty and environmental degradation, coupled with the proliferation of nuclear weapons are by now obvious to all of us.

An important contribution to a common vision of the future is the concept of sustainable development introduced in the report of the World Commission on Environment and Development. It implies that basic needs for food, clothing, shelter and jobs must be met in such a way that it does not compromise the ability of future generations to meet their own needs. A number of critical objectives are implied such as: economic growth; changing the quality of growth; meeting essential needs for jobs, food, energy, water and sanitation; ensuring a sustainable level of population; conserving and enhancing the resource base; adapting technologies to environmental and developmental needs; managing environmental risks and uncertainties; and closer international co-ordination of economic, developmental and environmental decision making.

The achievement of these ambitious objectives will depend on the formulation, implementation and co-ordination of appropriate national and international policies. Global solidarity is essential. Not only the kind of solidarity which is based on charity, but also solidarity in its original sense; a realization of commonality of interest, leading to the establishment of more effective political alliances and working towards shared goals.

233

THE INHERITANCE

In the 1980s economic and social problems related to population, poverty, unemployment, uneven income distribution, environmental degradation and overexploitation of natural resources were aggravated and became more interlinked and globalised. New critical issues emerged, such as the debt problem. The scientific and technological revolution combined with the increasing globalization of markets and enterprises created both opportunities and problems.

For the OECD countries, the long period of steady growth and financial stability from the end of the Second World War came to an end in the early 1970s. For the industrialised countries as a whole, OECD now forecasts economic growth of 2.5 to 3 per cent for 1989 and 1990. Growth prospects and possibilities for the 1990s will depend on the kind of policies implemented nationally and internationally. It is especially important that the problems of unemployment can be effectively dealt with.

The 1980s will be remembered as a decade of crisis and depression for many developing countries. Decreases in per capita income and employment losses in a number of developing countries were more widespread and lasting than those of Europe and the United States during the Great Depression of the 1930s. The lack of economic growth inflicted severe hardships on people and had a negative effect on the resumption of the growth process. Hard-core poverty increased.

The picture is, however, diverse. Some developing countries, especially in East and South-East Asia, have weathered the difficult 1980s remarkably well. China, India and some newly industrializing Asian countries have done better than they had during previous decades. The stronger growth of these countries increases their responsibility and influence in world affairs. Their outlook apparently is global rather than regional.

The debt crisis was caused partly by domestic factors in the debtor countries, and partly by international developments and policy changes in industrialized countries. Total external debt is estimated by the IMF to have doubled from $650 billion in 1980 to $1 280 billion in 1989. The debt overhang has been accompanied by a sharp fall in overall net financing flows to developing countries. For the group of middle income countries there has been increasing net outflow in recent years. Official Development Assistance (ODA) has stagnated during the 1980s. Private flows have been substantially reduced.

Another feature of the 1980s -- largely caused by economic developments in developed countries -- has been the fall in primary commodity prices in real terms to the lowest level since the 1930s. This contributed significantly to the severity of the debt crisis. For African countries 60 per cent of their export revenue is derived from exports of primary commodities. For Latin American countries the figure is 50 per cent. The commodity dependence also means that an adjustment strategy focusing first and foremost on increasing primary commodity exports is unlikely to solve the debt crisis and create the required sustainable growth.

Protectionist pressures in particular in the OECD countries have increased. This has been caused mainly by the economic downturn and increase in unemployment in the first half of the 1980s. A successful outcome of the Uruguay Round is therefore essential.

The rapid growth of world population has continued although rates of growth have slowed down in many countries, including China and India. At the end of the 1990s, more than 6 billion people will be living on our planet and by 2010 another billion will have been added. The distribution of this population increase is uneven. On one extreme, the population of industrial countries will increase very little beyond its present total of one billion. In some of these countries the population will even decrease. On the other extreme, in many developing countries the populations are increasing more rapidly than ever before and are likely to double to 2 billion, or almost 30 per cent of the world population by the year 2010. The rapid increase of these populations hampers economic development, and lack of development is one of the factors preventing birth rates from declining.

Poverty is in itself an increasing burden on the environment and is closely linked with desertification, soil erosion, deforestation and loss of species. Global environmental problems such as climatic change will have increasingly serious effects on the development potential of large parts of the Third World and present major challenges to international co-operation and to the necessary partnership between governments, multilateral institutions, industry and other economic decision-makers.

CHANGING PERCEPTIONS

Past developments and major challenges for the 1990s have reminded us of the growing global interdependence. If we are to avoid crisis management as a standing item on the agenda for the 1990s, perceptions and priorities will have to change. Otherwise we shall be exposed to frequent shocks, such as, for example, the worldwide stock market crisis in the autumn of 1987 which gave us a strong reminder of the globalization of financial markets.

There is an increasing realization of the economic cost of armaments and military conflicts. In Southern Africa, for example, SADCC nations have calculated that their annual economic losses because of war and destabilization, largely caused by the Apartheid regime in South Africa, are twice the amount of ODA flowing to the region every year.

A positive development over the last few years has been the improvement in East-West relations. It is uncertain how this will affect North-South relations. One possibility is that the resources and surpluses of the West would be used to further improve East-West relations and that fewer resources will flow South. Another and more dynamic scenario would imply that increased East-West exchanges and trade would stimulate economic development globally and generate more re-source transfers to and trade with the South.

The UN system has passed through a difficult period. There now seems to be greater understanding of the fact that the functioning and standing of the UN is closely linked to the political relationship between the superpowers as was the case already back in 1945. Recent progress has positively affected the standing of the UN system and helped to pave the way for its successful peacemaking efforts. When the system is fully used and supported by the member countries, it can function efficiently and constructively.

Last but not least, among policy initiatives that may have wider impacts on discussions and actions in the 1990s is the South Commission. It is the first time that the countries of the South have established their own high-level development commission exploring avenues for the solution of global development problems as well as for closer South-South co-operation.

TASKS, POLICIES AND INSTITUTIONS FOR THE 1990s

In order to manage global interdependence in a more sustainable and equit-able way, we must agree on ways to improve multilateral discipline and utilize in-ternational organizations more effectively. The competent forums must to a greater extent deal with the international effects of national policy making, acting as effec-tive instruments for analysis, discussion and negotiation and giving support, en-couragement and guidance to the policy dialogue with member governments. Increased international co-ordination and co-operation of national policies would constitute a practical step towards the management of global interdependence.

The precondition: an early solution of the debt crisis

The debt overhang of the heavily indebted developing countries presents an untenable situation for the countries concerned and a decisive constraint on growth and stability in the world economy in general. It also represents a threat to demo-cratic development. The debt-distressed countries have lost a decade or more of development already, and the effects of falling investment levels will be felt for a long time. The political, economic and social strain on the populations of the debt-ridden countries clearly necessitates urgent action. An early solution to the debt crisis is therefore a precondition for any development strategy for the 1990s.

The first phase of the debt strategy from 1982 onwards concentrated on debt re-schedulings and stabilisation programmes with domestic austerity policies and import contraction as central elements. In 1985 the debt strategy entered the second phase with the Baker initiative, focusing on new lending in support of growth-oriented structural adjustment policies. These developments, and particularly the Baker plan, have provided the basis to build on.

I believe we now have a golden opportunity to achieve a solution as we are moving to a third phase of the debt strategy. The content of the policies designed over the next few months will therefore be crucial.

First, favourable global economic environment and trade policies are important for a successful resolution of the debt crisis. No debt strategy can succeed unless export markets grow strongly and if the debtor countries are given the necessary access to the markets of the industrialised countries. This is particularly important now as policies in the developing countries are increasingly set in the direction of more outward-looking, open economies. For the industrial countries to restrict access would not only undermine the ability of debtor countries to grow out of their debt problems, it could well turn back the policies of many countries to inward-looking, isolationist approaches to development. This would be to the disadvantage of the whole world economy, not least the OECD countries themselves.

In addition to the necessity of market access, economic growth in the OECD area is of the utmost importance, not least for commodity exporters with no alternative source of export earnings. For instance, it was estimated by the OECD in 1986 that 1 percentage point higher OECD real growth increases export values of debtor countries by an annual average of between 2 to 3 per cent, leading to a strong improvement in the key debt-servicing ratios of developing countries. This would in turn stimulate their imports and thereby also exports and growth in OECD countries. Another simulation shows that a decline of 1 per cent in the level of dollar interest rates would, by 1990, make as large a contribution to managing the debt problems as $24 billion worth of new lending. This corresponds two-third of total ODA for DAC-countries in 1987.

Secondly, one of the most worrying long-term effects of the debt crisis is the falling investment levels aggravated by the increasing net outflow of financial resources from many debtor countries. Restoration of productive investment is, therefore, a crucial element in a new debt strategy. In most developing countries the domestic savings rate will not be sufficiently high to cover their investment needs for the foreseeable future. Consequently, they will continue to depend on financial transfers from the industrialised countries, especially in the form of direct investment, official lending and concession assistance. The goal must be the restoration of credit-worthiness and normal debtor/creditor relations. In this connection it is important to underline that for many of the debt-distressed countries, and particularly the poorer ones, a return to commercial lending is very far off indeed.

Thirdly, a further element in a new strategy is the continuation of adjustment policies. However, such policies must be economically, socially and politically sustainable. This means that the programmes must be carefully designed and based on the characteristics and capacities of the individual countries, with special attention being paid to the needs of the poorest part of the population. The programmes and the financing packages must also be set in a medium-term perspective in order to achieve the structural improvements needed. Structural change takes time.

Fourthly, it is increasingly being recognised that the debt crisis will not be solved unless debt reduction and debt service relief play a larger role. Thus, it is possible that the policies I have outlined above will only be effective if the debt overhang is reduced to manageable proportions. This is certainly true for the poorer countries, particularly in Africa, for which a start has already been made in the Paris Club. For the middle-income countries various market-based debt reduction schemes are increasingly being advanced. It seems, however, that such existing schemes will only be of limited importance in relation to the total debt overhang.

I believe therefore that the time has now come to develop a comprehensive set of debt reduction measures for both the poorest and the middle income countries.

For the poorest debt-distressed countries the Paris Club relief measures should be developed further as far as bilateral official debt is concerned. Realistically speaking, it is doubtful if much of this debt will ever be repaid. It is, therefore, important to tackle the burden-sharing problem between creditors which should pave the way for large debt reductions or re-schedulings on IDA-terms for countries undertaking recovery programmes.

The amount of private debt varies for these countries and it would seem that in certain cases debt buy-back schemes may be implemented by donors. Especially African debt is being sold at considerable discounts on the secondary market, thus making it possible to retire large sums of debt at relatively small costs.

A considerable part of the poorest countries' debt is owed to multilateral institutions. Servicing of non-concessional loans (i.e. IBRD and AFDB) has become a heavy burden for countries which are now IDA-only recipients. A scheme based on a Nordic proposal to soften interest payments on such loans has been taken up by the World Bank. We would expect this and similar schemes to be extended in the future.

The debt of the middle income countries is largely owed to private creditors. These creditors must unquestionably bear the main burden for an extension of the debt reduction schemes already in practice. These schemes could play a more important role in reducing the debt overhang, and creditor governments should actively encourage such measures through for instance national regulatory policies providing new incentives for debtor/creditor agreements.

Many proposals have been advanced for new debt facilities or institutions sponsored by creditor governments which would take over the claims now held by banks. The role of the existing financial institutions in such schemes and thereby the role of the international community at large, is one of the questions which need further deliberation. We should bear in mind, however, that the purpose of such arrangements should be to oil the machinery -- to enable the debtor and the creditor to reduce the debt overhang -- rather than to finance the losses. Seen in this perspective, the cost involved would probably be minuscule compared to the potential global benefits of bringing the debt threat within manageable proportions.

Improvement of global macroeconomic co-operation and co-ordination

Attitudes towards and practices of international co-operation and co-ordination of general economic policies have improved in the second half of the 1980s. We should utilise this momentum for further improvements within the established multilateral organisations in the 1990s.

We all recognise, at least in principle, the increasing global economic and political interlinkages and interdependence. It is therefore in each nation's interest to take increasingly into account the international and global consequences of their policies. The results will be better for all if policies could be co-ordinated to a larger extent.

A substantial reduction of mass unemployment in Europe should now become an urgent priority of economic policies. The momentum of the creation of a single market has revived investments and growth prospects for Europe. A proper combination of macroeconomic, structural and liberal trade policies should be established along the lines of the growth strategy suggested by the EEC Commission. As stated there, the participation of the social partners in the elaboration and implementation of this strategy seems important

It is generally recognised that the new US administration has to face up to the challenge of the "twin deficits". Lower Federal deficits and increased private saving in the United States will not only reduce the US external deficits and thus global payments imbalances. It may also make the surpluses of Japan, Germany and NIEs increasingly available to developing countries. From a world development point of view, financial surpluses in OECD countries should increasingly be used for investments in developing countries.

The OECD should play an important role in several ways. First, its analytical apparatus could to a larger extent be utilised to study global economic interlinkages in order to work out co-ordinated policy strategies. Secondly, the present system of country examinations could be extended to put increased emphasis on the international and developmental consequences of each member country's policies. Today, for example, economic policies, aid policies, agricultural policies, environmental policies are examined regularly but in different and quite separate committees. One should adjust and co-ordinate these sectoral examinations so that an overview of the international consequences could be monitored and improved in a more systematic fashion. This should be further explored in the 1990s.

On the global level the OECD could contribute substantively to the building of common perceptions necessary for negotiations in the IMF, the World Bank and the UN as a whole. The IMF regularly examines member countries' economic policies.

Building on an analytical base created by these organisations, a global system of monitoring and examination of economic policies and their international impact could be established, in order to achieve more concrete and coherent solutions to the economic, developmental and environmental problems of the 1990s. A special responsibility rests of course with the largest industrialised nations, but this system should also ensure real participation in the global co-ordination process by the developing countries.

The international trading system

It is important that the developing countries are given the opportunity to participate in the international division of labour through a liberal and global trading system. In addition, special and preferential treatment for developing countries will still be necessary, in particular for the least developed. Such a trade policy, together with mechanisms to solve the debt crisis and the institutional improvements in macroeconomic co-ordination mentioned above, represent the decisive elements if future development strategies are to succeed.

There has been a disturbing growth in protectionism in the 1980s which to a large extent is due to inadequate structural adjustment policies in the industrialised countries. The effects have been felt globally, and not least in the developing countries. For instance, a recent study by the IMF and the World Bank indicated that protectionism in the industrialised countries costs the Third World twice as much in lost export earnings as they receive in development assistance.

It is therefore clear that the Uruguay Round of multilateral trade negotiations is of critical importance if we are to further develop an open and equitable trading system. The outcome of these negotiations is also likely to affect the future development between the regional integration processes which can be observed, and the global trading relations. If it fails, the possibility that the weakest of the developing countries could be de-linked from the world economy and the emergence of regional and protectionist trade fortresses could become a reality.

International commodity co-operation

Although the relative importance of commodities is decreasing for most developing countries, it still is crucial to the economies of many of these countries and particularly to the poorest.

Producer-consumer co-operation to stabilize prices through market interventions will still be relevant for some commodities. Generally speaking, however, the conclusion one can draw from the experiences over the last 10 to 15 years is first and foremost that our goals for commodity co-operation have to be shifted from price stabilization to other measures. The Final Act from UNCTAD VII indicates the way to follow: increased activities in diversification and long-term development measures for the various commodities on the one hand, and increased market transparency and discussion of common problems among producers and consumers on the other. Oil with its current market uncertainties is in our view an example of a commodity for which an organised producer consumer co-operation of the type mentioned would be desirable.

Sustainable development

Sustainable development has become generally recognized as a goal and a guiding principle for the international community. The Toronto Economic Summit (June 1988) stated that it is imperative to provide for sustainable and environmentally sound development.

Thus environment and development have come to the top of the international political agenda and will increasingly have to be pursued at all levels. The policy measures to promote such a development must be placed in a broad North-South context and elaborated against the background of the prevailing imbalance of international economic relations and the lack of equilibrium in the global production, consumption and emission patterns.

As regards the integration of environment and development at the national and local level, additional resources from the international community must be mobilised, in particular for the poor countries which are besieged by other pressing domestic problems as well.

The larger ecological issues -- the ozone layer, global heating and the sustainable utilization of the tropical forest -- are tasks facing mankind as a whole. The World Commission of Environment and Development presented some innovative ideas on how to mobilize additional financial resources, e.g. revenues from the use of international common and natural resources. These and other approaches to this end are needed and warrant further consideration.

A system of development contracts

The severe problems facing the poorer developing countries represent an important challenge to the international community. This is amply illustrated in the UN analysis of the world economy to the year 2000 which predicts a particularly strong deterioration in the relative incomes of the least developed countries.

The 1980s has been the decade of structural adjustment programmes in developing countries. These programmes were initially short-term in nature focusing on stabilisation measures to improve the balance of payments situation. The burden of responsibility for programme success was put on the adjusting governments, even though the likelihood of adjustment success in many cases depends fundamentally on the trade and economic policies adopted in other countries. For this reason adjustment programmes should be replaced with more comprehensive "Development Contracts", which could be defined as a comprehensive instrument for the financing of a medium-and long-term development plan prepared by the developing country itself (with outside technical support where appropriate).

Experience from adjustment programmes has taught both developing and industrialized countries that all parties involved must be committed to the "Development Contract" once it has been agreed upon. The recipient government as well as the other contracting parties must agree to follow the policy framework laid down as long as the assumptions about external economic forces do not necessitate revisions.

A feature of "Development Contracts" that distinguishes them from adjustment programmes is the commitments to be made by the participating donors and banks. This can be arranged in a number of ways. Participants would very often have to include the major industrialised countries, major developing countries, the Bretton Woods institutions and the appropriate international organizations within and outside the UN (UNCTAD, GATT, UNEP, UNIDO etc.).

One possibility is to prepare a financing package composed of IMF loans for balance of payment support, Development Bank loans for sectoral adjustments support, bilateral grant elements for basic needs components, co-financing from a bilateral donor and export credits for the imports of special foreign products and capital goods and services required. Some of the financing should be quick disbursing, whereas other should require conventional project cycle reviews. Burden-sharing should be arranged on the basis of explicit assumptions about the roles to be played by the participating parties.

The institutional machinery could be an improvement of the present consultative groups and round tables. Arrangements would have to ensure a balanced and fair partnership and a central role for the developing countries in question. The overall co-ordination of the political and economic aspects of the system of the "Development Contract" should be carried out within the UN system.

Such a comprehensive system must be based on larger and more predictable flows of concession resources. In this connection the attainment of the 0.7 per cent ODA-target for the donor community as a whole, is not only necessary but a minimum target for the 1990s.

A comprehensive peace and development plan for sub-Saharan Africa

In Sub-Saharan Africa a complex web of problems seem to be accumulating. Despite a few bright spots, economic development falls further and further behind. A fragile environment is in danger of being destroyed. The traditional systems for social security break up and are not replaced with new ones. The interaction of low economic growth and high population growth in relatively new state formations threatens stability and viability.

The international community has attempted to help by promising higher resource transfers, especially for countries which follow certain development policy prescriptions. But whereas many African governments have courageously followed the prescriptions, often at great social and political cost, concessionary resource flows have not reached the levels promised and export revenues have dwindled because of disastrously low commodity prices. The mid-term review of the UN Programme of Action for African Economic Recovery and Development (UNPAAERD) which ends in 1990 draws attention to the "continuing gravity of the economic situation in Africa" and calls for stronger action towards implementation of the programme.

One development obstacle in Africa to my mind is severely underestimated: the direct and indirect economic effect of wars and unrest. This important factor is clearly beyond the reach of normal technical assistance programmes. Solutions must be sought in the political and diplomatic field. There is, however, an urgent need for diplomacy and development to be linked, perhaps particularly in the present situation in Africa. Development efforts are difficult per se, but they become nearly hopeless pursuits alongside military conflict.

A particularly serious problem is the apartheid regime in South Africa. It is responsible for massive human rights violations domestically. Its overt warfare, war by proxy and destabilisation activities have inflicted immense human misery and economic damage in the neighbouring countries. The SADCC conference in Arusha last year named South African military aggression "The major obstacle to the realisation of the full potential of the region's transport and communication system..."

It is necessary to follow up the process of détente with renewed peace and development efforts in Africa. Conflicts must be settled, and it is as important to prevent future conflict by tuning energies to reconstruction and development. My suggestion could be sketched out as follows:

-- The UN system should be fully used to bring African conflicts to the conference table and to stop bloodshed. In particular, for Southern Africa an early priority would be for the international community to agree on comprehensive and mandatory sanctions to put pressure to bear on the South African regime to eradicate apartheid.

-- Integrated in the concrete processes of conflict resolution would be the elaboration of reconstruction plans for tackling immediate social

243

needs in the areas involved. Reconstruction would be dovetailed with medium to long-term development plans for these areas. Such plans would be prepared on the basis of three important tenets which I feel capture an emerging consensus on broad directions for African development: i) determination of strategies by the African peoples themselves, through their legitimate representatives; ii) emphasis on development of Africa's human resources, in particular the resources of women; iii) inter-African co-operation, aiming at conflict prevention through developmental or other measures would be given special attention; and iv) the OECD countries should take an initiative in the UN to form a Consortium which would provide funding, on the basis of additionality, for the elements of the above plan.

CONCLUDING REMARKS

Solutions to the challenges of the 1990s will require decisive action, but why should the rich and powerful inhabitants of the globe be convinced that the necessary measures should be taken?

The obvious answer is that they will have to solve the problems for the sake of their own security and economic welfare. The threat to security has traditionally been the cause of war between nations. In future we may see a change in the instruments of power, a different type of violence across international borders, emerging from resignation and despair. This threat must be met through international co-operation East-West-North-South.

The concept of security is not just a question of military conflicts. We shall perhaps in future come to consider the explosive forces of poverty and environmental degradation and the proliferation of nuclear arms to be the most dangerous threats. Prevention of environmental deterioration must rely on strengthened international organizations, and one should consider developing elements of supranational authority. By surrendering part of their formal national decision making power in certain fields individual nations may, in solidary co-operation ensure effective control over, for example, climatic change. The only element of supranationality of the UN system today lies in the Security Council. In my opinion, this is the direction in which we should move in order to deal with the environmental problems and the poverty problems of the globe. It is in this context that the idea of a UN Ecological Security Council has been launched. Environmental and economic aggression are problems of equal importance to military aggression.

I believe there is a growing need for a more binding international co-operation in the 1990s. A North-South summit under the aegis of the UN could explore the basis for a more effective system of global macroeconomic co-ordination between industrialized and developing countries.

In this connection, I see an important role for the OECD. Developmental and environmental challenges of the 1990s could be a major theme at the OECD Ministerial Council Meeting in 1990. To prepare for such a ministerial discussion in 1990, a broad integrated evaluation in the various OECD committees could start as soon as possible. The Ministerial meeting of the OECD next year could then become an important step in preparing for a North-South summit.

DISCUSSANT'S CONTRIBUTION

by

Chinua ACHEBE

Dr. Soedjatmoko has presented impeccable arguments for a world development strategy for the next decade based on growth, sustainability and solidarity. It would be presumptuous of me and indeed quite superfluous to add anything to what he has said about growth and sustainability.

I think, however, that the third component of his subject, that is *solidarity,* is deeply problematic and can use a brief moment of further reflection. This is not to say that I have spotted any defect in this presentation. On the contrary, I think he has made all the right points. But I do wish to elaborate on an aspect of the matter which is of great moment to us in the Third World and Africa in particular.

Dr. Soedjatmoko has told us that no country North or South, East or West, can achieve its major objectives in today's world by acting alone but in co-operation, regionally or globally. This awareness, he seems to say, is forced upon us by inescapable economic, demographic and ecological considerations. Our survival, it would seem, depends on acting out the basic tenets of human co-operation and solidarity. But to do this, to act out these tenets, "requires profound changes in conceptions of the state of the international order". Again he argues that our moral horizon and our loyalties and commitment will have to transcend the tribe, the ethnic community, the nation, and should encompass the whole of humanity including future generations." *Transcend the tribe, the ethnic community, the nation.* For avoidance of doubt (as lawyers say) I would seek his and your permission to add the word *race* -- a word we hardly admit into polite society, such as this. Transcend race, tribe, ethnic community, nation.

But to get back to the main line of the argument, what are the prospects for this new, enlarged vision which would inspire our actions towards greater co-operation and solidarity?

The auguries, alas, are not too good. Dr. Soedjatmoko puts it bluntly: "the international community is in no mood to take such ideas seriously." Elsewhere he says: "The chances of effective policies that would lead to the resumption of resource transfer to the Third World will remain very small for a long period."

Why is that so? We hear of something called "aid fatigue"; we hear of western disenchantment with Africa for failing to develop in the last twenty-five years; we sense mounting irritation among our friends with our endless problems, and a growing desire to cut links with us. And one is moved to ask why there was no fatigue during the century-long colonial linkage (in the case of Angola, 500 years). Why do we hear so little about the massive transfer of resources of those times? I know for example that even while the more celebrated Marshall Plan was pouring help into Europe, Britain also managed through the so-called Marketing Boards to ensure that the high prices commanded in the world market by tropical cash crops like cocoa, groundnuts, palm produce, rubber, tea, coffee benefited African farmers far less than they did the metropolitan economy. In Nigeria the albatross of the Marketing Board tied round the farmer's neck by Britain in the immediate postwar years has only now been removed -- long after market prices of those crops had collapsed and most farmers abandoned their farms.

What I am saying is not very pleasant but I am afraid it needs to be said here. The Marshall Plan was wonderful and all that, but it was within the family. Harold Macmillan was not joking when he said that those United States were really United Europeans. Africa is a horse of a different colour. "An African is my brother but my junior brother" said the great European missionary doctor, Albert Schweitzer.

The fact that Africa has not lived up to the rosy expectations of the 1960s is a matter for disappointment not only for our European and American friends but even for ourselves. But we have travelled quite separate routes to disillusionment. We have not believed for instance any of that talk about all the excellent training we received for democracy and development under colonial rule having been betrayed. We know that no such training for democracy took place nor could have taken place. Democracy is not bestowed by dictatorship, colonial or otherwise. But at the same time *we* thought that freedom from foreign rule would unleash its own innate momentum for indigenous development. Seek ye first the political kingdom, said Nkrumah, and everything else shall be added unto you.

That was not to be, for two main reasons. First the terms of emancipation were frequently far more crippling than anyone realised in the heady atmosphere of independence celebration. Second, the late 1970s and 1980s were to prove devastating to the fragile economies and policies of the new nations far beyond the most generous allowances made by reasonable doubt and caution.

None of this is intended to minimize the contribution made to our disasters by our own corrupt and inept leadership, but this culpability should be seen in relation to external factors which are often powerful enough to tell us who our leaders shall be.

Against this background what are the prospects for that largeness of vision which Dr. Soedjatmoko proposes to affluent nations if they are going to take on the burden necessary to rescue the wretched of the earth from crushing poverty to sustained growth.

I don't see any sign of that vision replacing the traditional view of the poor by the rich. The poor are poor because they do not work hard enough or are in some other way defective in character. What they need is a stiff dose of missionary exhortation and occasional acts of charity. And they already get plenty of those.

Meanwhile the streets have become less and less safe to walk in. The rich cut the last links with the poor and retire behind the high walls of their mansions. They install guard dogs at their iron gates and hope to sleep of nights. But it is quite futile.

Dr. Goran Hyden's paper referred with reservation to a decision by some African intellectuals (including my humble self) meeting in Kenya and proposing a cutting of links with the developed world. We did not propose it; we only recognised it.

DISCUSSANT'S CONTRIBUTION

by

Dragoslav AVRAMOVIC

The excellent papers prepared by Ms. Arizpe, Rector Soedjatmoko and His Excellency Minister Stoltenberg permit a focus on the critical issues ahead. I have chosen to discuss two: the debt problem and the commodity problem.

THE DEBT PROBLEM

The transfer of resources from the main debt-affected countries (17 Highly Indebted Countries in World Bank terminology) to their creditors on loan account -- the difference between the countries' loan receipts (disbursements in their favour) and their debt service payments (amortization and interest) -- shot up to $31.1 billion in 1988, one-third higher than in 1987 and the highest ever since this perverse international resource movement started in the early 1980s. The cumulative total of this negative movement over the six years from 1983-88 was a staggering $135 billion (1). The UN Economic Commission for Latin America and the Caribbean (ECLAC), applying a broader concept of resource flows (loan receipts *plus* direct foreign investment *vs.* amortization and interest *plus* profits) arrives at an even more formidable cumulative total of resource outflows from the Latin America and Caribbean region of $178.7 billion over the seven years 1982-88 (2). A continuation of this movement is inimical to growth, is not sustainable, and it does not reflect solidarity -- to use Professor Emmerij's definition of the objectives for the future and the main themes of this session of the present Conference.

On present indications, an organised solution to the debt problem is not an immediate prospect. Proposals for the establishment of a debt refinancing facility which would buy debts at a discount related to market prices and transfer the benefits to the debtor countries, are under discussion in the Group of 7 (main industrialised countries), but an agreement is not in sight as some key creditor countries have difficulty with the concept of "transferring risks from the market to the governments." "Voluntary debt reduction" agreed to by creditor banks is under way, mostly through the exchange of debts for direct investment in debtor countries ("debt-equity swaps"). In some important countries, however, these swaps have been suspended (Brazil, Mexico), mainly because of their inflationary effects --

251

they represent premature debt repayment which comes on top of current debt service which is already heavy enough. Some countries are also engaged in buybacks of their own loans at market prices, mostly for cash; but since most debtors are short of cash, such transactions are limited. It should be possible to obtain cash from public lending institutions in developed countries for this purpose -- and this has been done in several instances, mostly for the poorest countries -- but the scope has been limited.

There are hopes that the World Bank and other international development finance institutions (IDFIs) might issue guarantees for "exit" bonds issued by debtor countries in exchange for their bank debts, at reduced prices for the latter to capture the discount, such guarantees to cover perhaps a part of future debt service on such "exit" bonds. The problems here are resource limitations of IDFIs and "prudent management of risks", as well as, perhaps, the "transfer risk theory" mentioned above. A further constraining factor is that only debts owed to banks are covered by debt reduction schemes; those owed to governments (except in the case of the poorest African debtor countries) and international agencies are outside these schemes. For all these reasons, a recent analysis by Morgan Guaranty Trust, after examining the likely size of the debt subject to reduction and the likely extent of such reduction, concluded that, "the cash flow relief achievable by debt reduction is too often overrated -- unless the reduction assumes massive proportions and involves debt forgiveness on the part of bilateral and multilateral agencies that also are major creditors to these countries." (3) In this analysis, the yearly debt service cash flow relief (reduction) is estimated at $7 billion for 15 "Baker plan" countries. (This is almost the identical group as the world Bank's 17 "highly indebted" countries.) The reduction of $7 billion represents some 22 per cent of the resource outflow from these countries of $31 billion (4). It is equivalent to only 14 per cent of their aggregate debt service payments in 1987.

It is an essential point of debt theory that debt servicing capacity over the long run cannot be assured unless output grows sufficiently fast to enable a smooth reconciliation of competing claims on it by domestic consumption and investment, and from foreign capital (as debt service). Over the short run, belts can be tightened, but the short-run -- the tolerance of the taxpayers -- is limited. As matters now stand, investment in debt-affected countries has been cut sharply, probably by one-third on average, affecting both these countries' current output and their capacity for future growth. Inflation is rampant, while real wages and consumption have been falling for the last six years. The tolerance of taxpayers is wearing thin. A cut in annual debt service of $7 billion, spread over 17 countries will not be sufficient to restore the growth momentum and fill the pipeline with working capital. It would not suffice for Brazil (or Mexico) alone. Furthermore, it will take time to work out the debt reduction arrangements, probably years judging by past experience.

Under these circumstance, even a temporary arrangement sharply to reduce the outflow of resources from debt-affected countries is needed. A scheme of this nature was submitted to the *Conference on International Debt: Practical Solutions,* organised by the University of Brasilia and the Third World Foundation, held in the Brazilian capital from 2nd-5th May 1988. The Conference supported the scheme, a first outline of which was given to the South Commission in January 1988. For a first period of six years (phase 1) it would include:

-- Postponement of amortization; and

-- Splitting of interest payments into three parts: i) payment in foreign exchange (say, 2 per cent on outstanding loans); ii) payment in local currency (say, 3 per cent); and iii) deferral of the balance of interest (say, 3 per cent) and its conversion into a new loan due in foreign exchange.

Specific proportions of the interest split would vary from country to country, depending on the circumstances of each case. The arrangement would apply to all non-concessionary debt, with two exceptions: trade credits and those creditors whose ongoing disbursements exceed a country's debt service, with appropriate adjustments in cases of partial coverage. Debt service would be resumed fully in foreign exchange as the temporary six-year arrangement (phase 1) ends; while debt servicing terms in the follow-up (phase 2) would be partly determined by measures taken in phase 1 to raise the debtor country's creditworthiness. It is suggested that countries benefiting from the interim arrangements establish a collective insurance fund to guarantee future interest payments which would be fully payable in foreign exchange. (The fund, which would be established immediately at the beginning of phase 1, with premiums, being paid by the beneficiary debtor countries, would continue in existence in phase 2. Alternatively, insurance might be possible to obtain through MIGA -- the World Bank insurance affiliate, or else in the open insurance market, depending what is cheapest and feasible.) As the existence of insurance would upgrade the value of the debts through greater security, the basic requirement of the theory of debt reorganisation -- exchange of reasonable equivalents -- would have been met, and it should then be possible to negotiate an improvement in loan terms, including a lasting reduction in the rate of interest.

Annual savings in debt service for the 17 countries would exceed $20 billion and may run up to $30 billion over the six-year period of phase 1 (5). The essence of the scheme is to enable a quick recovery in affected developing countries, after almost a decade of stagnation and decline. Phase 1 should be a part of a broader programme of each beneficiary country aimed at reconstruction, effective stabilization, increased investment and resumed growth. It may call for additional capital inflow.

There is no conflict between the efforts at debt reduction and the proposed arrangement to cut the transfer of debt service sharply for an interim period. This arrangement does not reduce the assets of the creditors, but is aimed at transformation of debt service payments so as to facilitate the position of the debtors in short order.

THE COMMODITY PROBLEM

In recent circumstances, in country after country, the adjustment objectives have been vitiated by price collapses on the export market or by a collapse of supply, which have strongly affected the debtor country's earnings and thus its budgetary and investment objectives. This has been a general case in developing countries, but it has affected the African countries with particular violence in view of their pronounced dependence on commodities, as a proportion of their total exports and national incomes. It then follows that unless ways are found to reduce adverse commodity fluctuations or mitigate their effects without incurring heavy debts, the adjustment is frequently almost bound to fail, however well conceived it may be in terms of domestic efforts and external financial support. Furthermore, as the analysis in a recent work by the UN Economic Commission for Africa on its perspectives beyond recovery has shown, the economic outlook for Africa is gloomy over the medium term and difficult over the long run without an improvement in export commodity prices. One of the key tasks of transformation and modernization is to reduce the relative dependence on primary exports, while achieving a sustained and productive exploitation at satisfactory wages of Africa's valuable assets in commodities. This holds for most other primary producers in the developing world as well.

The recent ratification of the Agreement on the Common Fund for Commodities provides an opportunity to consider a renewed approach to the commodity problem. Experience has shown that it is difficult to agree on an international commodity action when the effort is limited to price stabilization. There are also difficulties of implementation. It is urgently necessary to explore the feasibility of action covering most aspects of a particular commodity -- investment, processing, marketing, promotion, price stabilization, diversification, research -- in an attempt to work out a comprehensive, pragmatic, flexible and financially sound solution, which should minimize commodity surpluses and shortages and provide satisfactory average returns to producers. Such an approach would call for the preparation, by commodity, of a specific project and a financing plan involving support by several international financing agencies -- regional and worldwide -- on a consortium basis. Hopefully, over time, commercial sources of finance would also be attracted.

I am not underestimating the complexities and potential difficulties of this approach, but after many years of involvement in commodity affairs, I feel that all efforts need to be made to cope with the commodity problem in some comprehensive way. Perhaps as soon as the Common Fund has entered into force it may be requested to draw up a proposal along these or similar lines. Perhaps the Commission on Primary Products in Africa, recently agreed to by the UN General Assembly, could make efforts in this direction. Perhaps some of the existing international financing agencies could try to explore the possibilities. If the concept appears promising and feasible, one can then prepare specific project proposals for several vulnerable commodities in the near future. Success in a commodity endeavour of this kind is critically dependent on the solidarity and co-operation of producing countries. International financing agencies may be interested in financing such projects as they would complement, on an international basis, the individual country programmes these agencies are currently supporting. A well-designed commodity initiative, implemented with discipline, would assist the balance of payments of all producers.

A recent illustrative analysis, prepared by the International Food Research Institute in Washington DC, has shown that the aggregate expansion of Africa's cocoa production involved in all structural adjustment programmes may lead to a decline in aggregate export value of these countries over the medium-term as it may reduce prices more than proportionately (6). Would it not be better to prepare a world cocoa project instead of individual country projects *seriatim*? Perhaps cocoa, now in trouble, is the best case to try the feasibility of the comprehensive approach to the commodity problem suggested here.

NOTES AND REFERENCES

1. The World Bank, *World Debt Tables, 1988-89 Edition*, volume I, page XVII, December 1988. The 17 countries are: Argentina, Bolivia, Brazil, Chile, Colombia, Costa Rica, Côte d'Ivoire, Ecuador, Jamaica, Mexico, Morocco, Nigeria, Peru, Philippines, Uruguay, Venezuela and Yugoslavia.

2. ECLAC, *Preliminary Overview of the Latin American Economy 1988*, Table 15, page 22, 3rd January 1989.

3. "LDC Debt Reduction: A Critical Appraisal", *World Financial Markets*, 30th December 1988.

4. The $7 billion figure is arrived at by Morgan by assuming that all commercial banks would reduce their long-term claims on the 15 debtors by 30 per cent (roughly the fraction at which US money-centre banks reserved on average for their LDC exposure.) The face value of the aggregate amount of long-term claims of $240 billion would be cut by some $72 billion. At an interest rate of London Interbank Offered Rate (LIBOR) -- around 9 per cent -- plus a spread of 1 per cent, the debtors would save some $7 billion in annual interest charges. (The total of the "Baker 15" is estimated by Morgan at $500 billion: $240 billion in long-term debts to banks; $45 billion in short-term debts, mostly to banks and trade-related: and the remaining some $220 billion owed to official creditors and, to a lesser extent, suppliers and other lenders who may be covered by official guarantees.)

5. See AVRAMOVIC, Dragoslav *Debt Problem: What Next?* study submitted to the Brasilia Conference, revised 18th August 1988, page 12 (mimeo).

6. "Commentary: Demand-side Constraints and Structural Adjustment in Sub-Saharan Africa", in *IFPRI Report*, Volume 10, Number 4, October 1988.

DISCUSSANT'S CONTRIBUTION

by

Joseph KI ZERBO

We have been invited here to talk frankly about issues of concern to the entire planet, and I think that through encounters like this one we shall little by little manage to come closer to our common goal. Yesterday, I mentioned the motto of the Centre de Recherche pour le Développement Endogène, "one does not develop, one develops oneself". I should like to relate that to Louis Emmerij's metaphor of the train which transports much of the human race at very high speed -- a TGV -- while others have trouble holding on and getting on board, and still others are left behind on the platform.

This reminds me of a contribution I made to a UNESCO conference in Addis Ababa on education in Africa where there was much talk about school enrolment rates. In 1961, UNESCO had set its sights on providing schooling for the entire African continent within the next 20 years, and I remember being one of the few people at the time who said that Africa's main problem was not school attendance rates but educational content and orientation. That is to say, curricula. I even found myself saying that we could be likened to people travelling on a train in Africa. Today we are talking about increasing the speed of the train -- but if the rails are pointed towards the edge of a cliff, we are not doing much of a favour to those inside it by making it go faster! The first priority is to change the direction of the rails. I think this still holds true today, and I would use exactly the same arguments where the character and shape of relations between the South and the developed countries are concerned. If "structural adjustment" continues to function within the same old mould, it means that the South must fall purely and simply into line with the North.

In present-day Africa, some sort of adjustment is needed, but it should be self-adjustment and not an exogenous adjustment which imposes a set of constraints or requires entry into a voracious market. Some African heads of state who had put their faith in the market have now turned against it, having learnt that despite responding to calls to step up production, once prices start dropping you are as badly off as you were before. Again, if you practise less government intervention while there are still no businessmen of any consequence to create a private sector, you are obviously in many cases going to come to grief.

With aid and trade it is the same story. In the case of aid, we all know that right now the flow of capital, at least in overall terms, is directed from South to North, since the so-called "recipient" countries in the South are sending capital to the "donor" countries in the North to pay off their debts. I personally object to the term qualifying "poor" countries as recipients, mere receivers of the alms doled out to them.

Some of these things will have to change -- present arrangements are not immutable and little by little we can transform them. The image of the train, as I say, is instructive -- with people running behind to catch up. I believe we have here a new version of Rostow's famous "stages", or the stage theory taught at the time of Stalin. Real backwardness exists with respect to what one might or should be if one made the best use of the opportunities available -- it is backwardness with respect to oneself. So-called backwardness in the other sense cannot properly speaking be remedied. Someone made a simple calculation: if the population of the Sahel were equated with the population of the United States in terms of energy, calorie, protein, goods and services consumption, it would take 14 billion Sahelians to balance out the people of the United States.

This is an obvious absurdity. Translated into reality, it would be the end of the world. Either that, or the North would have to change its lifestyle...which, by the way, has seriously damaged the environment. True, the poor also attack the environment because of their very poverty, but the damage they do is less serious than the misdeeds of the industrialised countries -- take the example of the deterioration of the ozone layer or careless toxic waste dispersal.

So, I do not think backwardness can be eliminated under the existing system. What we must have is true development, the end of maldevelopment, for all. I define development as the raising of the self to a higher level, aided by others, but relying mainly on oneself. On that plane, material means are not the top priority. The top priority concerns the conditions for making development possible -- how do you achieve these conditions? Rates of development can differ greatly, that is not important. What is wrong with accepting different rates? If we are all aiming at the same destination, just as all roads lead to Rome, the destination being the development of *each one of us,* I do not see why different speeds should not be allowed. In any case, there is no other solution. History is full of advances and retreats, swift accelerations followed by backward moves.

The problem is therefore not one of speed, nor even of multi- or bipolarism, it lies elsewhere and I shall return to this point.

At one stage, bipolarism benefited the developing countries. President Nasser, for one, profited from the tensions of the Cold War. Bipolarism has admittedly given rise to terrible local conflicts in the countries of the South, but there is nothing to suggest that multipolarism would put an end to them. We have to be careful when talking about polarity that we do not wind up gazing at the Pole Star -- all locked in the same, unvarying direction!

The problem is not whether to board the train or not -- if everybody clambered on it would break apart. The problem is that some act as the locomotive while others are only wagons. I return to the train image because many races, many countries still have wagon status only. With things as they are, they are likely to retain this status for a long time to come.

It is a cold fact that certain countries, certain continents are left by the wayside, have been uncoupled from the train. In order to understand this better we should think historically.

Africa became uncoupled back in the 15th and 16th centuries, and that is where one has to look first. It was at that time that Africa took a different track, because it suffered a major population loss. Similarly today, it is suffering a collective "brain drain", with the massive exodus of its intellectuals and researchers to the North. The uncoupling was never a deliberate choice, it was rather an imposed isolation -- which, for certain countries in Africa, has had its beneficial side. Isolation is not inevitably bad: it can lead to the discovery of unsuspected energies in oneself. You will remember that, in what is today Zimbabwe, industrialisation was set in quite rapid motion during the boycott of Ian Smith's regime. During the Second World War, too, when isolated Africa served Europe as a staging area, African countries began to industrialise up to a point. The question we have to ask therefore is: why a single track?

I put this question to economists in particular, because they seem incapable of jettisoning the rational positivism and determinism inherited from the 19th century physical sciences. No matter that revolutions have since occurred in the same natural and physical sciences, these attitudes, in force since Bacon, Descartes, Galileo and Newton, and central to the political economics of Adam Smith, still prevail today unchanged. This unequivocal science has given way to a science of complexity, irreversible reactions, indeterminism and randomness -- these are what dominate today's physics. It is a world of open systems, with all the opportunity and risk that they imply. In the absence of a single destination for everyone, we must try to understand the conditions under which change can occur, and I should like to end by outlining what for me are the most important of these conditions.

The first is co-responsibility. We hear a lot of talk about interdependence and solidarity. Interdependence seems to me to be a static, cold and almost mechanical notion, whereas co-responsibility implies commitment, an idea at once political and ethical. I believe this principle should now guide the different regions of the world, since it is the one which will enable us to meet the serious challenges facing the planet. Thorvald Stoltenberg has spoken about the environment and a Security Council for the environment. I am in absolute agreement with him.

The world is lagging behind the realities which are at present shaping it. We have 19th century governments for what will soon be 21st century problems, and that is the greatest contradiction of our time. Where Africa is concerned, co-responsibility requires democracy. In mentioning democracy for Africa, we are not condemning heads of state, we are condemning structures unsuited to development in Africa. The citizenry must be free to play its part; heads of state must do more than simply manage survival and oversee poverty: they must attempt to change Africa so that it can rise to its rightful place in the world.

The second prerequisite for change is integration. There is a tendency in the world towards polarisation, the case of Europe and the coming single European market being the most obvious example. Some form of integration is essential for Africa, and for the world, and it should lead to a kind of solidarity that will give new meaning to the adventure of the human race on earth. I do not agree with the view of the world as a global village -- it is too bucolic when you think of all the dramas rending the planet. I prefer to compare it to a space ship, more in keeping with the poignant state of planet earth today. It is a space ship voyaging through the cosmos, on which we should all be united, but on which attitudes and institutions trail behind logistics and technology. We can properly speak of two different speeds in this connection: technology, invented by men, goes extremely fast, while our attitudes and institutions advance very slowly. The TGV exists but unfortunately we travel aboard institutions which lag far behind and must catch up.

To be effective, Africa needs its countries to draw together, in order that the continent may count for something in negotiations and avoid the pitfalls of bilateralism. It is also a requirement for science. There is little future for real science in Africa under the present nation-state structure. It is not possible to study the problems of a river catchment area or of the Lake Chad basin, for example, within the framework of a single country. The same holds true for initiatives against malnutrition, locust infestations, epidemics and other plagues.

The countries of Africa must work together in both science and economics. Africa will not exert its full weight until a genuine African bloc exists, and such a bloc will exist only if it is continental in scale. If the OECD wants to have a talking partner of any consequence in Africa, it can and must help us. I am not advocating a return to tribal structures, but we must go beyond the States we know today, using them to reach out to something continental and using them also to reach down into the popular roots, the communities which alone can supply the cultural, and economic, contribution of Africa.

The third of my prescriptions for change is research, a vital necessity for Africa. At the present time, 85 per cent of the research dealing with Africa is conducted outside of the continent.

Africa must internalise its research. If it does not, we shall be like people who walk around with their brains beside them -- a continent without a brain. The first step in development must be local research; otherwise we shall resemble a computer separated by thousands of miles from its software. The absence of indigenous research is the reason why Africa does not take off and seems to be stalled on the ground. Something has broken down in Africa -- throwing billions of dollars at us will not change anything. Africa must learn to become whole again. Research is not something immaterial; it is carried out by a continent for itself. We are not just walking digestive tracts, and Africa is more than just a client for international soup kitchens. We must build ourselves from the ground up with every level of personality: infrastructure, logistics, and superstructure, including the brain. There is an African proverb which says, "You forget how useful your buttocks are until you get a boil on them." For a long while Africa was considered useful precisely because of its problems and because it was needed. Increasingly, however, there is a feeling that Africa can get lost, be abandoned and cut adrift, that it does not matter and the world will continue to get along very nicely. Wrong, quite wrong! The friends of Africa should take this situation very seriously, because no continent will succeed alone. Africa today is slipping back -- soon, with the technological revolution and the biotechnologies in particular, even its raw materials and commodities will no longer be needed.

Africans must face up to this situation clearly, and their friends must help them to do so. The African continent must survive this period of mortal danger in order to supply, not only commodities, but other resources grounded in the essential question of who we are. This is the basic challenge, the answer to which will enable Africa to provide an impressive capital increment to mankind's common heritage.

Chapter VII

FURTHER COMMENTS ON THE QUESTION OF ONE WORLD OR SEVERAL

A COMMENT FROM A
NON-GOVERNMENTAL ORGANISATION PERSPECTIVE

by

Brian McKEOWN

I would like to begin by congratulating the OECD Development Centre on its 25th Anniversary. The work of the Development Assistance Committee and of the Development Centre have made a major contribution to development cooperation over the last quarter of a century. The scrutiny by the DAC of the quantity and quality of Member States' ODA Programmes and the research and outreach activities of the Development Centre have ensured that the development issue has occupied a secure place on the agendas of the OECD countries. That it is often too far down the agenda poses a challenge to us all for the future.

The theme of this seminar is "The Next Decade: Interdependence in a Multipolar and Two-Track World Economy". Papers by your very eminent contributors have sketched the future of the world economy. They present a picture of a future in which perhaps three quarters of the countries of the world in North America, Western and Eastern Europe, East and South East Asia, Latin America, plus India, China and the Soviet Union, will participate in a dynamic international economy. The remaining one quarter of countries particularly in Sub-Saharan Africa will be left behind and will hardly participate in this multipolar economy.

How does this vision of the future fit with the panorama as seen by NGOs? Clearly, there is some overlap. The NGOs as well as the official donor community have increasingly had to concentrate their efforts in Sub-Saharan Africa. Development has indeed been derailed, as UNICEF puts it, there and in many other parts of the Third World. In Sub-Saharan Africa NGOs increasingly find themselves called on to pick up the pieces after the destruction levelled on Africa by the debt crisis, the terms of trade crisis, and the internal crisis of development policies. We encounter the human face of these macro issues in our projects and programmes with grass roots groups. Although the mandate of my organisation stresses long term development and supporting micro-projects to assist people to shape their own futures, we have been increasingly drawn into relief and welfare projects in recent years. The overwhelming number of applications we receive from Sub-Saharan Africa currently are for basic needs projects, primarily for food, water and health care. Of late we have noted that the same trend is becoming evident in applications from Latin America too.

The statistics are grim: according to UNICEF in Africa and much of Latin America average incomes have fallen by between 10 per cent and 25 per cent in the 1980s; the average weight-for-age of young children, a vital indicator of normal growth, is falling in many of the countries for which figures are available; in the 37 poorest countries for which figures are available, spending per head on health has been reduced by 50 per cent and on education by 25 per cent over the past few years; in almost half of the 103 developing countries from which recent information is available, the proportion of 6- to 11-year-olds in primary schools is now falling.

The human cost is enormous. Nutrition, health, education are increasingly unavailable to millions of children. This is seriously marking an entire generation and the effects of the present denial of adequate nutrition, health-care and education must have a serious effect on the developmental potential of many countries and peoples. The major cause of this development disaster has been summed up as a retreat from the march of human progress on the part of nine hundred million people or one sixth of the world's population.

For most of the countries of Africa, Latin America, and the Caribbean, almost every current economic indicator suggests that development has been halted or reversed. Per capita GNP has fallen seriously in these areas, debt repayments have risen to a quarter or more of export earnings, their share of world trade has dropped, and the productivity of labour has declined in each year throughout the 1980s.

Much of this development crisis can be explained by the indebtedness of Third World countries and the collapse in commodity prices. The hostile international environment of the last decade is also a factor. The OECD countries must be cognisant of the fact that this environment is a product of their fiscal, monetary, and trade policies.

Similarly, as many of your papers recognise, we see that there are very many people in many of the NIEs who are not benefiting from the economic growth that is occurring. It is salutary to recall Louis Emmerij's warning that "while the slow track may apply to perhaps a quarter of the world's nations, it probably applies to half the world's people". From our perspective, then, it is worth repeating that, while the economic performance of the Newly Industrialising Countries may give room for hope, this hope must be matched by a recognition that their performance in the area of human rights leaves much to be desired. The Philippines has been singled out in some of the papers read here as the exception in the ASEAN group by virtue of its poor economic performance. This exception does not apply, however, in the area of human rights where the Philippines has much in common with its neighbours in the Newly Industrialised Country category.

This fact reminds us that good economic performance is not an end in itself but only a means to improving the well-being of the people who make up that economy. This well-being encompasses not only freedom from want but all the other basic freedoms enshrined in the United Nations Declaration on Human

Rights, such as the rights to life, freedom and security and freedom of movement, thought and religion.

When we broaden our perspective to take account of social and political realities as well as the economic dimension, there are in addition to poverty in Sub-Saharan Africa and Bangladesh and mal-distribution of income in many of the NIEs, other problems caused by political and social factors.

For example, war and the effects of war are to be seen all over the Third World. All of the 25 major wars currently being waged are in the Third World. Apart from the appalling loss of life -- 17 million people have been killed in wars since 1945 -- millions of people have been forced to flee their homes. There are, for example, 3 million refugees in Central America and Mexico, victims of war in El Salvador and Guatemala.

The refugee problem in Southern Africa is but one aspect of the tragic situation there. Apartheid in South Africa is a major cause of the poverty and destruction in the region. For example in Mozambique, while humanitarian assistance to refugees and others, emergency relief, and technical training remain part of our effort, socioeconomic development projects are problematic to say the least. It is part of the strategy of the South African backed MNR to destroy the social infrastructure in Mozambique. For example, over 2 000 primary schools have been destroyed or shut down because of the war, and over 700 small local clinics have been destroyed or looted. Teachers and health workers have been kidnapped and in some cases killed. In South Africa itself, over 2 200 people were killed between September 1984 and January 1987. Not surprisingly then, our partners look to us, not only for material assistance but for legal aid, leadership training and above all for solidarity with them in their struggle. A key demonstration of this solidarity must be our "conscientising" our own politicians and public to the plight of our partners and lobbying our governments to exert pressure for change. We in the OECD countries have to acknowledge our complicity in the South African situation. South Africa's major trading partners are OECD countries. With some exceptions we have failed to apply progressive, mandatory sanctions as a tangible protest against South Africa's apartheid and its destabilisation of Southern Africa.

Another area of the world where politics prevents development is Indo-China. For over a decade now Vietnam and Kampuchea have been denied ODA from the European Economic Community and most Western countries. This is despite the fact that these are among the poorest countries in the world. Trocaire, and other NGOs consider it inexcusable to deny assistance to people in need on political grounds. In Vietnam we find ourselves involved in projects and programmes that are more appropriate to official donors. For example, last year, over half the funds from the CIDSE Indo-China Programme which Trocaire co-ordinates, was spent on emergency aid and curative medicine. The food shortage is due in part to the absence of bilateral aid for pest control and irrigation systems.

A normalisation of relations between the OECD countries and Vietnam is a prerequisite for development. The Kampuchea problem appears to be on the verge of resolution. Hopefully, the OECD countries will do all in their power to assist the peace process. Hopefully, this will pave the way for a renewal of government to government links, an inflow of bilateral aid and a strengthened input from the multilateral agencies. A concerted effort is required by the whole OECD group to facilitate peace and development for the poorest of the poor in Indo-China.

For NGOs these economic, social and political aspects are indivisible. Why is this so? First because our concern is with integral human development -- "development of the whole man and of every man" in the words of Populorum Progressio. Second, because we have learnt that in some situations funding small-scale, income-generating projects may seem to make sense on the basis of an economic analysis but may be rendered impossible by political factors. For example, the involvement of my own agency in Central America over many years taught us that there are situations in which the basic preconditions for socioeconomic development projects do not exist. Where the roots of poverty lie in institutionalised, structural injustice the conditions necessary for full human development do not exist. Trocaire supported numerous socioeconomic projects in countries like El Salvador, Nicaragua and Guatemala in our early years of operation. But the experience was chastening. Partners in rural co-operatives and training schemes were terrorised, and, in many cases, murdered. Development involves change. In many Third World situations a reordering of social and political relationships is a prerequisite for socioeconomic progress.

For all of us, however, the overriding concern remains that, as Mahbub Ul Haq put it in his paper "despite the spectacular economic growth record of the developing world as a whole in the past quarter of a century, the number of people living in absolute poverty still exceeds one billion". What can we do about this awful challenge?

NGOs like my own see three avenues of assistance. First, by our work on the ground we try to help in a practical way to overcome obstacles and promote development. Our primary concern is to assist peoples to fashion their own development. A constituent part of this work involves showing solidarity with people constrained by poverty, social injustice and political oppression. Second, we advocate on behalf of the voiceless in the Third World structural change in the world economy in favour of developing countries. Third, we try to raise awareness in our countries of the situation in the Third World and awaken our people and politicians to their responsibilities in justice.

As NGOs, we are keenly aware that we cannot, nor do we want, to substitute for governments. In terms of resource transfers to developing countries the NGOs in the OECD countries transfer roughly the equivalent of one-tenth of official aid. It is clear to us that only governments have the resources to make a major impact on poverty alleviation.

For this reason, we are concerned about the performance of our governments in relation to ODA. We see this as vital in providing practical help to the Third World, and also as an index of commitment to a more equitable world order. Only four OECD countries have met the United Nations target of 0.7 per cent of GNP per annum as ODA. In my own country, Ireland, we have seen the

ODA/GNP ratio fall from 0.25 per cent of GNP in 1985-86 to 0.18 per cent currently. Economic stringency is blamed and the only commitment is to resuming progress "as soon as economic circumstances permit". Such vague aspiration is in marked contrast to our governments stance when arguing for transfers to Ireland from the EEC. As we have said on many occasions, we accept the principle of the duty of the strongest to help the weakest in the EC context where we stand to gain. It is not right that we should then abandon this principle in our dealings with our weaker partners in the world community. It is also at odds with the wishes of the general public, even at a time of austerity. When public expenditure cuts were at their most severe a survey carried out for Trocaire showed that 72 per cent of respondents supported government aid to the Third World, and over half wanted ODA maintained at current levels or increased. In Ireland, as elsewhere, public support for ODA is motivated as Richard Jolly put it, "by some sense of solidarity and humanitarian concern for poverty".

This public commitment to poverty alleviation offers the best hope for better ODA performance in the future. It will underpin assistance to the poorest of the poor for, as Colin Bradford remarks, the response of the world community to the least developed "will have to rest on a rationale other than self-interest".

The challenge to us all is clear. There is an urgent need to renew what Philip Ndegwa calls "the development commitment". I am confident that the Development Centre will make a major contribution to this task.

A COMMENT FROM THE SAHEL CLUB PERSPECTIVE

by

Anne DE LATTRE

Following the severe drought which afflicted the Sahel countries in West Africa in the early 1970s, the OECD countries markedly stepped up public development aid in their direction and, in the past 15 years, these countries have become the biggest recipients of aid in Africa.

Meanwhile, the drought and its frequently tragic consequences inspired studies on the Sahel situation and its medium and long-term prospects. Together, the Permanent Inter-State Committee for Drought Control in the Sahel (CILSS) and the OECD Club du Sahel were actively involved in these studies.

However, in spite of increased public aid, in spite of the proliferation of private aid projects, in spite of the analysis and research efforts and in spite of the efforts made by the Sahelians themselves, the situation has hardly improved in this region. The main unfavourable trends, namely the high population growth rates compared to those of production, environmental deterioration and rampant urbanisation, were not reversed. Indeed, they worsened and new problems appeared, such as macro-economic imbalances and indebtedness.

The OECD countries which are helping the Sahel were concerned about these trends. They therefore requested CILSS and the Club du Sahel to step back from the day-to-day situation, and undertake a futures study of the Sahel countries based on sound retrospective analysis and providing substance for a study on potential scenarios for the future of Sahel during the next quarter of a century. The team responsible for the futures study was led by Jacques Giri, who drafted the entire report. It attempted to answer the question in the minds of all those concerned about the future of the Sahel: are these countries moving towards increasing dependence or are they liable to embark on structural transformation?

The future scenario which seemed the most likely and was finally selected, was that of increasing dependence. However, the point was made that this probable scenario was by no means inescapable. Efforts were made to find ways out of the increasing dependence scenario: the awareness of more and more Africans, the thrusts of popular initiatives and autonomous attempts by the populations to set up their own organisations, and the support objectives and procedures of certain NGOs. Finally, the authors agreed that structural transformation rested with the Sahelians themselves -- they will be the main architects -- and, to a lesser but by no means negligible extent, with those trying to help them. Will the Sahelians and those helping them be able to seize the opportunities for structural transformation?

BRIEF RETROSPECTIVE ANALYSIS

How was the present crisis brought on and why did it set in? In a retrospective analysis prior to reviewing future prospects, the authors tried to find an answer.

With reference to the 1960s, the years of independence, they pointed out that the Sahelian societies and economies at the time were rural and traditional. Colonisation had sowed the seeds of change, and the ensuing changes led to imbalances in population growth, urbanisation, new values, and the emergence of new social classes, including a new political class moulded by the colonial education system and Western culture. In colonial times however, and during the first few years of independence, these imbalances were not sufficiently spectacular to be noticed.

In 1960 and subsequent years, power shifted to the new Westernised political class. Whether socialist or liberal, the policies of the new governments were inspired by a Western type of development model.

The choice was obvious for the Westernised élites. It met the aspirations of part of the population. The retrospective study showed that the priorities were:

-- To find the hard currency needed to import consumer goods from the West;

-- To develop industry, the symbol of modernity;

-- To construct the infrastructure that was needed for exports, mining and industry;

-- To develop the social services along Western lines;

-- To develop the institutions needed to build modern nation-States.

The State acted as a basic driving force behind the conception and implementation of this model of development. It tried to train, structure and organise the population so that it would respond to State initiatives.

Between 1960 and 1970, these policies led to different levels of development in different countries, and even to a certain amount of prosperity.

From the 1970s, external shocks disrupted this development, exposing internal weaknesses and contradictions:

-- Drought demonstrated that since independence food crops had been neglected as much as they had been during the colonial period. Food crop cultivation was still extensive, insufficiently productive and vul-

271

nerable. But times had changed. The production system was no longer capable of meeting the needs of a rapidly expanding population -- whence the deteriorating environment -- a growing urban population -- whence the increasing structural food deficit -- and drought -- whence the endemic emergency situation;

-- The oil shock and slump in commodity prices led to the deterioration of terms of trade. The Sahel countries occupied a marginal position on world markets; their output and productivity were growing less fast than the world average. They lost market shares to more efficient countries;

-- Fluctuations in the dollar rate and higher interest rates worsened the impact of external shocks.

Under the effect of these shocks, the internal conflicts which were already latent during the colonial period and which developed considerably after independence, became clearer:

-- The need to construct a modern westernised economy and the role that the State had assumed in this connection brought high taxation on the incomes of producers;

-- Overtaxed countries pulled out of the official market; agricultural production stagnated; modern industry, which was also overtaxed, stagnated or even shrank; the informal sector developed to allow the growing urban population to subsist;

-- The emphasis laid on the social services and on the building of a modern nation-state swelled the public sector out of proportion with the production sector. The developing school system, which had been designed and set up on western lines, nurtured the expansion of the public sector, which became the principal outlet for school leavers.

This situation led to:

-- Ever stronger pressure on incomes from productive activities, and hence even greater introversion of producers;

-- The establishment of a *de facto* free exchange zone in West Africa: an economy based on unofficial trade and financial networks filled the gaps of the production economy;

-- Increasing recourse to foreign aid of all kinds, and hence growing dependence;

-- Disproportionate external indebtedness.

The conclusion of the retrospective study was as follows: the State and foreign aid had failed to involve the unresponsive community in the attempts to develop along western lines. Social interaction did not bring self-sustained growth

272

but an increasingly dependent economy. As time went by, the situation in the Sahel countries was becoming more and more critical.

THE ROLE OF FOREIGN AID IN THE CRISIS FACING WEST AFRICAN SAHEL COUNTRIES

In the current crisis experienced by the West African Sahel countries, the role of foreign aid is by no means negligible. An attempt has been made to analyse these factors in the futures study.

First, external aid agencies did not question the model of development along western lines selected and implemented by the Sahel countries at the start of independence. Far from heeding the real conditions in Africa, they encouraged this model. They convinced the Sahelian States -- which were only too eager to be convinced -- that they could lead their countries towards industrial development, cash crops, and integration in European and world markets. They did not understand that the development of food crops, the protection of a vulnerable environment, small-scale decentralised industry, a large range of craft activities, and expanding regional trade in foodstuffs and manufactured products tailored to the requirements of low income populations and manufactured locally constituted the main steps in sound and healthy development which could have involved all Sahelian populations. Nor did they help to set up cost-effective systems for training, education and health, which might have promoted the entire Sahelian society.

Not only did external aid agencies fail to dispute the western-style model of development, but they failed to challenge their partners from the political class and administration on the role of the Sahelian State as the driving force behind the conception and implementation of the model. On the contrary, public aid largely backed up this conception and implementation.

The aid agencies did not realise or failed to see that the governments which had taken over from colonial power were rooted in a tradition foreign to Africa, their values were not those acquired by western countries through the painful vicissitudes of a long history -- these being still disputed and fragile. They failed to see, or refused to see, that Sahelian States and their customers were taking possession of a substantial share of the levies on rural populations and production activities, as well as a significant share of external aid, and that they were becoming increasingly isolated from the population, which did not identify with them. When the international co-operation community realised what was happening, it was unable to modify a system of which it had become a prisoner, and whose disadvantages were compounded by immediate political and economic considerations, conflicting aid policies, competition between such policies and the commitments entered into by the aid agencies.

WHAT IS THE ANSWER?

It will not be easy to reverse the unfavourable trends affecting the Sahel, and this will take time. The Sahel countries are burdened with major natural, political, economic, technical and social handicaps. It is by no means certain that a balance can be found with the current pattern of frontiers, and, in addition to their own handicaps, the Sahel countries also face external ones.

The process of change must therefore be set in motion, and to this end, ideas carry more weight than means. It is therefore urgent to bring home a few truths.

THE SAHEL IS IN THE HANDS OF THE SAHELIANS

The first home truth is that the Sahel rests in the hands of the Sahelians. In a world order which remains governed by war, what a people cannot achieve on its own will never be achieved on its behalf. This harsh truth is overshadowed by demagogic ideas, illusions fostered by technocratic powers, often cynical political power games, the interests and the emotional responses of public opinion moved by the suffering of the Sahelians. These factors combine with one another and are nurtured by the tendency of the Sahelian States and their customers to opt for the easy way out. It is up to farsighted Sahelians, of whom there are many more than might be suggested, to bring home the truths that might spark off political and social change in their countries.

IF EXTERNAL AID IS NECESSARY, UNDER WHAT CONDITIONS SHOULD IT BE USED?

It would be unfair to say that aid to the Sahel countries has been useless. Among its benefits the following may be mentioned:

- Mitigating the consequences of natural disasters. Nowadays, a much improved infrastructure, a degree of organisation, acquired experience and monitoring and emergency systems prevent famine in the Sahel countries;

- Improved rural and, above all, urban infrastructures, which are having a major impact on living conditions;

- Some expansion, albeit too slow, in agricultural production. The efforts made to combine cash and food crops are encouraging. Small scale livestock production, vegetable growing, fish farming, new crops and fruit growing are developing in the Sahel, whereas 10 years ago such diversification was still unknown;

-- More widespread education and human skills. Investment in human resources will yield results in the future.

It should also be noted, however, that in the past 10 years the following has been observed:

-- Massive food aid, even where it not was not justified, with a view to meeting the interests of the urban class, mainly the political class and its customers. The food aid volume has discouraged African farmers from producing more;

-- Increased balance-of-payment aid in different forms to meet excess consumption relative to domestic production; this aid has encouraged imports and the extension of unofficial trade in West Africa, which has now become a huge free exchange area in fact if not by right;

-- A steady increase in aid to the public and semi-public sector, which is constantly expanding through the many "development" projects, which mostly foster "development" of the administrations concerned to the detriment of that of productive activities;

-- Aid to lighten the burden of external aid contracted for financing unproductive projects as well as excess public and private consumption.

In the Sahel, co-operation has become political and humanitarian, in other words survival co-operation, and it can be safely asserted that aid could achieve far more with fewer means.

But what are the prerequisites?

-- First a change in the mentality, behaviour and attitudes of the Sahelians and their governments, since external co-operation can only be a response to demand by the Sahelian communities. It can only provide support for implementing the wishes of these communities. These must tend towards redefining the role and tasks of government, decentralisation of political power and freedom of organisation of the population;

-- And then a change in the mentality, behaviour and attitude of external aid agencies. Do they wish to promote structural changes in the Sahel or are they easily satisfied with its growing dependence?

A COMMENT FROM A GLOBAL POINT OF VIEW

by

Ferdinand VAN DAM

International economic structures are rapidly changing: Europe is progressing towards integration, the EC and the Council for Mutual Economic Assistance (CMEA) have decided to hold negotiations, Brazil and Argentina have agreed to set up a common market, Japan and the United States are considering a free trade agreement, and these are but a few examples. Everybody is preparing to take these innovations in their stride: companies are merging, government ministries are opening information desks and fees for admission to conferences devoted to the subject are rising exponentially.

All this will have considerable consequences for developing countries and will to a large extent determine their future position in the world economy. However, this seems to have escaped the notice of the politicians who are concerned with development, both inside and outside parliaments. When vague discussions took place 10 years ago on the subject of a possible new international economic order they were falling over one another to show the greatest concern and declare their support. Now that something is really happening to the economic structures of the world they are almost all as silent as the grave.

Various questions may be asked in the light of the changes which are now taking place in international economic relations. What forces are causing them? What shape will the new order have? Finally, what does it all mean for the position of developing countries?

CAUSES OF CHANGE

In recent decades a number of related trends have become visible, including a decrease in the growth of trade and the formation of economic blocs; the first steps have also been taken towards the conclusion of trade agreements between different blocs. A number of factors have contributed towards these trends (1).

Firstly, the location of production and the location of consumption are increasingly one and the same. This is caused primarily by changes in production processes. For example, in many sectors of industry wage costs now constitute a

276

smaller part of total production costs. This means that for the industries concerned it is not longer profitable to move production to low-wage countries; many companies are therefore returning production to the industrialised countries. Ohmae estimates that average wage costs in western industrialised countries have fallen from around 25 per cent of total costs ten years ago to between 5 and 10 per cent today (2). Drucker cites as examples the smaller integrated steel plants in the United States where wage costs have been reduced to ten percent and the larger textile factories where they have dropped to between ten and twelve percent (3).

An additional factor is that the application of improved technology has considerably reduced the use of raw materials per production unit. In the metal industry it has been halved in many cases. This means that there is no longer so much to be gained by processing raw materials at the primary production site.

Finally, aspects such as design, servicing and marketing have become increasingly important in today's competitive world. Such activities can best be undertaken in the place of consumption, so again production and consumption can best be located together.

Secondly, the continuation of the traditional pattern of the international division of labour and the concomitant international trade presents problems. The traditional division of labour came about in the colonial era and has continued *de facto* since de-colonisation. Seers asserts that the maintenance of this pattern costs too much in terms of aid, uncollectable debts, unprofitable investments and a military presence (4). Just as the colonial system was abandoned because of the heavy financial burden it entailed, so he believes the neo-colonial system will have to be relinquished. A number of actual developments support Seers' assertion: the volume of aid is no longer increasing, fewer commercial loans are being made to developing countries and there has been a drop in private investment in those countries too.

Seers relates his views to the United Kingdom in particular and advocates abandoning the links with former British colonies in favour of greater alignment with the EC. He also believes this is necessary because of the increasing competition faced by western industrialised countries from exports of industrial products from the the Third World, against which the West has only been able to protect itself by forming blocs protected by external tariffs or other trade barriers.

The notion of the neo-colonial division of labour was replaced in the seventies by that of interdependence, with which it is synonymous. The idea was that rich and poor countries would all benefit from increasing specialisation of production and trade. They would become mutually dependent, the Third World's constituting a major market for the rich countries' high technology products.

This dream was spoilt by two things. First, it soon became clear that developing countries were able to develop their own high technology products much more rapidly than had been anticipated. China, for example, is now launching commercial satellites into space for developed countries, for which it charges a great deal of money. Secondly, the debts of the developing countries have increased considerably, particularly since 1975. These debts compel many developing countries to use most of their export earnings to pay interest and repay loans. This means that they must reduce their imports, thus putting an end to the ideal of interdependence which had been propagated by the OECD.

Thirdly, serious doubts have arisen as to whether maximum economic growth can be achieved only by outward-looking trade policies. In discussions on the choice between inward-looking and outward-looking policies the emphasis has shifted from opting in favour of one or the other to establishing criteria for an optimal combination -- different for each country -- of production for export and production for domestic consumption. This can mean that countries such as Taiwan and Singapore benefit from labour-intensive production for export while China and Brazil have to gear their production capacity primarily to the domestic market. Countries and economic blocs with a population of 200 million or more flourish perfectly well on the basis of a largely autarkic economy. Furthermore, it is not possible for large numbers of countries to adopt the development strategy followed by the countries of eastern Asia, simply because demand on the world market would be insufficient to absorb the resulting flow of labour-intensive export products.

Fourth, there are a number of reasons why the markets for exportable goods will grow more slowly in the future. In this connection it is important to note that the world economy is now growing at a rate far below that of the period 1950-80. It is very much open to question whether the growth rate will eventually increase again because in historical terms today's rate can be regarded as "normal" and that of 1950-80 as exceptionally high.

An additional factor is that the population of the rich countries is hardly increasing at all; indeed population figures are expected to fall in the next few decades in a number of European countries. This will not only affect the size of the market but also the nature of the goods required. Zero population growth is accompanied by aging of the population and an elderly population is likely to devote additional spending power to non-importable services rather than to industrial products.

The final factor affecting the future size of markets is the agreement reached by the United States and the EC to limit agricultural overproduction. This should result in higher international prices for agricultural products which will stimulate production in developing countries; this will in turn mean that the latter will import proportionately less.

Fifth, a need has arisen for greater control of changes in international economic patterns. Such modifications result from the rapid changes in production processes and the mobility of the factors of production. The rate of change has partly increased because of the fact that recent technological developments are more application-oriented. This means that new technologies can be incorporated into production processes in a fraction of the time which would have been required 20 years ago (5).

These changes in pace lead to the rapid relocation of production processes, with the resulting loss of capital and increase in unemployment. The latter is a particular problem in Europe because labour is traditionally not very mobile. These developments cannot be controlled or their speed reduced worldwide, because the necessary instruments do not exist. Control through trade barriers in particular can only be achieved at national level or by economic blocs.

NEW PATTERNS

What will the new pattern of international economic structures look like? Until recently it was difficult to give a sensible answer to this question because few definite steps had been taken. The last two years have seen a radical change in this respect. Things are taking clear shape now as regards both the formation of blocs and the conclusion of interbloc agreements.

There are seven relevant blocs, each comprising either several countries or a single, very large country.

North America

Discussions have been going on for a number of years in the United States about the desirability of forming a free trade zone with Canada and Mexico. The first concrete steps were taken in 1987 with the conclusion of a far-reaching trade agreement with Canada and a more limited agreement with Mexico. Economic integration of the three countries would appear to be an obvious step in the long term: together the three countries occupy the whole of the North American continent, they have long common frontiers and there is already *de facto* integration. With regard to the latter, the majority of Canadians live near the border with the United States and the Canadian economy is geared increasingly to the needs of its larger neighbour: 80 per cent of Canadian exports now go to this market. The results of recent parliamentary elections in Canada have secured acceptance of the free trade agreement. The relationship with Mexico is more complicated. On the one hand there are close economic links with the United States, but on the other there is friction, largely in connection with such matters as migration, debts and drug trafficking. It is difficult to solve these problems on an interstate basis and would perhaps be easier in an intrastate framework. Dr. Henry Kissinger said recently: "The issues that we face in Mexico are almost all domestic in character" (6). Further economic cooperation between the United States and Mexico would appear to be probable. George Bush advocated a free trade agreement during his presidential election campaign. The new Mexican President, Carlos Salinas de Gortari, is acting cautiously: he will prevent US domination and is seeking to relate a trade agreement to debt relief.

South America

The nucleus of economic integration in South America is formed by the accords concluded between Brazil and Argentina in 1986 and further elaborated in May, July and November 1987. The accords are contained in twelve protocols aimed at the liberalisation of trade, measures to promote investment and binational businesses and a common policy on energy, biotechnology and aircraft-construction. In 1988, Uruguay, which lies between the two countries, also acceded to the accords. During an evaluation in April 1988 it was established that implementation was proceeding slowly and decided that they should be upgraded and given the status of conventions. Additional agreements have also been made to liberalise freight transport. In November, Brazil, Argentina and Uruguay agreed to achieve full economic integration by the year 2000. Besides the conventions involving Brazil, Argentina and Uruguay a trade accord was concluded in July 1988 between eleven Latin American countries -- the three already mentioned, plus Mexico, Chile, Colombia, Venezuela, Peru, Bolivia, Ecuador and Paraguay. The accord covers trade in goods, currently valued at $8 billion, for which the countries concerned have agreed to reduce tariffs.

Europe

The EC is endeavouring to liberalise economic transactions completely by 1992.

CMEA

In 1987 the CMEA adopted a working programme which provided for further economic integration of the member states. Given the current unpredictable developments in the Eastern bloc it is difficult to estimate the extent to which it will be successful and the speed at which progress will be made towards this objective.

China

The report "Discriminate Deterrence" which was drawn up in January 1988 by the Pentagon states that it is expected that in 20 years' time China's economy will be the third largest in the world, after those of the United States and Japan (7). Under the terms of the treaty with the United Kingdom, Hong Kong will become part of China in 1995. China also claims sovereignty over Taiwan. It is unclear whether this claim will ever be realised and if so, when.

India

Although growing less rapidly than China, India is developing into a major economy on account of its large population, the surmounting of its food production problems and the gradual setting in motion of industrialisation.

Japan

Besides the above there are a number of developing countries with economies of some importance with regard to which it is unclear whether they will seek to join an existing bloc, form blocs of their own or continue to operate on their own. For example, Turkey and Morocco have repeatedly expressed a desire to join the EC.

It is equally unclear what the pattern in East Asia will be in the years to come. In 1967 ASEAN (the Association of South-East Asian nations) was set up by a number of rapidly developing countries with the intention of achieving a certain degree of economic co-operation. Few results have as yet been forthcoming. Membership is limited to the southern countries of East Asia (Indonesia, Malaysia, Singapore, Thailand and the Philippines) which do not complement each other very well in economic terms; as a result there is no basis for practical integration. Indonesia occupies a special place within the ASEAN group because of its size and population growth. It is estimated that its population will number 340 million by the year 2005, after which it will stabilise (8).

Japan's future role in East Asia is uncertain. Since Mr. Takeshita became prime minister the country has repeatedly put itself forward as a spokesperson for the region (9). It is not clear whether this will have any economic consequences. In the meantime trade between Japan and the other countries of East Asia is increasing rapidly. The growth of imports into Japan from Korea, Taiwan, Hong Kong and Singapore has increased from 27 to 50 per cent in the last two years. Korea now imports more from Japan than from any other country and Japan is Korea's second largest export market, after the United States.

THE CONCLUSION OF INTERBLOC AGREEMENTS

In 1988 a new phenomenon has made an appearance; this involves the conclusion of agreements between existing blocs. Such agreements differ in nature and intensiveness but all of them aim to limit or prevent economic conflict between the blocs concerned and to enable them to benefit from each other's markets and production factors. The most important steps which have been taken so far are described below.

The United States and Japan

There has been conflict between Japan and the United States for many years, Japan's being accused of dumping goods on the American market while keeping its own market too closed. After long negotiations bilateral agreements have been concluded between the two countries on such subjects as trade in agricultural products and semiconductors and access for the United States to the Japanese construction market. At the beginning of the eighties it began to be felt that the two countries should set up an economic partnership, as Mansfield called it (10). The reasoning behind this is that economic conflicts are damaging and risky for both parties, that negotiations for each individual market take too long, that Japan and the United States both have to cope with an increasingly protectionist EC, that a number of topics can best be dealt with as part of a package (non-tariff friction, movement of capital, intellectual property rights) and that therefore a more general form of co-operation must be sought. In January 1988 the idea of a Japanese-American free trade agreement was given new momentum during Mr. Takeshita's visit to Washington. It was agreed that both governments would conduct a study of the advantages and disadvantages. In Tokyo this is being done by the Ministry of Finance and the Ministry of Trade and Industry and in the United States by the International Trade Commission. The proposal for co-operation has in recent months obtained the support of Henry Kissinger and Cyrus Vance (11). James Baker, who has little faith in the Uruguay Round, also advocates bilateral agreements with the United States' major trading partners. George Bush has pledged support in vague terms for an agreement with Japan.

The EC and the CMEA

After ignoring each other for decades, a declaration was signed on 27th June 1988 in which the two organisations officially recognised each other's existence. On 26th July, the EC ministers announced that they were in favour of talks with the Soviet Union about an economic accord after Moscow had indicated that it would like to conclude a far-reaching economic and technological cooperation agreement with the EC. Talks started at the beginning of November. In recent months German, Italian, French and Dutch banks have promised the Soviet Union some $11 billion in loans.

Japan and China

On 29th August 1988, after eight years of negotiation, Japan and China concluded an accord on investment protection. Under its terms Japanese investments in China will be treated in the same way as those by Chinese companies. None of the investment accords which China has previously concluded has gone so far. Japan is already China's most important trading partner (apart from Hong Kong) and provider of capital. Japanese investments in China have lagged behind in comparison. Japan has provided a loan of $6.5 billion to China to finance infrastructural projects in the framework of the investment accord.

THE POSITION OF DEVELOPING COUNTRIES

The question is what effect the formation of blocs and the growing tendency to conclude interbloc agreements will have on the position of developing countries. In concrete terms, how will their export opportunities and their chances of attracting investment be affected?

The factors which give rise to the formation of blocs -- production at the place of consumption, the abandonment of traditional patterns of division of labour, the adoption of more autarkic policies by large countries, slow market growth and the need for controllability -- by their very nature all have a negative effect on the exports of third countries. The same can be said of the formation of blocs as such. Free internal trade protected by external tariffs or other trade barriers encourages production within the bloc. Furthermore, the process of integration will inevitably lead to protectionism beyond that of which an individual member would be capable. After all, in order to achieve integration the member states must agree about such matters as the level of external tariffs and environmental criteria and there will always be a tendency to adopt the tariff or the standard of the member state with the most stringent requirements.

Integration is difficult to achieve, not only economically but also from the legal, social and political point of view. As a result those involved are likely to become inward-looking. If aid is to be provided or preferential measures taken, these are likely primarily to benefit the economically least developed member states of the bloc itself. In the EC this means Ireland, Portugal and Greece. As a result the Third World is lost from view.

The conclusion of interbloc agreements, which in fact amounts to a further increase in the size of blocs, will only intensify these factors and increase the negative effects they have on the export opportunities of third countries.

The formation of blocs also makes it harder for third countries to attract investment. The seven blocs listed above (disregarding the potential expansion of the Latin American bloc from 3 countries to 11) account for approximately 90 per cent of total gross world income. This means that the markets lie within the blocs, which will therefore attract the capital which is available for investment. The remaining ten percent is concentrated largely in a small number of countries which are not part of any bloc (Indonesia, Turkey, South Africa, Korea, Saudi Arabia and some European countries), which means that little is left for investment in the developing countries which remain.

It should be noted that counter-forces and frictions do exist. For example, the slow rate of economic growth, the levelling off of population growth and the aging of the population in Europe and the United States (and to a certain extent in Japan too) will mean that markets will expand less in the future. A further factor is that India, China and the CMEA have a structural lack of capital and will have to import capital from third countries.

The conclusion of interbloc agreements provides, as it were, a made-to-measure solution to this kind of counter-force and problem. An agreement between the EC and the CMEA means linking EC capital and EC technology to CMEA markets and raw materials. The same applies to links between Japan and China. The natural consequence is that the conclusion of interbloc agreements further reduces the opportunities third countries have to attract investment.

To return to the question of what all this means for developing countries, it is convenient to divide such countries into four categories.

The first group comprises the very large countries which constitute a "bloc" on their own, such as India and China, and developing countries which form part of a bloc, primarily Argentina, Brazil and Uruguay in the South American bloc and Mexico in the North American bloc. All these countries have a measure of protection and benefit from the formation of blocs as do all other members of blocs.

The second group comprises developing countries which are not full members of a bloc but have increasing links with one. In South America these are the eight countries which have taken the first steps toward a free trade agreement together with Argentina, Brazil and Uruguay. These are potentially "protected" countries.

The third group comprises countries which maintain links with blocs which are largely one-sided, for example the numerous developing countries which have association agreements with the EC. These are one-sided because the EC may unilaterally limit or terminate the free access of products from the associated countries if they are competing too strongly with the EC's own products. One consequence of this is that the volume and structure of exports from the associated countries to the EC have hardly changed since the association agreement was concluded.

The fourth group comprises countries which have no links with blocs. Some are doing very well, such as Korea and Indonesia, but the majority are in deep trouble, such as Bangladesh, Burma and many African countries.

From the point of view of the development issue the formation of blocs and the conclusion of interbloc agreements is a threat to the third and fourth groups of developing countries, which together have a population of about 1.5 billion people, about 30 per cent of the world's population. For that reason Prince Claus of the Netherlands has advocated that the GATT Uruguay Round should formulate standards and criteria for the formation of blocs as such and for trade between blocs and between countries not linked to a bloc in order to secure the position of countries in categories three and four (12).

Prince Claus spoke on the subject in March 1988. Since then the formation of blocs and the conclusion of interbloc agreements have gained momentum, whereas it seems likely that the Uruguay Round will take years. Standards and criteria which may be formulated in the course of it may therefore come too late. It would be preferable if the blocs and the individual countries concerned took the consequences for the third and fourth groups of developing countries into account from the beginning, and if this could also be done in concluding interbloc agreements. If this is not done these countries will become structurally marginalised and this will severely damage their development prospects.

NOTES AND REFERENCES

1. Trade figures: *World Development Report 1988*.

2. OHMAE, K., *Triad*, Veen Utrecht, 1985, p. 19.

3. DRUCKER, P.F. "The Changed World Economy", *Foreign Affairs*, vol. 64, No. 4, 1986, p. 768.

4. SEERS, D. "Wanted -- A New Map of the World", and "A Different Kind of Fortress Mentality", *The Guardian*, 28th May and 16th July 1982.

5. OHMAE, *op. cit.*, p. 24.

6. KISSINGER, H., VANCE, C. "An agenda for 1988", *Newsweek*, 6th June 1988, p. 17.

7. FITCHETT, "China seen as a new economic power", *International Herald Tribune*, 13 January 1988.

8. World Bank, *World Development Report 1988*, Oxford Unversity Press, 1988, p. 274.

9. RICHARDSON, M., SMITH, P.L., "Japan, changing image, moves into role as Asia's advocate", *International Herald Tribune*, 27 June 1988; BURGER, W., "Japan reaches out", *Newsweek*, 12th September 1988.

10. FARNSWORTH, C.H. "Idea of US-Japan Accord on Free Trade Gains", *International Herald Tribune*, 16th August 1988.

11. *Idem.*

12. Address by Prince Claus on 25th March 1988 in New Delhi at the General Conference of the Society for International Development.

Chapter VIII

DEVELOPMENT AT THE CROSSROADS

HUMAN RESOURCES AND THE CULTURAL DIMENSION

by

Federico MAYOR

I must confess that I hesitated before accepting the kind invitation to address the specific issue "human resources and the cultural dimension of development". Discussing such apparently "soft" issues as culture and human development within the OECD Development Centre, the recognised powerhouse of "hard" economics, implies taking a risk. It was only after reading the very excellent and balanced papers contributed to the Symposium by some of the most outstanding international development and financial specialists, that I was encouraged to take this risk and accept the invitation. Economists, "die-hard" as they are -- and have to be -- in matters of international finance, have gradually become more sensitive to the views of other social scientists when it comes to enriching the dialogue on international development.

The international development community, at the crossroads of intellectual and development co-operation between the industrialised and the developing world, will need to do more in the urgent task of clarifying and operationalising the contributions which human and cultural resources can make to solving the two major issues before us: the growing marginalisation of one quarter of the world's population and the need for converging international policies to assist poor countries in achieving equitable and sustainable development; and the requirements for both developed and developing countries to find more intelligent human responses to the global environmental changes we have unleashed. For this we need to combine imagination, political will and resources. One of the reasons why this has not yet happened can possibly be explained by the fact that the emergence of a less economistic and a more diversified and balanced view of the development challenge is of rather recent origin. It was only in 1985 that the World Bank published its authoritative and very promising book *Putting people first* (1).

Two years later in 1987, UNICEF followed with its often-quoted report *Adjustment With a Human Face: Protecting the Vulnerable and Promoting Growth* (2). Since then, there have been many statements -- including from the international financing agencies -- to support this change in emphasis in the development dialogue. Allow me to quote, in this connection, Mr. Conable, President of the World Bank, who in a recent statement affirmed that "development, in the final analysis, is about human aspirations and the individual's realisation of his or her potential, and (that) poverty, which is at the centre of the development drama, and

289

which destroys lives, human dignity and economic potential, must be fought with resolution and overcome with sustainable growth".

Going in the same direction is the continuing, but still inconclusive, debate within the United Nations family in the framework of preparing the international development strategy for the Fourth United Nations Development Decade. A consensus regarding a balanced mix of priorities which include human resource development, the global fight against poverty and sustainable economic growth of a new quality is being eagerly awaited.

It is important to focus on the issue of human and cultural development within the context of poverty in both the developing and within the relatively well-off nations. In many of the poorest countries, the repercussions of the economic and financial crises on the vulnerable individual can no longer be easily defined in terms of an interruption in development. They have taken on the dimensions of a "disaster", a set of events which outstrip an individual's, a family's or a society's capacity to cope with them. Poor people everywhere have always understood that economic progress tends to benefit others and to leave them more vulnerable than before to forces they cannot always identify, let alone control. It is our belated recognition of this tragic outcome that now promotes traditional values and the cultural dimensions of development to more prominent places in the development debate. Can any human community, however, preserve the cultural values essential to its identity and integrity while changing its social conditions to improve the quality of life of its people? In UNESCO, we have learned from experience that it is mainly through improving the relevance and quality of learning processes that we can assist children and adults in reducing their vulnerability to crisis. Human resource development should therefore focus on widening the opportunities for quality formal and non-formal education and training, enabling children to "leap" from survival to mastery over immediate want and, eventually, to adulthood and citizenship with the capacity to solve problems, to act autonomously and to hold public agencies and private entrepreneurs accountable for their uses of society's resources.

While the renewed international policy dialogue on the importance of learning as a major impulse for human and cultural development provides a beginning of hope for the long-term, in the short-term, observable trends in the sociocultural sectors remain a major cause of concern. The economic crisis and structural adjustment policies adopted in an increasing number of countries have often had a proven negative impact on the financial and material resources available for the social sectors, including education, and on the fate of the poor.

The short-term human and social costs of these trends are already becoming clearly visible while their serious detrimental effects on the future potential for the indigenous development and self-sustained economic growth of developing countries may well prove to be irreversible.

Adjustment policies have often resulted in a decrease in the resources available for human development as agriculture, technology, environment and economic infrastructure have replaced education and other social sectors as a focus of more immediate concern by governments and aid agencies. In periods of financial crisis, long-term social and human issues have lost out to more immediate economic and productive investments in job-related training. This is confirmed by UNESCO statistics which show that primary education has, during the first half of the 1980s, taken a turn for the worse in many developing countries. Even when primary school enrolments continue to grow -- generally still the case -- progress towards universal primary education can no longer be taken for granted. Worse still, the financial resource base for paying teachers and maintaining the quality of educational services is becoming increasingly precarious. These problems seem to affect not just the poorest and "Least Developed Countries", but many better-off countries as well. It seems no longer possible to uphold the credo of the 1960s and 1970s that all developing countries are firmly set on the course towards full primary education for all. On the contrary, a determined international effort will be needed to cope with the educational fallout of the economic crisis and of adjustment policies, and to help developing countries regain the educational momentum they have lost. UNESCO, the World Bank, UNICEF and UNDP, have just adopted a joint strategy and programme of action in the fields of primary education and literacy in response to and in support of national and local initiatives in this area.

The strategy, which will become fully operational in 1990, is being conceived within the wider framework of an increase in social concern among the financing agencies. In designing the joint plan of action, it is not realistic to expect that compensatory social and educational development programmes will succeed in counterbalancing the negative social and human impact fully. Investment in the non-economic sectors and in the capabilities of the poor should therefore not be seen merely as mitigating the social cost of adjustment, but as an effective and priority area for a new quality of sustainable growth in purely economic productivity terms.

Convincing the economic decision-makers will not be easy. The recognition that expenditures on human resources development are not only necessary in themselves and go to the very heart of development, but that they also yield essential returns of an economic nature, has not yet been fully incorporated into economic development planning, nor into analyses of the allocation of increasingly scarce resources available to the social sectors. Such considerations will need to be integrated into the main streams of social science research and its application to development.

A few words are in order here on UNESCO's attempts to link its work in the area of development studies and co-operation with its constitutional mandate in the fields of culture, and the creation and dissemination of knowledge.

The question of how civilisations can be advanced through a better interlocking of culture and economics is the central issue of cultural development today, both in the industrialised and in the developing countries. Economics has no meaning except as a dynamic contribution to and beneficiary of culture.

Like biological organisms, cultural value systems are not static, they must constantly assimilate change and adapt to new circumstances. Cultural values, networks of meaning, loyalties and patterns of living should define what are the proper ends and the suitable means of development and not be manipulated by planners as aids or obstacles to achieving development goals modelled on those of industrialised societies. Ultimately, both economic and social development represent means to a larger end: the fostering of human fulfilment resting on a secure sense of cultural integrity.

The slogan "poverty anywhere is a menace to prosperity everywhere" is just as true, whether it be applied to cultural or to economic poverty. The present conditions of the international system are causing people in the developing countries to become not only poorer in economic resources and in knowledge, but also poorer in the self-confidence and self-respect with which they could continue to create knowledge. Mobilisation, self-reliance and initiatives for poverty alleviation have therefore to be backed by confidence in what people already know and have already learned to do. This is why the focus on culture and on the preservation of people's knowledge is central in the fight against poverty. The equivalent of the loss of genetic diversity and of species due to the destruction of natural habitats is, in the realm of human development, the loss of the diversity of knowledge, of the capacity to create new knowledge and of cultural traditions.

For this we must encourage governments to work closer with people's and grassroots movements and citizens' organisations with a view to exploring the role of cultural value systems and collective behaviour in shaping the preferences and the directions of resource management of communities confronted with the consequences of externally inspired models of modernisation.

As an international agency we must also face the challenge of lifting the focus of the discussions from the project level to the policy level, graduating from grassroots experiences all the way to ministerial levels, while preserving the positive human values underlying people's participation in small-scale projects. As Johann Galtung has so wisely remarked: "While small is beautiful, some big is necessary".

In our efforts to support the new paradigm of social justice, to reverse the increasing gap between the "two humanities" -- the rich and the poor -- and to reduce the distance between the "two cultures" -- human capital and human potential -- the role of the distribution of knowledge and information and of the nature of knowledge networks in decision making has often been neglected. New technology and new data handling techniques seem further to bind the users to the international knowledge and research system dominated by the industrialised nations, and to block knowledge from the non-metropolitan systems from reaching end-users. The distances between the centres and peripheries of knowledge seem to be widening. The world of information, knowledge research and publications is unequal, and a recognition of these inequalities as an integral part of the human gap is necessary.

I am fully conscious of the fact that, in the international response to the "frontier" issues in human resources development, economics has tended to dominate culture, despite the fact that the international consensus of scholars and the

292

ethical vision of diplomats regarding social and cultural priorities is often the reverse. Nonetheless, I also have reason to remain optimistic.

Views on the importance of fostering human creativity and potential are converging between governments and development specialists entrusted with the preparation for the new International Development Strategy. They also accord well with the objectives of the World Decade for Cultural Development which started in 1988 and in which UNESCO is the lead agency.

We can observe a consensus emerging among scholars that development ethics, ecological wisdom and insights into the rich diversity of cultural potential must go together; otherwise, there is no future for development. We should search jointly for ways and means of integrating this conviction into national and international decision-making processes.

Finding an international response to the growing dualism in world economic development is hampered by the fact that we have not yet completely understood how our collective resources, knowledge and cultural values can be mobilised for new forms of management and action. Promising international trends which can support such a response are basically known: new technologies offer prospects of an international division of labour and a pattern of exchange of goods and services which can lead to a more equitable global distribution of income and employment; the intensified cultural interaction among nations and the increasing international mobility of people have resulted in more creative, multicultural societies which could form the basis for greater international human solidarity. Still, the gap between our increased understanding of the inter-relatedness of the real world and existing national development strategies seems to be wide indeed. While we have made progress in creating a holistic vision regarding the contemporary human crisis, we still lack the organisational capabilities we need to define the interlinked nature of the solutions and projecting the paths out of this crisis.

While institutions like ours are needed to give a forum to all peoples for mutual education, for sharing of experiences, for airing different views and for formulating new norms of international behaviour, we risk becoming marginalised if that global function is confused with the capacity to manage and act. For this we must bring the main non-governmental forces: the international scientific community, religious and cultural movements and the private sector -- the belatedly recognised major actors in real international relations -- into the international decision-making processes in ways that reflect their real role. This presents a major challenge in terms of imaginative organisation, creative management and new partnerships. It also implies new international income streams and transfers which, in terms of magnitude, need to go far beyond existing forms of official development assistance and multilateral co-operation.

This brings us to the last issue on the agenda of the symposium. How can international organisations assume an expanded role in times when global and international factors are becoming more and more important, while financial resources are stagnating or declining? A partial answer to this question relates directly to the future relations between the OECD and UNESCO in matters of intellectual and development co-operation. While the past record of co-operation between our two agencies has been professionally respectable, it has been rather modest in scope, mainly the *ad hoc* initiatives of professional staff in our two agencies. The challenge before us now is: how can the "whole" of our co-operation in the future become bigger than the sum of its component parts, so that jointly, we can have a more visible impact on development trends in poor countries.

Let me put it a different way. If, indeed, the views of the symposium were to go in the direction of strengthening the links between the Development Centre's work and the activities of other parts of the OECD, as has been suggested by Dr. Emmerij in his introductory paper, then this would provide a unique opportunity for the OECD and UNESCO to strengthen their mutual co-operation with Member States within a more comprehensive framework.

If such an initiative were to materialise, it could provide a much needed concrete example to the world of how the rhetorics about human development and about rethinking international co-operation and international governance can, through the convergence of technological, political and ethical notions of rationality, be translated into more flexible, sensitive arrangements for national and international decision making in matters of development. The combined knowledge and wisdom in matters of development accumulated by the two Organisations for over more than four decades should make it possible to arrive jointly at technically sound development strategies which are politically feasible and morally acceptable, and at ethically sound development investment choices which are technically efficient and politically possible. This is the gauntlet thrown down for future international co-operation. I look forward to picking it up with you.

DEVELOPMENT AT A MAJOR TURNING POINT IN TIME

by

Jacques LESOURNE

It is extremely difficult to sum up in a few pages -- from one of the many possible angles -- a symposium so ambitious in scope, so varied in content, and so enriching in terms of the quality of the papers and discussions. All the more so, since the underlying question is one of life and death for human beings and since in any talk of development, the sweeping comments which reduce a global process to a single dimension must be avoided at all costs.

Somewhat arbitrarily, I shall place the subjects discussed under four main headings: a major turning point, the diversity of development, policies in the 1990s, and ethical issues.

A MAJOR TURNING POINT

Despite the differences in terminology, most of the statements reflected the same conviction on the part of all the participants that humanity was at a turning point, as evidenced by:

-- The rise in the world's population from 5 billion at present to 10 to 12 billion by the middle of the next century.

-- The migrations to the urban capitals of the South and to developed countries which will accompany this population increase.

-- The emerging changes in man's relationship with the ecosphere.

-- The globalisation of the world economy, which does not simply mean growth in international trade, but also the expansion of many kinds of interlinking systems and the appearance of so many new actors on the transnational scene.

-- The gradual replacement of yesterday's strategic bipolarity and economic monopolarity world by a multipolar world in which the power structures are more difficult to describe.

Whatever benefits they may bring in the long term, these changes obviously raise a number of basic issues:

-- The complexity of the world political and economic situation is such that the intellectual and political elite no longer knows where to turn.

-- The growing interdependence of societies in no way prevents the world from continuing to be a dangerous place, as the various countries are still a potential threat to one another.

-- The way the world is organised politically, with governments that are too small to tackle big problems, does not permit the emergence of a real steering system, since intergovernmental co-operation can develop only slowly. In particular, the political leaders in democracies, lobbied on all sides, have very little room for manoeuvre and take into account the impact of their decisions on the rest of the world only if the resistance of public opinion in their own countries is not too strong. (On this point, it seems to me that policy decision mechanisms in developed countries received far too little attention at the symposium, given that the appreciation of world problems by their citizens is to be a prior requirement for a change in the policies of these countries.)

-- Multipolarity gives rise to various forms of regional organisation, but while some do not believe that this trend can lead to generalised protectionism, others fear that it may contribute to a split-up in the world economy, perhaps into three areas centred on the United States, the European Community and East Asia, or into two areas, with one centred on the Pacific including Japan, South East Asia, China and the Americas, and the other grouping Africa, West Asia and the Indian continent around Eastern and Western Europe. The question remains open. However, I consider that the additional factors must be borne in mind: first, the future of *perestroika* in the USSR is still extremely uncertain; and second, the European Community can adopt only a compromise -- and, therefore, reasonably open -- trade policy, while at the same time the unification of its market will facilitate its penetration by non-Community firms.

In this context, how is the Third World's performance to be judged? Opinions on this subject varied widely from one participant to another as a result of a twofold complexity of the Third World:

-- An all-round complexity making the existence of malnutrition, poverty, despair and violence compatible with the fact that never in the history of mankind have the lives of so many human beings changed so much and so fast, as reflected in the dramatic climb of social indicators recalled by R. Jolly;

-- A geographical complexity in which countries with rapid economic growth co-exist with others where per capita income is stagnating and

296

even declining, with consequently an increasingly greater divide between various Third Worlds which are, moreover, rediscovering their historical roots.

These findings and these questions concerning the long term should not overshadow the major imbalances affecting the world economy as it enters the next decade: the United States balance-of-payments deficit, the Japanese surplus and that of the newly industrialising economies, and Latin America's and Africa's debt. These imbalances were referred to throughout the symposium, but three remarks concerning them seem necessary in the first part of this synopsis:

-- If we believe at all in the significance of prices as indicators of the relative scarcity of resources, we cannot but worry about the microeconomic effects of macroeconomic imbalances. Choices by economic agents are guided by three series of basic prices: exchange rates, real interest rates and the wage costs of various skills. These prices tend to be deflected from their true values in many ways: i) with the exception of the United States because of the dollar's status, any balance-of-payments deficit subjects a country to external pressures, while a surplus reflects gains in market shares and purchases of assets abroad; ii) the present debt of certain countries -- particularly in Latin America -- is partly due to the poor internal allocation of available capital in the period when it was possible to borrow abroad at a real negative interest rate; iii) the various kinds of rigidity on labour markets -- in Europe but also in certain Third World countries -- contribute to the creation of "classical" unemployment and to preventing the maintenance or development of certain economic activities in these countries.

-- Noting the current level of surpluses, Saburo Okita and other speakers proposed the creation of a programme for the transfer of public and private capital to developing countries, but, in the case of private funds, guarantees seem necessary for risks to be reduced and subsidies desirable for the return on capital to be improved.

-- Finally, what are the conceivable scenarios for world macroeconomic trends over the next decade? The projections generally suggest either a soft landing with a gradual reduction in imbalances, or the development of moderate protectionism starting with some control of imports in the United States. A third scenario, however, seems conceivable: since the start of the 1970s the world economy has experienced a series of major fluctuations in which each imbalance has been eliminated by governments or markets only at the cost of a new imbalance in the same or in another field. There is nothing to preclude such a possibility in the future with, for example, a sharp fall of the dollar.

As for the Third World's debt, the problem will be discussed in the second part of this synopsis below.

THE DIVERSITY OF DEVELOPMENT

Economists, historians, sociologists, administrators, politicians and philosophers have been thinking for decades about development. Yet how fragile are our certainties. Even if it is agreed, as was the case at the Symposium, that development is a global process which can in no way be reduced to a single dimension (the economic, for example), and still less be explained on the basis of a single discipline.

At this stage, therefore, a few comments on the symposium discussions would be in order:

-- On the subject of development, extrapolations are dangerous, especially in the absence of in-depth analyses. Consider Argentina, which at the start of this century was the most developed country in Latin America, or Iran which 15 years ago was considered by some to be on the threshold of a major industrial advance. Decline and takeoff often appear rooted in the distant past. A European could hardly overlook the case of Spain which marked time from 1700 to 1950 before making a powerful comeback in the last quarter of the century. Joseph Ki Zerbo was right to mention in this respect that sub-Saharan Africa probably started to fall behind around the 15th century.

-- Relatively little can be done to speed up development unless social conditions are right. Luigi Coccioli said that Italy's tremendous effort for the Mezzogiorno succeeded in raising per capita income in the South from only 53 to 58 per cent of the figure for the North. Conversely, if the Marshall Plan was successful, it was probably because the human basis for reconstruction in Europe was there.

-- We thus have to be wary of the latest fads in the development field. They are frequently transformed into simplistic and extremist ideologies which often cruelly mark the life of nations. The current welcome emphasis on markets is no reason for disregarding their shortcomings, and highlighting the weaknesses of the State as a producer must not lead us to overlook the contributions government policies have made to development in certain countries. Conversely, the failure of many attempts to foist doctrinaire socialism irrespective of realities on societies with their own long-standing structures must be acknowledged. There is not just one possible development model, although this does not mean that all models can work.

-- The many roads to development give rise to a crucial question: in an interdependent world shaped by communications networks that tend to standardise aspirations, can the present differences in ways of life and standards of living last? Is convergence not a necessity, whether

298

as a result of an imposed redistribution or as the various countries in turn join the industrial economies' club? In other words, has decoupling or de-linking any meaning? The symposium discussions showed that these questions should be clarified, on at least two points: i) should we not dissociate the final target from the process? In other words, is the process intended to achieve the most rapid convergence the surest path to convergence? Should we or should we not temporarily accept some forms of de-coupling, for example in the case of a region such as sub-Saharan Africa? ii) the concept of decoupling is itself ambiguous, for relations between societies are multidimensional. Very limited trade in goods in no way rules out tourist flows or information transfers. De-coupling may be unintended or intended.

The symposium focused on development in three Third World regions: the newly industrialising economies of East Asia, Central and South America, and sub-Saharan Africa. Regrettably but understandably enough, the programme did not allow much discussion of the problems concerning the two nation continents of China and India, the rest of South Asia and the vast region running from Pakistan to Morocco whose development pattern is so important for the world's equilibrium.

We can never overemphasize what the world owes to the economic progress of East Asia. As stressed by Yung Chul Park, the world economy would be healthier if there were four Singapores, four Hong Kongs, two Taiwans and two South Koreas, but their very success is now placing these countries in a more difficult situation since they are up against competition and sometimes protectionism from developed countries on one side and, on the other, new competitors from the Third World are emerging. Like the OECD countries, they also have to take into account the impact of their economic policies on the rest of the world.

The 1980s have been very hard for South and Central America, but they have not quite cancelled out the effect of development over a number of decades. A new period of growth is therefore conceivable, if the debt problem can be at least partly resolved and if the way in which countries are run is improved enough to eliminate undesirable public expenditure. On this subject Helio Jaguaribe expressed his conviction that solving structural problems required the rallying of "a multi-class, left-of-centre majority able to back social modernisation and development projects based on a socially regulated, free market economy and a social democracy working at maximum efficiency."

The focus was obviously on the case of sub-Saharan Africa. Despite differences in their appraisals, most participants acknowledged that the impact of debt, the collapse in commodity prices and unfavourable environmental conditions were not enough to explain Africa's situation, and that the finger must also be pointed at the power structures and systems of government that had often borrowed more from the colonial period than from earlier political structures. Hence the question of whether we should be patient with or despair of Africa. In the light of the prospective study conducted on the Sahel by the Club of the same name, I would personally opt for patience. New prospects are starting to emerge south of the Sahara, in informal urban economies and in certain rural communities. Young people, particularly women, are behind these initiatives, but it will take time, perhaps a quarter of a century, for society to be really transformed.

It was on the basis of these findings that the symposium then considered the policies of the 1990s.

THE POLICIES OF THE 1990s

To what degree should Utopia and realism be combined in proposals? The first brings about changes in thinking and may some day permit policies that are unacceptable for the time being; however, there is a risk that it will prove counter-productive by creating bottlenecks in the system; it is the merit of the second that the scope for action is fully used, but often with timid and incomplete measures as the outcome.

Understandably hesitating between these two poles, the debate centred first on sub-Saharan Africa and then on the world and the Third World economy.

-- At present, sub-Saharan Africa can scarcely expect inflows of private capital. For a few agricultural commodities, it can hope for agreements between producers that could improve prices. Accordingly the main decisions concern the treatment of debt and the definition of the volume and kind of aid.

Many speakers were in favour of cancelling the African debt, since they considered that it could not be repaid in the foreseeable future.

The range of opinions on aid was wider. Although in any case the formulae for aid clearly had to be reviewed, its ineffectiveness and its misappropriation because of corruption led to some proposals for a reduction. I shall venture my own opinion: in the light of the Sahel prospective study, I greatly fear that Africa's situation will force the developed countries to maintain and even increase the volume of aid for a long time to come, but with a shift in the objective of this development aid towards survival (which would lead in particular to emphasizing infrastructure maintenance).

-- It is more difficult to sum up the relationship between the Third World and the world economy. I have noted somewhat arbitrarily some of the proposals made: i) better co-operation between international institutions and especially the strengthening of these institutions (but can they be strengthened in a world where political power is dispersed among such a large number of centres?); ii) the creation within the United Nations of a Security Council for environmental problems; iii) the co-ordination of industrialised countries' macro-economic policies in order to reduce the imbalances in the world

300

economy; iv) recycling a part of the Japanese and East Asian surpluses to the developing countries; v) measures to reduce the Latin American countries' debt service; vi) the extension of the open trade system on the basis of the GATT; vii) the conclusion of multi-annual development contracts between receiving and donor countries.

However, it does seem that government agreements are not the answer where technology transfers are concerned, since the only efficient vectors are transnational enterprises.

A three-day symposium could hardly be expected to redefine development policies. However, the discussions did make it possible to identify the possible chapter headings for these policies in the 1990s.

Another aspect, however, that of ethical questions at the start of the 21st century, constantly emerged from the discussion.

ETHICAL ISSUES

Ethical problems are as old as the hills, but are now taking a different form.

On one side, technical advances are modifying man's relationship with his own mind, body and family, with other species and with space.

On the other, the globalisation of human history is transforming man's relationship with the ecosphere, creating new ties between successive generations and making us think about the concepts of equity, freedom, participation and international security. Dr. Soedjatmoko aptly quoted André Malraux, "le XXIème siècle sera religieux ou il ne sera pas" (the 21st century will be religious or will come to nothing).

It is not enough merely to acknowledge the ethical dimension. It has to be carefully thought through, for nothing would be more dangerous than a composite ethic which assumed that environmental protection, the fight against poverty and efforts to reduce differences in countries' incomes are necessarily simultaneous operations. Mankind's resources are limited. Choices therefore have to be made, and most often the pursuit of one objective jeopardises the achievement of another. Taking an ethical approach in exploring the various possibilities of using the world's material and human resources to promote development cannot but contribute to greater awareness of planetary problems and to extending the scope of feasible policies. True, it will not make conflicts disappear as if by magic, but the possibilities of co-operation will be better used and compromise more energetically sought.

Annex

PARTICIPANTS

LIST OF PARTICIPANTS
OF THE SYMPOSIUM HELD IN PARIS, 6TH TO 8TH FEBRUARY 1989
TO MARK THE 25TH ANNIVERSARY OF
THE OECD DEVELOPMENT CENTRE

Professor Chinua ACHEBE (Nigeria)
Department of English
University of Nigeria
NSUKKA
Anambra State
Nigeria

Mr. Arne ARNESEN (Norway)
Secretary of State
Ministry of Development Co-operation
BP 8142 Dep
0033 OSLO 1
Norway

Ms. Lourdes ARIZPE (Mexico)
President, International Union of Anthropological and
Ethnological Sciences
Campestre No. 54
MEXICO, DF 01060
Mexico

Dr. Dragoslav AVRAMOVIC (Yugoslavia)
Bank of Credit and Commerce International
1667 K Street NW
WASHINGTON DC 20006
United States

Dr. Bashir BAKRI (Sudan)
Chairman
National Bank of Sudan (Private Bank)
PO Box 1183
KHARTOUM
Sudan

Professor Pierre BAUCHET (France)
Université Paris I
12, rue Pestalozzi
75005 PARIS
France

Mr. Andrew J. BEITH (United Kingdom)
Director
European Office
International Monetary Fund
64-66, avenue d'Iéna
75116 PARIS
France

Mr. Munir BENJENK (Turkey)
73, Cadogan Square
LONDON SW1
United Kingdom

Professor Elliot BERG (United States)
907 Duke Street
ALEXANDRIA, VA 22319
United States

Mr. Yves BERTHELOT (France)
Deputy Secretary General
United Nations Conference on Trade and
Development (UNCTAD)
Palais des Nations
1211 GENEVA 10
Switzerland

Mr. Jean BOISSONNAT (France)
Directeur des Rédactions du Groupe Expansion
25, rue Leblanc
75015 PARIS
France

Professor Colin BRADFORD (United States)
Strategic Planning and Review Department
The World Bank
WASHINGTON DC 20433
United States

Mr. G. Arthur BROWN (Jamaica)
Associate Administrator
UNDP
One UN Plaza
NEW YORK, NY 10017
United States

Professor Luigi COCCIOLI (Italy)
President
Banco di Napoli
Via del Giardino Theodoli
00186 ROME
Italy

Dr. Antonio M. COSTA (Italy)
Director General
Economic and Financial Affairs
Commission of the European Economic Community
Rue de la Loi, 200
1049 BRUSSELS
Belgium

Ambassador Dr. Heinrich-Dietrich DIECKMANN (Germany)
Auswaertiges Amt
Adenauer-Allee
5300 BONN
Federal Republic of Germany

Professor Habib EL MALKI (Morocco)
Université Mohammed V
Department of Economics,
Faculty of Law
BP 721 Avenue des Nations Unies
RABAT
Morocco

Mr. Daan EVERTS (Netherlands)
Executive Secretary
United Nations Capital Development Fund
One United Nations Plaza
NEW YORK, NY 10017
United States

Mr. Altaf GAUHAR (Pakistan)
Secretary-General, Third World Foundation, and
Editor-in-Chief of "South"
New Zealand House
80, Haymarket
LONDON SW1Y 4TS
United Kingdom

Dr. Dharam GHAI (Kenya)
Director
United Nations Research Institute for Social Development
Palais des Nations
1211 GENEVA 10
Switzerland

Ambassador Oddmund GRAHAM (Norway)
Ministry of Foreign Affairs
PO Box 8114, Dep
0032 OSLO 1
Norway

Mr. Patrick GUILLAUMONT (France)
Faculté de Droit et Sciences Economiques
Université de Clermont Ferrand
41, boulevard Gergovia
63002 CLERMONT FERRAND
France

Dr. Mahbub ul HAQ (Pakistan)
Senator
Parliament Building
PO Box 2006
ISLAMABAD
Pakistan

Mr. Kai HELENIUS (Finland)
Under-Secretary of State
Ministry of Foreign Affairs
PL 17600161
HELSINKI
Finland

Mr. Paul-Marc HENRY (France)
Ambassadeur de France
Président
Comité Français contre la Faim, Action pour le Développement
42, rue Cambronne
75015 PARIS
France

Mr. Stéphane HESSEL (France)
Ambassadeur de France
5 rue Alexandre Cabanel
75015 PARIS
France

Ambassador Erich P. HOCHLEITNER (Austria)
Director General for Development Co-operation
Ministry of Foreign Affairs
Ballhausplatz 2
1010 VIENNA
Austria

Professor Goran HYDEN (Sweden)
Department of Political Science
3324 Turlington Hall
University of Florida
GAINESVILLE, FL 32711
United States

Mr. Enrique IGLESIAS (Uruguay)
President
Inter-American Development Bank
1300 New York Avenue NW
WASHINGTON DC 20577
United States

Dr. Helio JAGUARIBE (Brazil)
Decano
Instituto de Estudos Politicos e Socials
R. Barao de Oliveira Castro, 22
Jardim Botanico
RIO DE JANEIRO
Brazil

Dr. Lal JAYAWARDENA (Sri Lanka)
Director
World Institute for Development Economics Research (WIDER)
Annankatu 42 C
00100 HELSINKI
Finland

Professor Dr. Paul R. JOLLES (Switzerland)
Président du Conseil d'Administration
Nestlé SA
1800 VEVEY
Switzerland

Dr. Richard JOLLY (United Kingdom)
Deputy Executive Director -- Programmes
UNICEF
866 United Nations Plaza
NEW YORK NY 10017
United States

Professor Joseph KI ZERBO (Burkina Faso)
President
Centre de Recherche pour le Développement Endogène
BP 3311
DAKAR
Senegal

Dr. Manfred KULESSA (Germany)
Chairman of the Development Policy Forum
Deutsche Stiftung für Internationale Entwicklung (DSE)
Reiherwerder
1000 BERLIN 27
Federal Republic of Germany

Mrs. Bjoerg LEITE (Norway)
Director General
Ministry of Development Co-operation
BP 8142 Dep
0033 OSLO 1
Norway

Professor Jacques LESOURNE (France)
Conservatoire National des Arts et Métiers
292, rue St-Martin
75141 PARIS Cédex 03
France

Ambassador Walther LICHEM (Austria)
Deputy Director General for Development Co-operation
Ministry of Foreign Affairs
Ballhausplatz, 2
1010 VIENNA
Austria

Professor Ian LITTLE (United Kingdom)
Nuffield College
OXFORD OX3 OPS
United Kingdom

Professor Angus MADDISON (United Kingdom)
University of Groningen
26, Meerweg
9752 JH HAREN
Netherlands

Ambassador Pekka MALINEN (Finland)
Pihlajatie 47-49 B 28
00270 HELSINKI 27
Finland

Mr. F.A. MALJERS (Netherlands)
Chairman of the Board of Directors
UNILEVER NV
BP 760
3000 DK ROTTERDAM
Netherlands

Mr. Rafael MARTINEZ CORTINA (Spain)
Vice Presidente y Consejero Delegado
Banco Exterior de España
Carrera San Jeronimo, 36
MADRID 28014
Spain

Professor J. MATON (Belgium)
Rijksuniversiteit-Gent
Gust de Smetlaan 11
9831 St. MATENS-LATEM (Deurle)
Belgium

Mr. Federico MAYOR (Spain)
Director General of UNESCO
Place de Fontenoy
75700 PARIS
France

Miss Fiona McCONNELL (United Kingdom)
Chairman, OECD Environment Committee
Central Director Environmental Pollution
Department of the Environment
Romney House
43 Marsham Street
LONDON SW1P 3PY
United Kingdom

Mr. Brian McKEOWN (Ireland)
Director
The Catholic Agency for World Development (TROCAIRE)
169 Booterstown Avenue
Blackrock
Co DUBLIN
Ireland

Mr. Mansour MOALLA (Tunisia)
Président de l'Institut Arabe des Chefs d'Entreprises
77 boulevard Ali Bourguiba
SOUKRA 2036
Tunisia

Dr. Bernhard MOLITOR (Germany)
Vice-Chairman of the OECD Economic Policy Committee
Ministerialdirektor
Bundesministerium für Wirtschaft
5300 BONN 1
Federal Republic of Germany

Mr. Philip NDEGWA (Kenya)
Chairman
First Chartered Securities Limited
PO Box 46143
NAIROBI
Kenya

Professor Göran OHLIN (Sweden)
Assistant Secretary-General in charge of
the Office for Development Research and Policy Analysis
United Nations
1 United Nations Plaza
NEW YORK, NY 10017
United States

Ms. Maureen O'NEIL (Canada)
Director
North-South Institute, Ottawa
77 Bloor Street West
TORONTO
Canada

Dr. Saburo OKITA (Japan)
Chairman
Institute for Domestic and International Policy Studies
Fukokuseimei Bldg.
2-2, Uchisaiwaicho 2-Chome
Chiyoda-ku
TOKYO 100
Japan

Dr. Yung Chul PARK (Korea)
Visiting Professor of Economics and Research Associate
Harvard Institute for International Development
One Eliot Street
CAMBRIDGE, MA 02138
United States

Professor I.G. PATEL (India)
Director
London School of Economics and Political Science
Houghton Street
LONDON, WC2A 2AE
United Kingdom

Mr. Tore ROSE (Norway)
UNDP - Vietnam
c/o Palais des Nations
1211 GENEVA 10
Switzerland

Professor Louis SABOURIN (Canada)
Directeur du Groupe d'Etude, de Recherche
et de Formation Internationale (GERFI)
Université du Québec
Membre de la Commission Pontificale Justice et Paix
4835 rue Christophe-Colomb
MONTREAL
Quebec
Canada H2J 3G8

Professor Ignacy SACHS (France)
Centre de Recherches sur le Brésil Contemporain
Ecole des Hautes Etudes en Sciences Sociales
54 Boulevard Raspail
75270 PARIS 06
France

Mrs. Marie-Angélique SAVANE (Senegal)
Présidente
Association des Femmes Africaines pour
la Recherche et le Développement (AFARD)
BP 3304
DAKAR
Senegal

Mr. Bengt SAVE-SODERBERGH (Sweden)
Under-Secretary of State
Development Department
Ministry of Foreign Affairs
Box 16121
10323 STOCKHOLM
Sweden

Professor Pu SHAN (China)
Institute of World Economy
Academy of Social Sciences of the People's Republic of China
5 Jianguomennei Dajie
BEIJING
People's Republic of China

Dr. Manmohan SINGH (India)
Secretary-General
The South Commission
17-19, Chemin du Champ d'Anier
PO Box 228
1211 GENEVA 19
Switzerland

Mr. Steinar SKJAEVELAND (Norway)
Resident Representative
NORAD
Royal Norwegian Embassy
PO Box 46363
NAIROBI
Kenya

Dr. SOEDJATMOKO (Indonesia)
Jalan Tanjung 18
JAKARTA 10350
Indonesia

Mr. Thorvald STOLTENBERG (Norway)
Minister for Foreign Affairs
PO 8114, Dep
0032 OSLO 1
Norway

Dr. Hans-Helmut TAAKE (Germany)
Director
Deutches Institut für Entwicklungspolitik
Fraunhoferstr. 33-36
1000 BERLIN 10
Germany

Mr. Albert TEVOEDJRE (Benin)
Président
Association Mondiale de Prospective Sociale (AMPS)
CP 56
1211 GENEVE 19
Switzerland

Mr. Carl THAM (Sweden)
Director-General
Swedish International Development Authority (SIDA)
Birger Jarlsgatan 61
10525 STOCKHOLM
Sweden

Professor Constantine VAITSOS (Greece)
University of Athens
Ypsilandou Street, 37
10676 ATHENS
Greece

Professor Dr. Ferdinand Van DAM (Netherlands)
State University of Leyden and Institute of Social Studies
Badhuisweg 251
THE HAGUE
Netherlands

Mr. Joseph WHEELER (United States)
Chairman of the OECD Development Assistance Committee
Château de la Muette
75116 PARIS
France

Mr. Maurice WILLIAMS (United States)
Secretary-General
Society for International Development (SID)
Palazzo Civita del Lavoro
00144 ROME
Italy

Ambassador Layachi YAKER (Algeria)
Special Adviser to the Director-General of Unesco
Member of the South Commission
3, rue Edmond Roger
75015 PARIS
France

Professor Montague YUDELMAN (United States)
Fellow
Conservation Foundation
1250 24th Street NW
WASHINGTON DC 20037
United States

NATIONAL DELEGATIONS TO THE OECD

AUSTRALIA	Mr. Ed VISBORD Ambassador, Permanent Representative
	Mr. Ronald McINNES Deputy Permanent Representative
AUSTRIA	Mr. Georg LENNKH Ambassador, Permanent Representative
BELGIUM	Mr. Juan CASSIERS Ambassador, Permanent Representative
	Mr. Gaston VAN DUYSE-ADAM Embassy Counsellor, Deputy Permanent Representative
	Mr. Werner VERTONGEN Financial and Economic Counsellor
CANADA	Mr. Michael BERRY Ambassador, Permanent Representative
	Mr. George HAYNAL Minister-Counsellor, Deputy Permanent Representative

	Mrs. Suzanne LAPORTE Counsellor
DENMARK	Mr. Henrik Munck NETTERSTROM Ambassador, Permanent Representative
	Mr. Eric HEDEGAARD Counsellor
FINLAND	Mr. Wilhelm BREITENSTEIN Ambassador, Permanent Representative
	Mr. Jorma PAUKKU Counsellor, Technical and Economic Co-operation
FRANCE	Mr. Marc BONNEFOUS Ambassador of France, Permanent Representative
	Mr. Didier FERRAND Deputy Permanent Representative
GERMANY	Dr. Klaus MEYER Ambassador, Permanent Representative
	Mr. Wolfgang BUCH Counselor, Co-operation Affairs
GREECE	Mr. Dimitris KOULOURIANOS Ambassador, Permanent Representative
	Mr. Vassili RAPANOS Deputy Head of the Permanent Delegation
ICELAND	Mr. Haraldur KROYER Ambassador, Permanent Representative
IRELAND	Mr. Tadhg O'SULLIVAN Ambassador, Permanent Representative
	Mr. Patrick CRADOCK Deputy Permananent Representative
ITALY	Mr. Luigi FONTANA GIUSTI Ambassador, Permanent Representative
	Mr. Paolo SANNELLA Counsellor
JAPAN	Mr. Hisashi OWADA Ambassador, Permanent Representative
	Mr. Masao KAWAI Counsellor, Development
LUXEMBOURG	Mr. Pierre WURTH Ambassador, Permanent Representative

NETHERLANDS	Mr. A.G.O. SMITSENDONK Ambassador, Permanent Representative
	Mr. Hans H.J. LABOHM Counsellor, Deputy Head of the Permanent Delegation
NEW ZEALAND	Mrs. J.C. TROTTER Ambassador, Permanent Representative
NORWAY	Mr. Thorvald MOE Ambassador, Permanent Representative
	Mr. Helge SKAARA Second Secretary
PORTUGAL	Mr. Fernando Augusto dos SANTOS MARTINS Ambassador, Permanent Representative
	Mr. José LAMEIRAS Counsellor, International North-South Relations
SPAIN	Mr. José Antonio LOPEZ ZATON Ambassador, Permanent Representative
	Mr. Miguel Angel de FRUTOS Embassy Counsellor
SWEDEN	Mr. Bo KJELLEN Ambassador, Permanent Representative
	Mrs. Anita MELIN First Secretary
SWITZERLAND	Mr. Eric ROETHLISBERGER Ambassador, Permanent Representative
	Mr. Anton THALMANN Embassy Counsellor, North-South Development, Budget
TURKEY	Mr. Mustafa ASULA Ambassador, Permanent Representative
	Mr. Haluk SIPAHIOGLU Counsellor
UNITED KINGDOM	Mr. J.W.D. GRAY, CMG Ambassador, Permanent Representative
	Mr. H.L. DAVIES Counsellor, Deputy Head of the Permanent Delegation
UNITED STATES	Mr. Denis LAMB Ambassador, Permanent Representative

Mr. Martin V. DAGATA
Minister-Counsellor

Mr. William B. ERDAHL
Development Assistance Adviser

COMMISSION OF THE
EUROPEAN
COMMUNITIES   Mr. Raymond PHAN VAN PHI
                                Head, Permanent Delegation

                                Mr. Juan Miguel MARCH
                                First Secretary

YUGOSLAVIA   Mr. Tomislav JANKOVIC
                                Ambassador

                                Mr. Nemanja JOVIC
                                Counsellor, Deputy Head, Permanent Mission

                        *   *   *

BUSINESS AND INDUSTRY ADVISORY
COMMITTEE TO OECD (BIAC)
                                Mr. Gerold PILZ
                                International Affairs
                                Hoechst Aktiengesellschaft
                                Frankfurt am Main
                                Federal Republic of Germany

TRADE UNION ADVISORY
COMMITTEE TO THE
OECD (TUAC)   Mr. John EVANS
                                Secretary-General

OECD SECRETARIAT

Mr. Jean-Claude PAYE
Secretary-General of the OECD

Mr. Gerhard ABEL
Director, Trade Directorate

Mr. Thomas ALEXANDER
Head of the Secretary-General's Private Office

Mr. Richard CAREY
Deputy Director, Development Co-operation Directorate

Mr. Serge DEVOS
Deputy Director, Trade Directorate

Mr. Helmut FUHRER
Director, Development Co-operation Directorate

Mr. James GASS
Director, Directorate for Social Affairs, Manpower and Education

Mr. J.-H. GUILMETTE
Head of Club de Sahel

Mr. John HACKETT
Former Director, Directorate for
Financial, Fiscal and Enterprise Affairs

Mr. David HENDERSON
Head of Department, Economics and Statistics Department

Mr. J. Wallace HOPKINS
Deputy Executive Director, International Energy Agency

Mr. Stephen JOYCE
Secretary-General's Private Office

Mme Anne de LATTRE
Adviser to the Club du Sahel

Mr. Bill L. LONG
Director, Environment Directorate

Mr. Quincey LUMSDEN
International Energy Agency

Mr. Wolfgang MICHALSKI
Head of the Advisory Unit on Multidisciplinary Issues

Mr. Derry ORMOND
Head, Technical Co-operation Service

Mr. Tsuneo OYAKE
Special Adviser to the Secretary-General

Mr. Tohiro TANIGUCHI
Deputy Director, Directorate for Science, Technology and Industry

Mr. Gérard VIATTE
Director, Directorate for Food, Agriculture and Fisheries

Mr. Pierre VINDE
Deputy Secretary-General

Mr. George WILLIAMSON
Head of Division in the Publications Service

Mr. Salvatore ZECCHINI
Special Adviser to the Secretary-General

OECD DEVELOPMENT CENTRE

Mr. Louis EMMERIJ
President

Mr. Jean BONVIN
Director of Co-ordination

Mr. Giulio FOSSI
Head of Programme, External Co-operation and Documentation

Mr. Dimitrios GERMIDIS
Head of Programme, Research

Mr. Christian MORRISSON
Head of Programme, Research

RESEARCH STAFF

Mr. Martin BROWN
Mr. Teruyuki IWASAKI
Mr. Charles OMAN
Mr. Helmut REISEN
Mr. Hartmut SCHNEIDER
Mr. David TURNHAM
Mrs. Carlienne BRENNER
Mr. Richard CONROY
Mr. Ian GOLDIN
Mrs. Winifred WEEKES VAGLIANI

**EXTERNAL CO-OPERATION
AND DOCUMENTATION
STAFF**

Mrs. Valérie DI GIACOMO
External Co-operation

Mr. Jacques SELETTI
External Co-operation

Miss Alice WATSON
Data Base

Miss Isabelle CORNELIS
Librarian

Mrs. Françoise BEUDOT
Sahel Antenna

SUPPORT SERVICES

Miss Catherine DUPORT
Administration

Miss Flora FEIGENSPAN
Secretary to the Advisory Board

Mrs. Michèle FLEURY-BROUSSE
Statistic and Computer Services

Mr. Colm FOY
Publications and Information

WHERE TO OBTAIN OECD PUBLICATIONS
OÙ OBTENIR LES PUBLICATIONS DE L'OCDE

ARGENTINA - ARGENTINE
Carlos Hirsch S.R.L.,
Florida 165, 4º Piso,
(Galeria Guemes) 1333 Buenos Aires
Tel. 33.1787.2391 y 30.7122

AUSTRALIA - AUSTRALIE
D.A. Book (Aust.) Pty. Ltd.
11-13 Station Street (P.O. Box 163)
Mitcham, Vic. 3132   Tel. (03) 873 4411

AUSTRIA - AUTRICHE
OECD Publications and Information Centre,
4 Simrockstrasse,
5300 Bonn (Germany)   Tel. (0228) 21.60.45
Gerold & Co., Graben 31, Wien 1   Tel. 52.22.35

BELGIUM - BELGIQUE
Jean de Lannoy,
Avenue du Roi 202
B-1060 Bruxelles   Tel. (02) 538.51.69

CANADA
Renouf Publishing Company Ltd
1294 Algoma Road, Ottawa, Ont. K1B 3W8
Tel: (613) 741-4333
Stores:
61 rue Sparks St., Ottawa, Ont. K1P 5R1
Tel: (613) 238-8985
211 rue Yonge St., Toronto, Ont. M5B 1M4
Tel: (416) 363-3171
Federal Publications Inc.,
301-303 King St. W.,
Toronto, Ont. M5V 1J5   Tel. (416)581-1552
Les Éditions la Liberté inc.,
3020 Chemin Sainte-Foy,
Sainte-Foy, P.Q. G1X 3V6,   Tel. (418)658-3763

DENMARK - DANEMARK
Munksgaard Export and Subscription Service
35, Nørre Søgade, DK-1370 København K
Tel. +45.1.12.85.70

FINLAND - FINLANDE
Akateeminen Kirjakauppa,
Keskuskatu 1, 00100 Helsinki 10   Tel. 0.12141

FRANCE
OCDE/OECD
Mail Orders/Commandes par correspondance :
2, rue André-Pascal,
75775 Paris Cedex 16   Tel. (1) 45.24.82.00
Bookshop/Librairie : 33, rue Octave-Feuillet
75016 Paris
Tel. (1) 45.24.81.67 or/ou (1) 45.24.81.81
Librairie de l'Université,
12a, rue Nazareth,
13602 Aix-en-Provence   Tel. 42.26.18.08

GERMANY - ALLEMAGNE
OECD Publications and Information Centre,
4 Simrockstrasse,
5300 Bonn   Tel. (0228) 21.60.45

GREECE - GRÈCE
Librairie Kauffmann,
28, rue du Stade, 105 64 Athens   Tel. 322.21.60

HONG KONG
Government Information Services,
Publications (Sales) Office,
Information Services Department
No. 1, Battery Path, Central

ICELAND - ISLANDE
Snæbjörn Jónsson & Co., h.f.,
Hafnarstræti 4 & 9,
P.O.B. 1131 – Reykjavik
Tel. 13133/14281/11936

INDIA - INDE
Oxford Book and Stationery Co.,
Scindia House, New Delhi 110001
Tel. 331.5896/5308
17 Park St., Calcutta 700016   Tel. 240832

INDONESIA - INDONÉSIE
Pdii-Lipi, P.O. Box 3065/JKT.Jakarta
Tel. 583467

IRELAND - IRLANDE
TDC Publishers - Library Suppliers,
12 North Frederick Street, Dublin 1
Tel. 744835-749677

ITALY - ITALIE
Libreria Commissionaria Sansoni,
Via Benedetto Fortini 120/10,
Casella Post. 552
50125 Firenze   Tel. 055/645415
Via Bartolini 29, 20155 Milano   Tel. 365083
La diffusione delle pubblicazioni OCSE viene
assicurata dalle principali librerie ed anche da :
Editrice e Libreria Herder,
Piazza Montecitorio 120, 00186 Roma
Tel. 6794628
Libreria Hœpli,
Via Hœpli 5, 20121 Milano   Tel. 865446
Libreria Scientifica
Dott. Lucio de Biasio "Aeiou"
Via Meravigli 16, 20123 Milano   Tel. 807679

JAPAN - JAPON
OECD Publications and Information Centre,
Landic Akasaka Bldg., 2-3-4 Akasaka,
Minato-ku, Tokyo 107   Tel. 586.2016

KOREA - CORÉE
Kyobo Book Centre Co. Ltd.
P.O.Box: Kwang Hwa Moon 1658,
Seoul   Tel. (REP) 730.78.91

LEBANON - LIBAN
Documenta Scientifica/Redico,
Edison Building, Bliss St.,
P.O.B. 5641, Beirut   Tel. 354429-344425

**MALAYSIA/SINGAPORE -
MALAISIE/SINGAPOUR**
University of Malaya Co-operative Bookshop
Ltd.,
7 Lrg 51A/227A, Petaling Jaya
Malaysia   Tel. 7565000/7565425
Information Publications Pte Ltd
Pei-Fu Industrial Building,
24 New Industrial Road No. 02-06
Singapore 1953   Tel. 2831786, 2831798

NETHERLANDS - PAYS-BAS
SDU Uitgeverij
Christoffel Plantijnstraat 2
Postbus 20014
2500 EA's-Gravenhage   Tel. 070-789911
Voor bestellingen: Tel. 070-789880

NEW ZEALAND - NOUVELLE-ZÉLANDE
Government Printing Office Bookshops:
Auckland: Retail Bookshop, 25 Rutland Stseet,
Mail Orders, 85 Beach Road
Private Bag C.P.O.
Hamilton: Retail: Ward Street,
Mail Orders, P.O. Box 857
Wellington: Retail, Mulgrave Street, (Head
Office)
Cubacade World Trade Centre,
Mail Orders, Private Bag
Christchurch: Retail, 159 Hereford Street,
Mail Orders, Private Bag
Dunedin: Retail, Princes Street,
Mail Orders, P.O. Box 1104

NORWAY - NORVÈGE
Narvesen Info Center – NIC,
Bertrand Narvesens vei 2,
P.O.B. 6125 Etterstad, 0602 Oslo 6
Tel. (02) 67.83.10, (02) 68.40.20

PAKISTAN
Mirza Book Agency
65 Shahrah Quaid-E-Azam, Lahore 3 Tel. 66839

PHILIPPINES
I.J. Sagun Enterprises, Inc.
P.O. Box 4322 CPO Manila
Tel. 695-1946, 922-9495

PORTUGAL
Livraria Portugal, Rua do Carmo 70-74,
1117 Lisboa Codex   Tel. 360582/3

**SINGAPORE/MALAYSIA -
SINGAPOUR/MALAISIE**
See "Malaysia/Singapor". Voir
« Malaisie/Singapour »

SPAIN - ESPAGNE
Mundi-Prensa Libros, S.A.,
Castelló 37, Apartado 1223, Madrid-28001
Tel. 431.33.99
Libreria Bosch, Ronda Universidad 11,
Barcelona 7   Tel. 317.53.08/317.53.58

SWEDEN - SUÈDE
AB CE Fritzes Kungl. Hovbokhandel,
Box 16356, S 103 27 STH,
Regeringsgatan 12,
DS Stockholm   Tel. (08) 23.89.00
Subscription Agency/Abonnements:
Wennergren-Williams AB,
Box 30004, S104 25 Stockholm Tel. (08)54.12.00

SWITZERLAND - SUISSE
OECD Publications and Information Centre,
4 Simrockstrasse,
5300 Bonn (Germany)   Tel. (0228) 21.60.45
Librairie Payot,
6 rue Grenus, 1211 Genève 11
Tel. (022) 31.89.50
Maditec S.A.
Ch. des Palettes 4
1020 – Renens/Lausanne   Tel. (021) 635.08.65
United Nations Bookshop/Librairie des Nations-
Unies
Palais des Nations, 1211 – Geneva 10
Tel. 022-34-60-11 (ext. 48 72)

TAIWAN - FORMOSE
Good Faith Worldwide Int'l Co., Ltd.
9th floor, No. 118, Sec.2, Chung Hsiao E. Road
Taipei   Tel. 391.7396/391.7397

THAILAND - THAILANDE
Suksit Siam Co., Ltd., 1715 Rama IV Rd.,
Samyam Bangkok 5   Tel. 2511630
INDEX Book Promotion & Service Ltd.
59/6 Soi Lang Suan, Ploenchit Road
Patjumamwan, Bangkok 10500
Tel. 250-1919, 252-1066

TURKEY - TURQUIE
Kültur Yayinlari Is-Türk Ltd. Sti.
Atatürk Bulvari No: 191/Kat. 21
Kavaklidere/Ankara   Tel. 25.07.60
Dolmabahce Cad. No: 29
Besiktas/Istanbul   Tel. 160.71.88

UNITED KINGDOM - ROYAUME-UNI
H.M. Stationery Office,
Postal orders only: (01)873-8483
P.O.B. 276, London SW8 5DT
Telephone orders: (01) 873-9090, or
Personal callers:
49 High Holborn, London WC1V 6HB
Branches at: Belfast, Birmingham,
Bristol, Edinburgh, Manchester

UNITED STATES - ÉTATS-UNIS
OECD Publications and Information Centre,
2001 L Street, N.W., Suite 700,
Washington, D.C. 20036 - 4095
Tel. (202) 785.6323

VENEZUELA
Libreria del Este,
Avda F. Miranda 52, Aptdo. 60337,
Edificio Galipan, Caracas 106
Tel. 951.17.05/951.23.07/951.12.97

YUGOSLAVIA - YOUGOSLAVIE
Jugoslovenska Knjiga, Knez Mihajlova 2,
P.O.B. 36, Beograd   Tel. 621.992

Orders and inquiries from countries where
Distributors have not yet been appointed should be
sent to:
OECD, Publications Service, 2, rue André-Pascal,
75775 PARIS CEDEX 16.

Les commandes provenant de pays où l'OCDE n'a
pas encore désigné de distributeur doivent être
adressées à :
OCDE, Service des Publications. 2, rue André-
Pascal, 75775 PARIS CEDEX 16.

72380-1-1989

OECD PUBLICATIONS, 2, rue André-Pascal, 75775 PARIS CEDEX 16 - No. 44837 1989
PRINTED IN FRANCE
(41 89 04 1) ISBN 92-64-13249-X